Operation
Just Cause

Operation
Just Cause

The U.S. Intervention
in Panama

*Edited by Bruce W. Watson
and Peter G. Tsouras*

Westview Press
BOULDER • *SAN FRANCISCO* • *OXFORD*

The information in this book is based on the research of the editors and authors and does not represent the positions or the policies of any agency or department of the U.S. Government. The information was derived from unclassified publications and sources and is intended to neither confirm nor deny, officially or unofficially, the views of the U.S. Government.

This Westview softcover edition is printed on acid-free paper and bound in library-quality, coated covers that carry the highest rating of the National Association of State Textbook Administrators, in consultation with the Association of American Publishers and the Book Manufacturers' Institute.

Published in 1991 in the United States of America by Westview Press, Inc., 5500 Central Avenue, Boulder, Colorado 80301, and in the United Kingdom by Westview Press, 36 Lonsdale Road, Summertown, Oxford OX2 7EW

Library of Congress Cataloging-in-Publication Data

Operation Just Cause : the U.S. intervention in Panama/edited
   by Bruce W. Watson and Peter G. Tsouras.
      p. cm.
   Includes bibliographical references.
   ISBN 0-8133-7981-4
   1. United States--Foreign relations--Panama. 2. Panama--Foreign relations--United States. 3. Panama--History--American invasion, 1989. I. Watson, Bruce W. II. Tsouras, Peter.
   E183.8.P2064 1991   90-22872
   327.7307287--dc20   CIP

Printed and bound in the United States of America

The paper used in this publication meets the requirements of the American National Standard for Permanence of Paper for Printed Library Materials Z39.48-1984.

10   9   8   7   6   5   4   3   2   1

To Jennifer Viola Bowen Watson

A wonderful daughter. Her love, concern, and support,
developing interest in foreign affairs and politics, her
enthusiasm for the heat of political discussion, and her
"people person" personality all have encouraged us of the
worth of this endeavor. May she keep up this enthusiasm and
interest and may she join us in some future work in the field.

Contents

Preface

In 1984 and 1985, Westview Press published <u>Military Lessons of the Falkland Islands War: Views from the United States</u> and <u>American Intervention in Grenada: The Implications of Operation "Urgent Fury,"</u> both of which I coedited with Peter M. Dunn. These were the first serious academic studies on these topics. This book should be considered as the third in such a series in that it offers one of the first comprehensive academic views on <u>Just Cause</u>, the December 1989 U.S. military intervention in Panama. The group of academic and professional authorities who present the material have great familiarity with the various aspects of <u>Just Cause</u>, so this book amounts to the first serious attempt to consider the operation in its political and historical perspective. The contributors present excellent positions for the reader to consider and give a comprehensive view of all of the factors and events that prompted the operation, all the various aspects of the operation itself, and the likely effects that the operation will have on regional and international affairs. Thus the book ties together the disparate elements that prompted the operation. Although more comprehensive examinations of <u>Just Cause</u> are expected to appear in the coming years, this book is intended for the serious researcher and attempts to provide the greatest amount of factual material that is currently available. It is hoped that this will assist those who will accomplish future studies on the subject.

The book opens with Panamanian and U.S. perspectives of the U.S.-Panamanian relationship. Professor Donald Mabry admirably presents a history of the relationship that demonstrates that the primary concern of the United States has been the Panama Canal. The resulting position was often characterized by a view that bordered on disdain for the Panamanians and that tolerated and even supported leaders who were judged on the basis of their ability to guarantee the canal's security rather than on their value to Panama or the needs of Panamanians. That the antidemocratic, corrupt records of some of the individuals ran against the U.S. public's sense of decency only made the problem more complex.

William H. Drohan presents the Panamanian view. Although the Panamanians did not build the canal and could not have built it, the canal offered both benefits and liabilities.

The expenses associated with its operation improved the standard of living. Conversely the canal and the Canal Zone cut a swath through the nation, guaranteed continued U.S. attention and periodic intervention in Panamanian affairs, and retarded the development of Panamanian politics. Over the years Panamanians came to view the canal as theirs and strove for complete control of the waterway. In the 1960s and 1970s Americans came to grudgingly accept a new reality concerning the canal and to realize that it would eventually be transferred to Panamanian control.

The focus of the book then broadens to consider drugs, another major factor in U.S.-Panamanian relations. Michael Hathaway presents a comprehensive analysis of both General Noriega's and Panama's involvement in the drug trade and in money-laundering. He concludes that their roles were very significant, involved millions of dollars, and that this, in itself, was a major cause prompting U.S. action against Noriega.

Part II of the study considers the events leading up to operation Just Cause, as well as the actual operation. Intelligence and indications and warning factors are analyzed by Susan Horwitz with the aim of determining how they contributed to the decision to launch operation Just Cause.

Professor Lorenzo Crowell's chapter begins Part III, details the military operation, and considers the adequacy of air power, logistical support, and medical evacuation procedures. The operation is then considered in the context of its contribution to U.S. joint operations. Here again, Just Cause appears to have been a success. Whereas in the action in Grenada (Urgent Fury) all the services insisted on taking part, creating a difficult multiservice force that was rife with command and control problems, the forces for Just Cause were chosen with care. The Army and Air Force were the major operating forces, with participation by the Navy and Marine Corps. The result was a controllable and responsive force continually under excellent command and control.

The command, control, and communications (C^3) factors are also examined by Michael Seitz, and here it is difficult not to make comparisons with operation Urgent Fury, the intervention in Grenada, and El Dorado Canyon, the U.S. operation against Libya. Urgent Fury suffered from critical problems in communications (in one instance commercial telephone lines had to be used because available communications were so inadequate and confused that they failed to fulfill their purpose). Likewise, command and control of the operation was very complex and burdensome. El Dorado Canyon amounted only to two isolated U.S. Navy and Air Force air strike operations with the only joint requirement being that the two reach their targets on time. Just Cause was an anomaly in that the United States had a sizable force stationed on the scene before the operation began. Nonetheless, it was a very complex operation and all indications are that C^3 was very successful, a vast improvement over Urgent Fury. Lean and responsive, C^3 provided the communications and direction needed to accomplish this very detailed military operation.

The book's consideration of the operations also includes assessments of air power, logistic support, civil affairs operations, and press access to information by Noris L. McCall, John W. Turner, Edward F. Dandar, Jr, and me. The endemic problem concerning press access centers on a military that is justifiably concerned for its forces and wants to restrict the flow of information to the public and a press that wants complete access to information in order to keep the public fully informed. Relations between the two were very bad during the Vietnam War, with the press deriding the "five o'clock follies" news briefings and the military questioning the moral purposes of a press that not only released information that the military considered endangered its troops but appeared to slant the news against U.S. forces fighting the war. The nadir in the relationship may have come in Urgent Fury, when the press, having been denied access to Grenada, rented boats and attempted to reach the island. Some of the boats were reportedly strafed by U.S. aircraft. The fact that there was little investigation of these claims infers that the strafing did not occur. Still, the fact that many believed that the incident could have occurred attests to the low state of press-military relations that existed at the time. In Just Cause, the military attempted to correct this problem. In the wake of the operation, complaints were heard, and the Pentagon conducted its own investigation, which revealed that problems still existed and that the press had been unjustifiably denied access to some information. Conversely, there were reports from military commanders that some of the press reporting unnecessarily endangered American soldiers' lives. From this we can conclude that there has been progress in solving the military-press issue but that a solution has not been reached. Thus Just Cause may someday be judged as a step that contributed to a solution.

Part IV considers the ramifications of Just Cause. Mark Sullivan assesses the current situation and concludes that U.S. actions and sanctions before the operation had severely disrupted the economy. Additionally, the disruption and damage caused by the operation itself amounted to a further liability. In the aftermath, Panama looked to the United States, possibly unrealistically, as a panacea for all of its ills. Meanwhile, Washington looked on Panama in the light of fiscal stringency and its perceived responsibilities toward Eastern Europe and its allies and clients around the world. The subsequent U.S. Operation Desert Shield in Saudi Arabia only exacerbated this problem of conflicting claims on the United States. Sullivan concludes that there is considerable distance between Panamanian expectations and U.S. perceptions and believes that the way that these two are resolved will govern future U.S.-Panamanian relations.

Dr. Alan Goldman and E. Maria Biggers then consider the international repercussions of Just Cause, and the study concludes with an assessment of the significance of the operations.

Finally, a chronology of the major events concerning the prelude, the operation, and the aftermath is provided by Lawrence S. Germain and me to help the reader understand the progression of events and assist researchers in their efforts.

In summary, Just Cause is both an intermediate step and a culmination. Its role in the ongoing history of U.S. combined operations, of U.S. military command, control, and communications (C^3) procedures, and of U.S. military-press relations, is that of an intermediary step that should lead to continued progress and eventual resolution of existing problems. More immediately, Just Cause may have been of value in the subsequent Operation Desert Shield in Saudi Arabia.

In its historical context, however, Just Cause might be considered to be either an intermediate step or a culmination, depending on one's perspective. Latin Americans might consider the operation to be an intermediate step--another instance of unwelcome U.S. interference in Latin American affairs. In this context, it is of little value to point out that the view is myopic and ignores U.S. sensitivity to drugs, that Noriega's actions were tantamount to pushing Washington to the wall, and that to not act would have involved a great loss of U.S. prestige both regionally and globally. Rather, it is more productive to recognize the misperception and work for its correction.

To most Americans, the operation is considered a culmination in which a complex set of issues deteriorated to the extent that efforts for a peaceful solution by the United States, the Organization of American States, and the United Nations failed, and a military operation was perceived as the only solution. Indeed, to many Americans, Just Cause proved the validity of Carl von Clasewitz's views in that it was the continuation of politics on a more violent level. Such a continuation is believed to be justified, given that peaceful solutions had failed, and the loss of life and destruction of property that occurred during the operation had been very low. At the conclusion of Just Cause, those with the latter view believed that it had been an isolated event that had resolved the Panamanian drug issue and would not have lasting effects on regional relations.

BRUCE W. WATSON

Acknowledgments

We must begin by thanking the contributors. The value of any work of this nature is always directly related to the ability, devotion, and dedication of its contributors. Ours are located in several states and pursue a variety of occupations. In all cases, we were impressed with the quality of their work and their attention to detail. The quality of this book directly reflects on their efforts.

We would also like to acknowledge our wives Susan Watson and Patricia Tsouras, and children, Bruce, Susan, and Ella Watson, and Ted, Peter, and Kate Tsouras. This work amounts to months of effort, and their support and understanding during that time is appreciated greatly.

We would like to thank Patricia Lanzara for her work in preparing the manuscript.

We have dedicated this book to Jennifer Watson. Jennie took a particular interest in its production and was instrumental in gathering and collating the materials for its chronology. We hope that this is merely the beginning of her career and that in the future she will make substantial contributions to our understanding of current affairs.

B.W.W.
P.G.T.

PART I

The Background (1905–1988)

1 Panama's Policy Toward the United States: Living with Big Brother

Panamanian nationalists eagerly point out that Panama existed before the settlement of Jamestown in 1607 and centuries before the United States intervened in November 1903 to help Panama gain independence from Colombia. Moreover, Panamanians had been transshipping people and goods across the isthmus since the early 1500s. The conquest of Peru was launched from Panama and most of the Spanish colonial South American empire was supplied from Spain through trade fairs held in Panama. When the Spanish empire collapsed in the early nineteenth century, Panama technically became part of Colombia, but the Colombian rule was light, for it was extraordinarily difficult to travel from one country to the other. Panamanian nationalists had sought independence from Colombia in the nineteenth century and unsuccessfully fought for Panamanian freedom in the Colombian civil war of 1899-1903. To them, the U.S. intervention in 1903 complicated the formation of a Panamanian national state. Thus, to Panamanians, the United States, at best, was a midwife and never the parent of Panamanian nationality.[1]

For Panamanians, relations between their republic and the United States have been duplicitous and unfair from the beginning of the independent republic. The Hay-Bunau-Varilla Treaty (1903) was an act of chicanery forced upon the fledgling nation by the United States. The temporary Panamanian representative to the United States, Phillipe Bunau-Varilla, a Frenchman, violated his instructions from the new Panamanian government to await the arrival of officials from Panama before negotiating a treaty. Instead, he wrote a treaty so generous in giving away Panamanian authority that John Hay, U.S. Secretary of State, quickly signed it before the Panamanian delegation could force changes. The new Panamanian government reluctantly accepted it, fearing either Colombian or U.S. military intervention if it did not.

Instead of being a liberator, the United States treated Panama as a conquered province. Washington established a military dictatorship in the Canal Zone; the Canal Zone Commissioner was always an active-duty U.S. military officer and Zonians, regardless of their nationality, had no political power. They did what the Commissioner wanted or were expelled. The zone was a military socialist society; the U.S. government owned virtually all but Zonians' personal possessions. Outside the zone, the United States controlled most of the public services in Panama City and Colon. Americans viewed Panamanians, even those of the elite class, as lesser people. Moreover, these Spanish-speakers resented the importation of English-speaking black workers from the Caribbean because of their language and ethnicity, a complaint compounded by the subsequent U.S. refusal to repatriate them once the canal was completed.

The U.S. actively discouraged Panamanian self-determination, for Washington saw its interest as maintaining a compliant Panamanian government. Foreign soldiers and foreign laws controlled the zone; Panamanians could be arrested by foreign personnel, tried in foreign courts, and punished by foreigners, all on Panamanian soil. The bifurcation of the nation by this foreign enclave prohibited Panama's integral development and, instead, skewed national development towards the cities of Panama and Colon, each a terminus of the canal. As these two cities grew, Panamanians wanted unused Zonian land converted into Panamanian-owned farms to produce food to feed the urban populations along the canal.[2]

Panamanians also criticized the 1903 treaty for treating Panama unfairly economically. Panama had no right to tax in the zone or fix the toll rates on the canal. The rent on the zone was fixed by treaty, thus making it extraordinarily difficult to change, and inflation reduced the value of the rent paid. The United States imported goods directly into the zone, both escaping Panamanian taxes and bypassing Panamanian merchants. Panamanians or black West Indians were paid at the "silver rate" whereas U.S. citizens were paid at the higher "gold rate."

Panamanian sovereignty has always been the source of friction between the two nations. Soon after the Hay-Bunau-Varilla treaty was signed in November 1903, Panamanians argued that the treaty's phrase "as if it were sovereign" only gave the United States "jurisdictional sovereignty" over the Canal Zone and that the zone was Panamanian. U.S. officials understood the distinction, although they usually ignored it, but the average U.S. citizen wrongly believed that the zone was U.S. territory and that Panama had yielded all rights in the zone in perpetuity.

Washington regularly intervened in Panamanian politics, usually through diplomats but too often through soldiers, to support favored local elites, those who supported U.S. policies because they benefitted most directly from them. Throughout the history of Panamanian-U.S. relations, the United States could always rely on those Panamanians who prospered from the U.S. presence. Until the military revolution of Omar Torrijos in 1968, presidents came from this group.

The fledgling Panamanian Army was disbanded in 1904 on the grounds that the U.S. Army was all the protection needed by the nation,[3] thus eliminating any Panamanian counterforce. In 1918, the United States intervened militarily in Panama

City and Colon to settle an election dispute. U.S. troops occupied Chiriqui province in 1918-21. In order to prevent a boundary dispute between Panama and Costa Rica in 1921, the U.S. threatened Panama by sending a battleship and four hundred marines. In 1925, U.S. troops, at the request of the now thoroughly demoralized Panamanian government, intervened in an election dispute. The United States was the final arbiter of Panamanian domestic political squabbles since only pro-U.S. politicians were allowed to stay in power. The threat of military intervention soon became sufficient to keep Panamanians in line.

From 1904, within months after independence, until they obtained some satisfaction in 1936, Panamanians pushed for official U.S. recognition of their sovereignty over the zone and better treatment of Panama. Washington conceded to some of their demands. In January 1936, the United States guaranteed Panamanians equal opportunity with Americans in the zone, a promise never completely fulfilled. In the Hull-Alfaro Treaty later that year, Washington renounced the right to intervene militarily to guarantee Panamanian independence and the right to maintain police in Colon and Panama City. The annuity was raised to $430,000 to offset the devaluation of the dollar in 1933. Panama obtained the right to control immigration. Most important, Article III stipulated that the Canal Zone was the sovereign territory of the Republic of Panama under the jurisdiction of the United States. The U.S. Senate, however, refused to ratify the treaty until 1939 and then only after Panama agreed to allow the United States to continue military intervention when the latter thought it necessary; Panama only nominally ceased to be a protectorate. Panamanian resentment flourished in some quarters as pro-Axis sentiment, which President Arnulfo Arias exploited for political gain until he was overthrown by the National Guard in 1941. A pro-U.S.government took his place.

Panamanians willingly supported the expansion of the U.S. military presence during World War II as an emergency measure, for they believed the war to be a just cause, but only with the understanding that the increased presence would soon end. In 1942, therefore, Panama leased defense sites to the United States for five years. When a renewal treaty, negotiated in 1947, ignored demands for better treatment of Panama, nationalistic riots erupted in Panama City. The Panamanian government quelled them with its National Guard, but not before the rioters turned their fury against the United States.

Chastened by these riots, Panama's government pressured Washington anew for a more favorable treaty, eventually getting one in 1955. Panama managed to obtain important concessions: it could now tax zone employees who were Panamanians; the United States gave up monopoly rights over railroad and highway construction and control of sanitation in Colon and Panama City; zone commissaries were restricted to selling only to U.S. citizens and to canal employees who worked and lived in the zone; Panamanians were granted a large share in supplying goods to zone markets; Panama obtained some zone land; and the rental annuity was raised to $1,930,000. In an informal, separate "Memo of Understandings Reached," President Dwight Eisenhower agreed to create equality of opportunity in the zone and end wage discrimination against the Panamanians working for the canal company. Panamanians mistakenly believed that this memo had the same force as the treaty.

The United States acted slowly, however, in implementing both the treaty and the memo, and anti-U.S. demonstrations marked the late 1950s. Nationalistic students demanded that the zone and the canal be returned to Panama. In May 1958, university students entered the zone under Operation Sovereignty to plant some fifty Panamanian flags as an assertion of sovereignty. Rebuffed in a brief confrontation, they withdrew. When they returned on November 3, 1959, American personnel resisted, and more than 120 students were killed or wounded, nine of them by U.S. soldiers. In 1960, President Eisenhower responded by opening skilled positions in the zone to Panamanians and ordering the Panamanian flag flown in parts of the zone.

Official relations improved under conservative President Roberto Chiari. He allowed the United States to expand the scope of its military programs in Panama. President John Kennedy began using the School of the Americas to train Latin American militaries in counter-insurgency warfare. Two of the most famous graduates of the school would be Omar Torrijos and Manuel Antonio Noriega. In addition, Washington stationed U.S. anti-guerrilla paratroopers in the zone. Panamanians were split on this new U.S. role in their country. Many rejoiced at the increased business, but nationalists and leftists objected to the increased U.S. military presence as a treaty violation and threat to Panamanian self-determination. Also, critics believed that the right-wing Latin American military officers trained at the school would suppress democratic movements in Latin America. They particularly feared improving the military skills of the Panamanian National Guard, for it had a long history of overthrowing governments. In part to pacify this resentment, Kennedy, in 1963, ordered that foreign counsels accredited to Panama be allowed to operate in the zone and that the Panamanian flag be flown jointly with the U.S. flag over civilian installations.

In 1964, Panamanian national pride provoked a serious confrontation between Panama and the United States. Panamanian students, although pro-U.S. in general terms, had long insisted that the United States recognize Panamanian sovereignty over the zone.[4] Zonian attitudes towards Panamanians had changed little since 1903, however. In January 1964, conservative American high school students refused to fly the Panamanian flag over their high school and flew the U.S. flag by itself in violation of U.S. law. Panamanian students, backed by public opinion, swarmed into the zone to assert Panamanian rights. During the riot which ensued, twenty-four persons (three of whom were U.S. soldiers) were killed and hundreds were injured. President Chiari demanded that the Organization of American States and the United Nations investigate what he called U.S. aggression and suspended diplomatic relations for four months.

President Lyndon Johnson and President Marco Robles agreed to negotiate three new canal treaties. Johnson, however, announced that the United States was also exploring the possibility of building a canal across Nicaragua or Mexico. Panamanian leaders got the message that they should accede to U.S. wishes lest Panama be stuck with a white elephant. The 1967 treaties were never ratified. They agreed to explore the possibility of a sea-level canal in Panama, to increase the Panamanian share of canal revenues, and to create a U.S.-dominated Panama Canal Commission to govern the zone and the canal. Further they would have allowed Panama to integrate the zone into the Panamanian Republic and to absorb the entire zone in 1999, to maintain the neutrality and establish joint defense of the canal, and to bring Zonians under the jurisdiction of joint Panamanian-U.S. courts. Once again, Panama demanded and obtained explicit recognition from the United States that it had sovereignty over the zone. Panama agreed to allow the U.S. military bases to remain until 2004.

To Panamanians, the United States never intended to meet their legitimate demands. When the terms of the treaties became known, the Panamanian National Assembly rejected them for giving Americans control over the commission and for allowing long-term leases on military bases. The leading candidates for the 1968 Panamanian presidential elections, David Samudio and Arnulfo Arias, roundly condemned the proposed treaties as a sellout to the United States. Robles' efforts to get further concessions from Washington failed, and the proposed treaties died.[5]

From the Panamanian nationalist's perspective, traditional Panamanian leaders were either stooges of the United States or simply interested in preserving their personal interests; thus, canal negotiations dragged on for years until the two nations finally agreed to terms unfavorable to Panama. Some believed that Arias was the U.S. candidate. Others resented the efforts of Robles' government to implement the U.S.-backed Alliance for Progress program proposed by Samudio; the program meant they would have to pay more taxes. Panamanian political elites contested with each other for the spoils of public office, and were more interested in preserving their privileged position within Panamanian society or vis-a-vis the United States than they were in furthering Panamanian interests. They had little interest for the well-being of the average Panamanian, who was poor, black or mestizo, and marginal within the Panamanian political system. Thus, by 1968, there was widespread dissatisfaction not only with Panama's inability to obtain more favorable terms from the United States but also with the nature of the political system; to many Panamanians, the two were intertwined. The only political force capable of effecting change was the National Guard, which historically had been the enforcement arm of the traditional elites.

Colonel Omar Torrijos, the commander of the National Guard, exploited this widespread dissatisfaction with the political system to overthrow the Robles government in a bloodless coup d'etat in October 1968, and created a populist, nationalistic military dictatorship. The Guard, composed mostly of blacks and mestizos, represented those sectors of the population that had not fared well in Panamanian history. Torrijos, a mestizo, started rural development programs, urban housing projects, and more equitable employee-employer relations through a new labor code, both to build popular support for his regime and to redress the grievances of the average Panamanian. He increased corporate and personal taxes to fund these programs. With U.S. technical advice, Panama instituted new banking laws in 1970 to make the country an offshore banking haven in an effort to generate new revenues. Torrijos' new constitution in 1972 institutionalized these changes and, more importantly, guaranteed that the Guard would be the nation's dominant political institution.

Torrijos moved quickly to reassure the Nixon administration that the reform program did not threaten U.S. interests, but he pressed the treaty revision issue. He recognized that Washington enjoyed a virtual veto power over Panamanian affairs, and that all efforts to reform Panama depended upon obtaining a new treaty from Washington. By 1970, Nixon agreed to restart discussions on the canal. Torrijos patiently waited as the negotiations proceeded through the 1972 American presidential elections, understanding that the canal issue was an explosive one in U.S. politics. By 1973, however, Panama faced serious economic difficulties, for revenues lagged behind expenditures. Washington did not sense the same urgency as did Torrijos, faced as he was with nationalistic demands to gain control of the canal and to resolve the sovereignty issue once and for all.

Torrijos forced Nixon's hand. He invited the U.N. Security Council to hold its March 1973 meeting in Panama City and arranged for the introduction of a moderate resolution supporting Panama's position on the canal. Thirteen of the fifteen council members voted for it. To block its passage, the United States had to cast a veto, only the third veto that it had cast since 1945. Torrijos had managed to focus world opinion on U.S. recalcitrance and embarrass the United States. Later, when Panamanian nationalists threatened to march into the zone and take control, Torrijos stated that if an angry mob marched on the zone he would lead it.[6] Serious negotiations then began, resulting in the joint "Statement of Principles" by Panamanian Foreign Minister Juan Antonio Tack and Secretary of State Henry Kissinger in February 1974.

Panama wanted more than Washington was willing to concede. By the Kissinger-Tack understanding, the United States agreed to a new treaty with a fixed termination date, to return the zone to Panama in stages, to give the United States specified rights to operate and defend the canal in conjunction with Panama during the life of treaty, and to guarantee that Panama would get a fair and equitable share of revenues. By March 1975 however, the two nations were deadlocked, for Panama refused to give the United States a forty- or fifty-year lease on military bases, to allow the United States to occupy as much territory as it wanted, or to allow the U.S. control of the canal to last as long as the Americans wanted.[7] Panama demanded complete control over the canal by the year 2000 and equal pay for equal work in the Canal Zone. The average Panamanian wage was $3,000 yearly while that of U.S. administrative personnel was over $12,000 and of U.S. manual workers, over $9,000. Panama demanded full control over police-fire protection and health and sanitation, and that the United States retain only the 4% of the zone's land that was used by the canal itself, and retain land sufficient for only three military installations.

By the mid-1970s, technological change had gradually made the canal less important. It and the zone no longer had as much economic and strategic importance, for the development of a two-ocean navy, nuclear submarines and carriers, long-range bombers and missiles reduced, if not eliminated, the canal's strategic importance and the necessity of maintaining military bases there. Further, the development of excellent ground transportation within the United States and the construction of gigantic ships reduced the commercial importance of the canal; by the 1960s, approximately 80% of the canal's traffic was Latin American. By 1975, only 16% of total U.S. import and export tonnage passed through the canal; in monetary terms, only 8%. The canal influenced less than 1% of the U.S. GNP.[8]

Moreover, Torrijos, unlike previous Panamanian leaders, saw the end of U.S. colonialism as the necessary centerpiece of his efforts to transform Panama into an independent, modern state, and he had both the popular support and National Guard muscle to implement his goals. Further, he supported the United States on other issues to demonstrate that Panama was a reliable ally. Even so, Torrijos had to tread lightly through the quagmire of Panamanian and U.S. politics. Domestic troubles mounted when the Panamanian economy ceased growing, the Guard showed signs of restiveness, and leftists criticized the proposed treaties as being too favorable to the United States, especially for granting too much military power to Washington. Ronald Reagan, in an effort to wrest the Republican presidential nomination from President Gerald Ford, made an issue of the proposed treaties, falsely asserting that the zone was sovereign U.S. territory. Torrijos patiently awaited the results of the U.S. election before pressing for consummating the negotiations.

Once Carter defeated Ford for the U.S. presidency, Torrijos successfully launched a well-financed campaign to convince the U.S. Senate to ratify the two treaties, signed in 1977. A U.S. public relations firm was hired to bombard

key Americans with pro-treaties propaganda, ranging from
published statements by military men, church leaders,
academics, and prominent political figures to speaking tours
by pro-treaties advocates. Throughout the campaign, Panama
and its friends insisted that Panama be allowed to achieve its
own destiny without U.S. interference. As Panamanian Foreign
Minister Gonzalez Revilla put it:

> It is very wise to bear in mind that the problem is
> one of abolishing a colonial enclave which in the
> three quarters of a century of its existence has
> imposed discriminatory practices, unequivocally
> prejudicial to human rights...[9]

Panamanians were alarmed by the De Concini Amendment to
the Neutrality Treaty, for it seemed to vitiate Panamanian
efforts to gain complete control over Panama. The amendment
gave the United States or Panama the right to act
independently of the other nation, restricted only by each
nation's constitutional requirements, to intervene militarily
to reopen the canal if it were closed or to insure its
operations if they were blocked. The Panamanian Independent
Lawyers Movement argued that the amendment was reproachable
and clearly gave the United States the right to intervene in
affairs that were solely of concern to Panamanians. Torrijos
complained to the United Nations,[10] and Panamanian students
took to the streets to protest the amendment. The issue
seemed resolved by a Senate resolution accompanying the
ratification which asserted that the De Concini amendment
"will not be interpreted as a right of intervention in the
internal affairs of the Republic of Panama nor of interference
in its political independence nor the integrity of its
sovereignty."[11]
    When the treaties were finally ratified in 1978,
Panamanians rejoiced, believing that they had finally achieved
full nationhood. They had accepted the original treaties by
a 506,927-245,112 vote in a national plebescite in October
1977, and the United States had weakened the De Concini
Amendment.[12] Such was not the case. Panamanians believed that
the Treaty Concerning the Permanent Neutrality and Operation
of the Panama Canal would mean that the United States would
no longer intervene militarily in Panamanian domestic
politics. In Article II both nations agreed that the canal
would be open to peaceful transit in times of peace and war,
and in Article IV stipulated that both the United States and
Panama agreed "to maintain the regime of neutrality
established in this Treaty." Each nation, on its own accord,
was permitted to take military action to prevent the closure
of the canal. When doubt arose as to what this meant in terms
of U.S. intervention in Panamanian internal affairs, Panama
obtained a joint statement of interpretation, a codicil to the
Neutrality Treaty, which asserted that "however, the United
States would not have the right, nor would it intend, to
intervene in the political processes or internal affairs of

Panama."[13] To Panamanians, this U.S. promise was co-equal with the return of the Zone to full Panamanian control.

Thoughtful Panamanians, however, openly criticized the new treaties for maintaining U.S. hegemony over Panama. To them, the Neutrality Treaty guaranteed neither Panamanian independence and neutrality nor the neutrality of the canal. The United States had asserted that the canal could not be defended militarily; yet, the treaties allowed Washington, at its own discretion, to maintain and utilize troops in Panama, and to do so even after the canal became wholly Panamanian in 2000. If the canal was militarily indefensible, no troops need be stationed in Panama; the presence of U.S. troops, instead, provided a constant threat to Panamanian sovereignty, served only the geopolitical interests of the United States, and invited attacks on Panama in time of war. What the canal needed, instead, was a strong, well-trained police force to protect it against sabotage. Instead, the United States had militarized Panama.[14]

To most Panamanians, however, the treaties were a national political victory that removed the principal irritant between the two nations. Panama was slowly but surely regaining control of its national territory, a process to be completed at midnight, December 31, 1999. The United States had agreed to cease military interventions in Panamanian domestic affairs. Panama insisted that the School of the Americas leave Panama, and it did in 1984. The United States quietly watched but did not intervene as Panamanian politicians used coups, elections, and vote fraud to gain power after Torrijos died in an airplane crash in 1981.

Former National Guard intelligence chief Manual Antonio Noriega emerged as the new Panamanian strongman in 1983. He reorganized all the nation's public security forces into the Panamanian Defense Forces (PDF), which he headed, thus insuring his personal control of the nation. Further, he justified enlarging the PDF on the grounds that it was necessary to protect the canal.[15] Presidents came and went, their tenure dependent upon their favor with Noriega. Noriega, like Torrijos, propagandized Panamanians that the military regime was under a "Pentagon umbrella."[16] He worked closely with U.S. agencies such as the Drug Enforcement Administration, Department of Defense, Central Intelligence Agency, and White House, supplying intelligence data to the United States and allowing Panamanian territory to be used by Americans and the Nicaraguan Contras as a base for the U.S. anti-Nicaragua policy. Noriega also conveniently ignored the fact that the presence of SOUTHCOM, with its mission of being the U.S. military command for Latin America, violated the treaties, for its purpose was explicitly more than the defense of the canal.

Some Panamanians expressed concern over such a policy,[17] but Noriega deflected much of this opposition with active Panamanian participation in the Contadora group, which opposed Washington's policy in El Salvador and Nicaragua. When a Panamanian nationalist immolated himself in front of the U.S.

Embassy in January 1984 to protest U.S. violations of the
treaties and its Central American policies, Panama's National
Legislative Council declared him a national martyr,[18] but did
little else.   In return for Noriega's support of the most
important U.S. policies, the United States ignored the
increasing brutality of his regime and its involvement in such
unsavory activities as drug trafficking and money laundering.

Noriega's special relationship with the United States and
his nefarious activities became widely-known in Panama in the
mid-1980s, converting perceptions of him from being a
nationalist hero to a thug dictator. Panamanians increasingly
became disenchanted, led by Noriega's most vocal critic, Dr.
Hugo Spadafora. Panamanians were shocked when Spadafora's
decapitated body was found just inside Costa Rica in September
1985, for such political violence was uncharacteristic of
Panamanian politics. The United States suddenly suspended
five million dollars in aid, and in 1986, relations between
the two nations deteriorated further.   Noriega refused
permission to the United States to train Contras in the zone.
Reports began circulating that he was providing aid to the
Soviet Union, Cuba and Nicaragua.   U.S. officials began
charging Noriega with substantive involvement in illicit drug
trafficking, money laundering, and arms trading.

Panamanian-U.S. relations worsened in 1987. In June,
retired Colonel Roberto Diaz claimed that Noriega had rigged
the 1984 presidential elections, ordered Spadafora's murder,
and engineered Torrijos' death. The revelations touched off
riots, and Panamanians attacked the U.S. Embassy with rocks
and paint to protest U.S. support of Noriega. The revelations
prompted the formation of the anti-Noriega National Civic
Crusade.   The U.S. Senate passed a resolution calling for
Noriega's resignation, and the Reagan administration suspended
military and economic aid, amidst charges by U.S. officials
that Noriega was an active participant in the drug trade.
Noriega clamped down on domestic opposition while marshalling
his forces to protest the American actions. The Panamanian
Legislative Assembly demanded the expulsion of the U.S.
ambassador and accused the United States of interventionist
aggression. About 500 demonstrators attacked the U.S. Embassy
and Consulate as well as American business establishments in
Panama City. Noriega obtained an Organization of American
States' resolution accusing the United States of unwarranted
intervention in Panamanian affairs. A summer 1987 Gallup poll
indicated that 75% of Panama's urban population wanted Noriega
to step down, and a July 1987 nationwide strike indicated that
rural areas had also quit supporting Noriega. Washington
suspended all military and economic aid.

Although the National Civic Crusade stepped up its
efforts to reduce or eliminate Noriega's power, Washington
inadvertently strengthened Noriega by allowing him to wrap
himself in the Panamanian flag. After two U.S. grand juries
indicted him as a drug trafficker in February 1988, Noriega
argued that "this is simply another aggression against Panama
by the United States."[19]

The U.S. Senate also branded Noriega as a drug trafficker.[20] Encouraged by the United States, President Eric A. Delvalle, who had been put into office by Noriega under dubious circumstances, ordered Noriega's dismissal as commander of the PDF but the Noriega-controlled Legislative Assembly dismissed Delvalle and appointed a pro-Noriega man as acting president. Washington continued to recognize Delvalle as the legitimate Panamanian president, however, and stepped up economic and diplomatic pressure on Panama. Noriega easily suppressed a March coup attempt by police chief Colonel Leonidas Macias. The Panamanian Roman Catholic Church, Panamanian civilian employees of the canal and U.S. military facilities, and many Panamanian opposition leaders opposed Washington's tactics. In early April 1988, the anti-Noriegan Authentic Panamanian (PPA) and Popular Action (PAP) parties opposed the U.S. policy of working to remove Noriega and stressed a national, popular solution. Roberto Eisenmann, an opposition leader living in Miami, explained that "we felt [U.S. officials] were giving away the store. Unfortunately, they were giving away our store."[21]

The U.S. government realized that it had to turn Panamanian public opinion against Noriega if it wanted to avoid further arousing Panamanian nationalism and pursued a dual policy to oust Noriega. The National Civic Crusade, which many saw as a U.S.-front organization, supported the sanctions, and worked closely with the Reagan administration to bring down Noriega. The Crusade demonstrated in the streets against the dictator, who responded with violent repression. Publicly, Congress held numerous hearings to publicize Noriega's involvement in drug trafficking and supported Executive Branch decisions to levy economic sanctions against Panama. Noriega, for his part, helped turn opinion against himself by publicly suppressing his domestic opposition with tough measures. Out of the public spotlight, administration officials tried to convince Noriega to leave voluntarily while also conducting psychological operations to weaken his support inside Panama. Reports that Noriega was seeking the active support of Fidel Castro, importing leftist guerrillas, and suffering from mental instability appeared in the Panamanian and U.S. media. Noriega, in fact, was seeking support from the Latin American left to counter U.S. pressure but, in doing so, he further alienated Panamanian nationalists, who wanted no foreign influence in their country. By November 1988, a poll taken in Panama indicated strong opposition to Noriega.

Panamanian public opinion definitively turned against Noriega and in favor of U.S. military intervention when he stole the May 1989 elections and ordered his minions to beat the opposition presidential and vice presidential candidates when they led a massive protest of the electoral fraud. Noriega's newly-constituted Dignity Battalions had overstepped the bounds of acceptable Panamanian political practice, and had done so in front of the international media. The Panamanian Roman Catholic Church denounced the regime for the fraud and violence, calling for Panamanians to withdraw their support of the dictator. The United States recognized the victory of opposition leader Guillermo Endara. Panamanians openly began suggesting that either a military coup or U.S. military intervention might be the only way to oust the dictator.

Elements of the Panamanian Defense Force failed to overthrow Noriega in October 1989. Noriega executed the ringleaders and reorganized the PDF to insure its loyalty. He also sought to neutralize other dissidents, some of whom fled to the zone and U.S. protection. The thug dictator seemed invincible. Elections, Organization of American States diplomacy, and an attempted military coup had all failed. Noriega was tightening his grip on the nation, strangling it for his personal ends. In December 1989, Noriega, growing bolder by his seeming ability to act with impunity, harassed U.S. personnel and had the national assembly assert that Panama and the United States were in a virtual state of war. For both the average Panamanian and for Washington, Noriega had gone too far.

Confronted with this intolerable situation, Panamanians welcomed Operation Just Cause even though U.S. military intervention did not meet the strict guidelines of the neutrality treaty. The only legal grounds for U.S. intervention are to prevent closure of the canal; the U.S. had specifically signed away all other rights to intervene. Noriega had not threatened to close the canal. By closing the canal during the invasion (the only time it has ever been closed), the United States gave the Panamanian government the right, under both Panamanian and U.S. law, to resist by military means. This issue was clouded, however, by the problem of which was the legitimate government of Panama.

Regardless of the legality or illegality of Operation Just Cause, Panamanians initially, at least, supported the invasion, the capture of Noriega,[22] and the installation of Guillermo Endara as the new president of the republic. By December 20, 1989, Panamanians had so despaired of ridding themselves of the tyrannical dictator that even usurpation of their nation's sovereignty seemed preferable to his continuance in power. Such a euphoric response was unlikely to endure, however, and more thoughtful Panamanians realized that not much had changed in U.S.-Panamanian relations since 1903, and the relationship between the two nations remained as unequal as it had been then.

Washington could and did manipulate the Panamanian economy at will even though doing so caused suffering for innocent Panamanians. Endara was as much a part of the U.S. colonial system as former presidents had been. In the disputed election of May 1989, he had benefitted from the expenditure of millions of dollars in U.S. funds. He and his vice president had been sworn into office on a U.S. military base shortly before the invasion and then had to be protected by the U.S. military for several days. While the Panamanian business and professional classes, from which Endara and his vice presidents come, clearly supported the new government, Endara's government had few ties to the majority of Panamanians--farmers, laborers, and the urban middle sectors. U.S. military forces were still the key to power in Panama, treaties notwithstanding. Panamanians realized that the longevity of the Endara government depended upon the U.S. military and U.S. economic aid. In short, Panama was a client state.

NOTES

1. Ricaurte Soler, <u>Pensamiento Panameno y Concepcion de la Nacionalidad durante el Siglo XIX</u> (Panama: Libreria Cultural Panameno, 1971), pp. 99-100.

2. Miguel Antonio Bernal, <u>Los tratados Carter-Torrijos: una traicion historica</u>, 2nd ed. (Panama: Edicones Nari, 1985), 34-35; and E. Bradford Burns, "Panama: A Search for Independence," <u>Current History</u> (February, 1977): 67.

3. Walter LaFeber, <u>The Panama Canal: The Crisis in Historical Perspective</u> (New York: Oxford University Press, 1978).

4. Daniel Goldrich, <u>Sons of the Establishment: Elite Youths in Panama and Costa Rica</u> (Chicago: Rand McNally, 1966).

5. LaFeber, pp. 147-148.

6. Ibid., p. 184.

7. "The Panama Canal: Old Myths and New Realities," <u>The Defense Monitor</u> (August 1976): 1-8.

8. Ibid.

9. Nicolas Gonzalez Revilla, Panamanian Minister of Foreign Affairs, Statement to the General Assembly, Organization of American States, June 15, 1977, published as United Nations, General Assembly circular #77-12182. See also, Marcos G. McGrath, C.S.C. (Archbishop of Panama), "The Panama Canal: A Test Case," in <u>The Panama Canal and Social Justice</u>, edited by Margaret D. Wilde (Washington: United States Catholic Conference, 1976), pp. 5-11.

10. J. Conte-Porras, <u>Del tratado Hay-Bunau-Varilla a los tratados Torrijos-Carter</u> (Panama: Biblioteca Jose Agustin Arango Ch., 1981), pp. 144-46. See G. Harvey Summ and Tom Kelly, eds., <u>The Good Neighbors: America, Panama, and the 1977 Canal Treaties</u> (Athens: Ohio University Center for International Studies, 1988) for an excellent account of the negotiation and ratification processes and Panamanian reactions to them.

11. Conte-Porras, p. 155.

12. Ibid., p. 142.

13. See Amendment (a,1) to the Neutrality Treaty, found in _Instrumento de Ratificacion de la Republica de Panama del Tratado Concerniente a la Neutralidad Permanente del Canal y al Funcionamiento del Canal de Panama_, and United States Department of State, _The Defense and Neutrality of the Panama Canal Under the New Treaties_. Special Report No. 37. (Washington: Bureau of Public Affairs, Department of State, 1977), p. 3.

14. Carlos Bolivar Pedreschi, "Las enmiendas y la intervencion norteamericana en Panama," _Matutino_, March 30, 1978, reprinted in Carlos Bolivar Pedreschi, _De la proteccion del Canal a la militarizacion del pais_ (Panama, 1987); and Bernal, pp. 76-78.

15. See Carlos Bolivar Pedreschi, "Carta sobre la Ley Organica de las Fuerzas de Defensa," October 21, 1983, reprinted in Pedreschi, _De la proteccion del Canal_, pp. 65-69. Pedreschi, one of Panama's most distinguished jurists, argues that the creation of the PDF was unconstitutional.

16. David Norman Miller, "Panama and U.S. Policy," _Global Affairs_ (Summer 1989), 136.

17. See Pedreschi, _De la proteccion del Canal_, 53-56.

18. _La Prensa_ (Panama), January 12, 1984.

19. Nancy Cooper, et al., "Drugs, Money and Death," _Newsweek_ (February 15, 1988): 32.

20. United States, Senate, Committee on Foreign Relations, _Drugs, Law Enforcement, and Foreign Policy: Panama_. Hearings before the Subcommittee on Terrorism, Narcotics, and International Communications, United States Senate, 100th Congress, 2nd sess., 1988; and United States, Senate, Committee on Foreign Relations, _Drugs, Law Enforcement, and Foreign Policy: The Cartel, Haiti and Central America_. Hearings before the Subcommittee on Terrorism, Narcotics, and International Communications, United States Senate, 100th Congress, 2nd sess., 1988.

21. Tom Morgenthau, et al., "Anatomy of a Fiasco," _Newsweek_ (June 6, 1988): 39.

22. See the Washington Post, December 27, 1989, for examples of Panamanian attitudes. Panamanian Archbishop Marcos McGrath, as quoted in _MacLean's_ (January 8, 1990): 17, said that he feared that a free Noriega would stir up trouble again.

2   When All the Old Bills Came Due: The Development of U.S.-Panamanian Relations Through 1989

From 1903, when the United States fostered Panama's independence from Colombia, to the end of 1989, the United States and Panama maintained a special, if unequal, relationship focused on a canal that lay entirely in Panamanian territory, but had been built and remained controlled by the United States. For Panama, the central issue in this relationship was to gain control of the Canal Zone, and, as drug trafficking in the hemisphere became a major concern in the 1970s, it became a second issue in Panama's relations with the United States. For its part, the United States had three major concerns, the foremost being the security of the canal. A second and related issue, spurred on by Castro's accession to power in Cuba, the later rise of a communist government in Nicaragua, and the Cuban presence in Grenada, was the stability of the entire Central American-Caribbean region. Finally, Panama's role in international drug trafficking became a third critical issue. In 1989, these issues came together to set the stage for Operation Just Cause.

THE HISTORICAL CONTEXT

To early Spanish explorers it must have seemed like an oversight of nature. With ships plying both the Atlantic and Pacific oceans to bring home riches, Spain's path between these oceans was blocked by a small thirty-mile strip of land, the Isthmus of Panama. For the Spanish, Panama would remain little more than a barrier to trade as long as they held the isthmus, since trade was the core of the Spanish imperial experience. Here the object of acquiring foreign possessions was to extract as much wealth as possible, and unlike the British colonies where a sizeable influx of settlers often produced middle class societies, the Spanish colonies attracted few permanent settlers. The result in New Spain would be a society in which most of the land and economic and political power remained concentrated in the hands of a Spanish minority, while the larger segment of the population was kept poor, landless, and politically insignificant. These two factors--its physical position as a barrier to inter-ocean trade, and the concentration of wealth and power in a minority of the population--would continue to shape Panama's development long after the end of Spanish rule in 1821.

Building a canal across Panama was considered as early as 1524, when Charles V of Spain ordered a canal route to be surveyed, but the project was abandoned, and until 1914, inter-ocean commerce was done overland across Panama.[1]

The other prominent factor of Panamanian history--the concentration of wealth and power in the hands of an oligarchy--would also persist into modern times. When Spanish rule ended in 1821 and Panama became part of Colombia, little changed for most of the population. Similarly, while the sharp rise in transits across Panama during the American gold rush brought increased wealth to those controlling the coastal port facilities and the railroad across the isthmus, these benefits were realized by only a few. Thus, Panama remained largely a barrier to be crossed, with little reason for travellers to linger en route. Although a French company attempted to build a canal across Panama in 1880, under Ferdinand de Lesseps of Suez Canal fame, the venture failed after twenty years of effort.[2]

While life for most Panamanians at the beginning of the twentieth century was much the same as it had been under Spanish rule, major changes would soon occur because of U.S. involvement. Alfred Thayer Mahan's book, The Interests of America in Sea Power, Present and Future, released in 1897, helped to focus the attention of a small but influential group of Americans, including Teddy Roosevelt, on a role for the United States in world politics. Shortly thereafter, that role was expanded considerably as a result of the U.S. victory in the Spanish-American War, which gave the United States territorial responsibilities in Cuba, Puerto Rico, and the Philippines. During Roosevelt's administration, the United States was frequently involved in Caribbean and Central American affairs. This conformed to his "corollary" to the Monroe Doctrine, which argued that since the Monroe Doctrine prevented European powers from intervening in the hemisphere, in cases where regional nations were unwilling or unable to correct flagrant wrongdoing, the United States "however reluctantly" might intervene.[3]

The United States intervened frequently under this concept, creating a legacy of hostility toward such interference that continues to influence U.S. hemispheric relations today. Of all such involvements, the one that had the broadest effects was the U.S. role in creating the nation of Panama and building the Panama Canal. While the two were intimately connected, they remained distinct, with consequences that would not completely emerge until the 1960s.

It began when the United States, in a period of expansion and concerned over its growing interests in two oceans, turned its attention to Panama. Negotiations with Colombia for a right-of-way ended in the Hay-Herran Treaty of 1903, which gave the United States a six-mile canal zone at a very modest fee. Political opposition in Colombia defeated the treaty but a revolution in Panama supported by U.S. interests helped to reopen the negotiations. In November, Panama declared its independence from Colombia, a U.S. naval ship deterred Colombian reaction, and the United States recognized the new nation. Negotiations for a new treaty took two weeks during which Panama was not even represented by one of its own citizens, but by a Frenchman from the earlier canal company. For $10 million and an annual rent of $250,000, the United States received complete control of a ten-mile canal zone through the isthmus. This zone cut the new nation in two, but Panama was in no position to argue. Building the Panama Canal took until 1914 and $387 million, but a canal connecting the Atlantic and Pacific oceans finally became a reality and a U.S. enclave bisected Panama.[4]

When the SS <u>Ancon</u> passed through the canal officially opening the waterway in August 1914, the route was an engineering marvel. Its construction had involved the largest earthen dam, canal locks, and gates ever built. U.S. pride in this achievement was tremendous and U.S. identification with the canal was so strong that even in 1976, when Ronald Reagan sought the Republican nomination for president, his statement of U.S. control of the canal was unequivocal.[5] The canal became an important feature of world commerce and defense of its approaches was an important element in Mahan's concept of U.S. sea power projection.

While the canal was a very great achievement and its importance to U.S. strategy and commerce was vital, it had one major vulnerability--it was immovably fixed in Panama. Over time, the new nation occupying the land left over on both sides of the Canal Zone developed a society of its own. Although this Panamanian society shared its historical development with the U.S.-controlled Canal Zone, Panama was treated as a very junior partner. The long-term interests of the two nations moved progressively further apart until, in 1989, the United States invaded Panama to ensure the security of the canal and to reestablish a democratic government. In the interim, unable to take its canal and go home, and unwilling to annex all of Panama, the United States concentrated on the affairs of the Canal Zone. U.S. policy toward the Panama that grew up on both sides of that zone was one of accommodation and benign neglect until, by 1989, a military dictatorship that had developed had become an intolerable threat to U.S. and Panamanian interests.

THE ISSUE OF THE CANAL'S SECURITY

Throughout the seventy-five years of U.S. administration of the Canal Zone, there were two Panamas. The Panama of the Canal Zone was a peaceful, prosperous world where life revolved around the canal's operations. U.S. laws prevailed and an American population of "Zonians" enjoyed many facilities, such as commissaries, that were restricted or denied to Panamanian employees until 1958. The other Panama, replete with governmental corruption and military coups, was largely ignored by the United States as long as it did not endanger the canal.[6]

Trade through the canal continued to grow until by the late-1980s some 12,000 ships passed through it annually. World War II emphasized its strategic significance for the U.S. Navy's worldwide operations, and at the height of the Vietnam War in 1968, more than 1,500 ships passed through the canal carrying troops and supplies. Because it was a major sea line of communication, the system of bases to defend the canal and U.S. concern for the security of its approaches increased steadily. Even when supertankers and the largest aircraft carriers grew beyond the canal's capacity, it still could accommodate New Jersey-class battleships.[7] While the United States viewed the canal as an important military and commercial asset, across the zone's boundaries, movements by Panamanian nationalists to end the U.S. administration of the zone began to surface in the 1930s.

Over the first fifty years of the canal's operations, a prosperous middle class Panamanian trading society developed and Panamanian resentment over the inequities between the two Panamas grew steadily. The first major U.S.-Panamanian clash occurred in 1964, in which the United States acceded to Panamanian demands that the Panamanian flag be flown in the Canal Zone. An attempt by several hundred Panamanian students to raise their flag at the zone's Balboa High School was met by a large crowd of Zonians determined to maintain the U.S. ascendancy in the zone. When the Panamanian flag was torn down it touched off four days of rioting, the worst clash up to that time. U.S. troops were used to control the rioting, which ended with 21 Panamanians and 3 U.S. soldiers dead, and as many as 300 Panamanians and 150 Americans injured. The Johnson administration's approach to the crisis was to initiate negotiations for a new canal treaty. To improve its negotiating position, Washington announced that it might build a new sea level canal in Nicaragua, which would greatly reduce the commercial value of the existing canal.[8]

Although negotiations did occur, the Johnson administration was preoccupied with the Vietnam War and domestic problems and no serious progress was made. Meanwhile, Panama changed leaders in the presidential elections of May 1968, when Arnulfo Arias Madrid, a nationalist leader, was elected president. Arias, however, was promptly ousted by Lieutenant Colonel Omar Torrijos. For the United States, concerned about the vulnerability of the canal, the coup seemed to improve the prospects for security considerably. As Jack Hood Vaughn, President Johnson's ambassador to Panama recalled, "the feeling at the time was that a deal cut with a military government would be much more to our liking than one with a democratic but hostile civilian government with Arnulfo [Arias] at its head."[9] Similarly, the editor and publisher of a leading Panamanian newspaper, La Prensa, J. Roberto Eisenmann, Jr., observed, "the American attitude in 1968 was that now we do not have to go through all that congressional nonsense in Panama."[10] However, Torrijos would prove to be a formidable champion of Panamanian sovereignty.

THE REGIONAL SECURITY ISSUE

Omar Torrijos, head of the Panamanian National Guard (later the Panamanian Defense Forces) was closely associated with the U.S. administration. During the 1968 coup he had reportedly taken refuge in the home of a U.S. military officer in the Canal Zone.[11] To a U.S. government concerned with the spread of communism from Castro's Cuba, the Torrijos regime was a hopeful development. He was anticommunist and, while there were problems with corruption in his military regime, U.S. officials were confident that, in time, the military would relinquish control to a civilian government acceptable and indebted to the United States.

But Torrijos proved to be an able and aggressive opponent. He came to power determined to recover control of the Canal Zone and played a skillful game of balancing his advantages as head of a sovereign state with his role as beneficiary of a special relationship with the United States. Sovereignty and strong domestic support allowed him to play the role not only of champion of Panamanian rights, but of Third World leader as well, boldly pushing his demands for the transfer of the Canal Zone. At the same time, he sheltered Panama against any aggressive intentions from Cuba behind his attachment to the United States.

When the treaty negotiations held in 1971-1972 showed little progress, Torrijos took the offensive in a successful bid for a U.N. Security Council meeting to be held in Panama City to discuss the "problems of colonialism and dangers to peace in Latin America." The U.S. Ambassador to the United Nations, George Bush, fought the idea vigorously, but to no avail.[12] The embarrassment that the United States suffered at this meeting, held in 1973, prompted new attention from the Nixon administration. Shortly after the Security Council session, President Richard Nixon said:

> For the past nine years, efforts to work out a new treaty acceptable to both parties have failed. That failure has put considerable strain on our relations with Panama. It is time for both parties to take a fresh look at this problem to develop a new relationship between us--one that will guarantee continued effective operation of the Canal while meeting Panama's legitimate aspirations.[13]

The negotiations under this new mandate had made some progress by 1976, but faltered over the issue of how long the United States would control the Canal Zone and the problem of the canal's defense. When the canal's stewardship became a partisan issue in the U.S. presidential election of 1976, highlighted by Ronald Reagan's statement of keeping "our" canal, progress halted to await the next administration's policies.

Throughout the Nixon and Ford administrations, Torrijos followed a two-tiered approach in his relations with the

United States.   He maintained the tempo of demonstrations
against the U.S. presence to strengthen Panama's position in
the negotiations. At the same time, he actively assisted U.S.
intelligence, and through his regime the United States was
able to obtain extensive information both about events in
Panama and in many other nations in the region. Panama also
became a base of operations for a wide range of U.S.
intelligence gathering operations, and the principal U.S.
contact in the Torrijos regime was a long-time Torrijos
intimate, Panama Defense Forces' G-2 (Chief of Intelligence)
Manuel Antonio Noriega.

       To some observers the apparent contradictions of U.S.-
Panamanian relations during the Nixon and Ford administrations
suggested a fairly simple scenario. The United States was not
averse to an increased share of control over the Canal Zone
for Panama as long as the canal and U.S. investments remained
secure, and U.S. intelligence gathering and regional security
operations in Panama were not disrupted.   On the Panamanian
side, Torrijos realized the economic and security value of the
U.S. presence in the Canal Zone. Although he might be forced
to take a strongly independent public stand, he was firmly on
the U.S. side. This was reflected in the increasing value of
the intelligence either provided secretly to the United States
through Noriega,   or   gathered through   U.S.   intelligence
activities based in the Canal Zone, which Torrijos discretely
ignored.   Thus it appeared that the best interests of the
United States would be served by accepting: the extreme
vulnerability of the canal if confronted by a hostile Panama;
the potential benefits of negotiating a new but still
favorable treaty regarding the canal and Canal Zone; and in
view of Panama's immense importance to U.S. regional and world
strategy,   the   greater   good   of   tolerating   annoying   but
acceptable displays of Panamanian independence that appeared
to be the price of continued Panamanian cooperation.   In
reality, the price would be considerably higher and a number
of extra items would appear on the final bill.

PANAMA'S ROLE IN INTERNATIONAL DRUG TRAFFICKING

       Against this background, the third major issue in U.S.-
Panamanian relations--Panama's role in international drug
trafficking--slowly came into focus in the 1980s.   The
association of prominent Panamanians with drug trafficking was
not completely new, since corruption in the Panamanian
military and government was systemic, involving many leading
officials and their families. Among these was Manuel Noriega.
       The drug trafficking issue was so closely interwoven with
the canal's security and regional stability that, for years,
none of the issues could be understood fully without reference
to the others, since an aggressive, opportunistic military
government was willing to deal with all sides at once and to
exploit neglect at every opportunity.
       Torrijos and Noriega became associated with drug
trafficking when the problem of Latin American drugs was still

the U.S. law enforcement issue of the 1970s, vice the national security threat of the 1980s. Floyd Carlson Caceres, once Noriega's personal pilot, told a U.S. Congressional Committee in 1987 that, "Panama's problems were the result of the military coup [of 1968]." He said that, starting with Torrijos, ties to drug traffickers had been formed to obtain financing and foreign friends.[14] Ambassador Vaughn, U.S. Ambassador to Panama during the Johnson administration, recalled in 1988 that he had known that Torrijos' brother, then Panamanian Ambassador to Spain, was involved in drug trafficking as early as the 1970s. He summarized the activities of the Panamanian military by saying, "From early on we were hearing reports from Panamanian bankers and other knowledgeable people on how the National Guard was moving in relentlessly on all sorts of nefarious businesses from drugs to arms."[15] After President Nixon declared a war on drug trafficking--a war that has been reaffirmed by each succeeding administration--the Panamanian role in drug trafficking might have been expected to have halted or at least to have disrupted the canal treaty negotiations. This, however, was not the case.

In 1971, the Bureau of Narcotics and Dangerous Drugs (BNDD), predecessor of the Drug Enforcement Administration (DEA), lured Joaquin Him Gonzalez, Panama's deputy chief of civil aeronautics and a drug trafficking suspect, into the Canal Zone and arrested him. His apprehension and prosecution proved more challenging than BNDD had anticipated because they had violated a U.S. agreement with the Panamanian government by failing to notify Panama that one of its officials was suspect. The arrest quickly became an international incident, creating divisions within the U.S. government. The State Department was concerned about its adverse impact on the canal negotiations and the Army was concerned over the possibility of rioting in the Canal Zone. The BNDD supervisor of the case later remarked that, "We were pretty naive" and "we had no idea of diplomatic protocol" in describing Gonzalez's arrest.[16]

There were other cases involving Panamanian officials and their families, often with ties leading back to Noriega. Official U.S. complaints were made directly to Torrijos, who promised serious action against drug corruption. Noriega, Torrijos' "man of action," began efforts against drug trafficking that resulted in a long series of U.S. commendations to him. These were described at length in a Panamanian governmental publication released during Noriega's regime entitled, Panama: Sixteen Years of Struggle Against Drug Traffic, that was used as a defense by Panama whenever the subject of corruption arose.

This situation offered little hope for improving drug control in Panama because Noriega was the point of contact for both the U.S. intelligence agencies and drug dealers. In 1976, as the United States conducted intelligence operations against Panama, Noriega, trained in intelligence by the United States, also spied, not only for the Americans, but on them as well.   The U.S. intelligence agencies' concerns over the matter were conveyed to then Director of Central Intelligence, George Bush.[17]

When Jimmy Carter entered the White House in 1977, one of his first acts was to issue Presidential Review Memorandum 1, calling for a quick review of the Panama situation.   He was determined to end what he perceived as an increasingly untenable U.S. hold on the Canal Zone.   Torrijos continued to pressure the Carter administration negotiators, and the issue climaxed on September 7, 1977, when new canal treaties were signed in Washington.   Under them, directorship of the Panama Canal Commission would be assumed by a Panamanian in 1990, and full control of the canal would be assumed by Panama at midnight on December 31, 1999.[18]

The new treaties, though controversial in the United States, increased U.S. prestige in Latin America and defused the Panama problem by providing a definite schedule for the canal's transfer.   Unfortunately, there was no means of peacefully transferring political power in Panama, and Torrijos remained in power, despite some pretenses toward democratization.   He soon began assisting the Nicaraguan opposition movement against Anastasio Somoza, a notorious dictator and one of the strongest supporters of the United States in Central America.   According to Jose de Jesus Martinez, Torrijos had decided as early as 1975 "to convert our country into a rear base for regional revolution and Martinez had personally helped ship arms to the Sandinistas and other Latin American insurgent groups."[19]   Caught between the public and the secret Panama, the United States, as Patricia M. Derian, Carter's head of the State Department's Human Rights Bureau described it, "operated on a see no evil, hear no evil, speak no evil basis."   This had been the case, she said, for twenty years.[20]   Problems in Panama would be minimized by U.S. officials because there were always higher interests, such as the security of the canal and U.S. bases in Panama.   This was reflected by Ambassador Moss, who said:

> Don't forget, no Panamanian official, including Noriega, has ever raised the question of what we do with the bases.... Under the treaty, the bases are there for only one purpose: to defend the Canal. But you don't need a four-star general and 10,000 troops and airplanes coming and going when the canal isn't being attacked by anyone.   So there was a great deal of permissiveness on the part of the Panamanians.[21]

When Ronald Reagan entered the White House in 1981 Torrijos was still following his course of buying U.S. tolerance with carefully measured cooperation.   He greatly enhanced his standing in 1979, for example, by sheltering the deposed Shah of Iran, when sanctuary in the United States became too much of an embarrassment.   But in Reagan's first year in office, the Panamanian situation took a sudden turn for the worse. Torrijos died in a plane crash in July and Noriega began to assume control. It required patience and skill to eclipse the other contenders, but by 1983, he was in full control. In spite of this, Noriega outdid himself. He continued his close relationship with the United States, careful to ensure his continued value to U.S. interests. He arranged assistance for the U.S.-backed Contras, who opposed the Sandinistas that Panama had formerly aided. "He let it be known that the U.S. agenda was his agenda: the U.S. game in Central America was the Nicaraguan war, not Panama, and Noriega recognized a real priority when he saw one."[22]

Noriega came to be seen, for all his unsavory past, as our man in Panama. Unfortunately, there were other problems. The Reagan administration's war on drugs became a major domestic policy issue. Noriega was fighting on both sides, providing assistance in disrupting drug trafficking operations, while making a handsome profit from the drug traffickers who could meet his price. And there were other offenses as well. Noriega and his regime were allegedly involved in money-laundering, alien smuggling, and evading the U.S. embargo on technology sales to communist nations.

Officially, U.S. comment was restrained. The National Narcotics Intelligence Consumers Committee's (NNICC) Narcotics Intelligence Estimate (NIE), the primary U.S. government statement on drug trafficking, did not even mention Panama until 1981. The 1983 NIE speculated that Panama may have surpassed the Cayman Islands as the preferred banking center for cocaine and marijuana profits, but in the 1985-1986 NIE there was still no condemnation of the Panamanian military regime. Rather, it reported that Panama had closed a bank owned by drug traffickers and had seized their assets in 1985.[23]

The brutal slaying of Noriega's rival, Hugo Spadafora, in 1985 was a major turning point. In Panama, the killing was attributed to Noriega, creating an opposition movement against him, and in the United States, anti-Noriega sentiment was aroused. This would combine with factors, including his program of increasingly blatant repression and electoral fraud, his involvement in drug trafficking and money-laundering, and Congressional probes concerning his illicit activities, to turn the United States against him. In February 1988, the United States indicted him for drug trafficking. The final break had come, but the indictment was unsuccessful to the extent that Noriega could not be brought into a U.S. court without resorting to force in Panama and the United States was unwilling to make such a move. Instead, it resorted to economic sanctions. Noriega believed that he had won another victory and his arrogance against the mounting opposition grew rapidly. Panama suffered economically, but Noriega retained power, possibly even strengthened by his successful defiance of U.S. power. The war on drugs, now a priority concern of President Bush, had suffered when it failed to prosecute Noriega after indicting him. It suffered further from the admission that a regime tied closely to the

United States was controlled by a key figure in drug
trafficking. This, coupled with the failure of U.S. pressure
on Colombia to extradite major drug traffickers to the United
States for trial, meant that the war on drugs had faltered
badly by mid-1989. President Bush was determined that Noriega
be removed from power. His participation in drug trafficking
was intolerable, and there was serious concern about the
wisdom of following the treaty timetable for Panama's assuming
control over the canal while Noriega remained in power. His
continued hold on Panama not only endangered Panama's
stability, but that of the region as well.

The initial planning for Just Cause moved ahead.
Whatever concerns there were for the vulnerability of the
canal or the political costs of moving against Noriega, the
continued demonstrations and violence in Panama in 1989
suggested that violence and bloodshed might increase
significantly, posing an even greater threat to the canal.
Through the summer and autumn, it became increasingly evident
that Noriega had no intention of relinquishing power and was
taunting the United States, inviting a confrontation. Despite
the liabilities, the necessity of his removal was obvious.
Equally obvious was the conclusion that such an undertaking
would require more strength than the Panamanian opposition
could provide without significant assistance. The commitment
of U.S. forces under the provisions of the canal treaty
dealing with the defense of the canal was deemed the only
remaining option by the end of 1989.

The United States is a nation of investors. In 1903 it
helped create Panama to achieve one purpose, to obtain a canal
connecting the Atlantic and Pacific oceans. Since then it had
continually found reasons not to resolve the problems
remaining from that first intervention. By 1989, these
included a threat to the stability of the Caribbean and Latin
American region; a threat to discredit the U.S. war on drugs;
and a threat to the continued operation of the canal.
Professor German Munoz summed up the Panama crisis in 1988
with a comment that would be even more applicable to the
situation a year later. "This is not a question of
Republicans or Democrats. They have all blundered, and now
we have to pay for it. The future is here and all the old
bills have suddenly fallen due."[24] On December 17, 1989,
President Bush authorized payment on the accounts, and on
December 19th, Just Cause delivered the first payment.

NOTES

1. Panama Canal Commission, The Panama Canal: Today and
Yesterday (Washington, DC: Panama Canal Commission, n.d.),
p. 2.

2. Ibid.

3. Bernard Bailyn, et. al., The Great Republic, 2d ed.

(Lexington, MA and Toronto, CA: D.C. Heath and Co., 1981),
pp. 704-707, 716-718.

4.   Ibid., pp. 718-719; and Bart McDowell, "The Panama Canal
Today," National Geographic (February 1978):   280-281.

5.   Panama Canal Commission, p. 2. Reagan said of the Canal,
"... we bought it, we paid for it, its ours, and we should
tell Torrijos and company we are going to keep it."   See:
John Dinges, Our Man in Panama (New York: Random House,
1990), p. 80.

6.   McDowell, pp. 282-283, 288.

7.   Panama Canal Commission, p. 2.

8.   Dinges, pp. 75-77.

9.   Larry Rother, "America's Blind Eye: The U.S. for Years
has Ignored Corruption in Panama," The New York Times Magazine
(May 28, 1988):   25.

10.   Ibid.

11.   Ibid., p. 28.

12.   Dinges, pp. 78-79.

13.   Ibid., p. 80.

14.   Rother, p. 26.

15.   Ibid.

16.   Dinges, pp. 53-55.

17.   Ibid., pp. 81-90.

18.   Ibid., p. 95.

19.   Rother, p. 26.

20.   Ibid., pp. 25, 26.

21.   Ibid., p. 29.

22.   Dinges, p. 207.

23. National Narcotics Intelligence Consumers Committee
(NNICC), Narcotics Intelligence Estimate 1983 (Washington, DC:
NNICC, 1983), p. 50; and National Narcotics Intelligence
Consumers Committee (NNICC), Narcotics Intelligence Estimate
1985-1986 (Washington, DC: NNICC, 1986), p. 101.   The
National Narcotics Intelligence Consumers Committee's (NNICC)

<u>Narcotics Intelligence Estimate</u> (NIE) should not be confused with the U.S. Intelligence Community's National Intelligence Estimate, also referred to as an NIE. The NNICC document is an unclassified annual publication. Its title was changed from <u>Narcotics Intelligence Estimate</u> to <u>NNICC Report</u> in 1987.

24. Rother, p. 26.

3   The Role of Drugs in the U.S.-Panamanian Relationship

"This scourge will stop."

George Bush, January 20, 1989

President Bush was not the first U.S. President to wage war on drugs. President Richard M. Nixon declared war on drugs in 1969, and Panama was a front in that war as well.[1] The Joaquin Him Gonzalez case, involving the deputy head of the Panamanian Civil Aviation Authority, and the Rafael Richard/Guillermo Gonzalez case, involving the son of a Panamanian diplomat and his friend, were the opening engagements on this front during the Nixon administration's war. These cases and their consequences raised drugs from a law enforcement issue to a foreign policy priority second only to the status of the Panama Canal in U.S.-Panamanian relations during the early 1970s.

The Him Gonzalez case caused an immediate diplomatic incident.[2] The Richard/Gonzalez case led to Moises Torrijos, the older brother of General Omar Torrijos, and involved heroin smuggling. Moises Torrijos was indicted on narcotics trafficking charges by a federal grand jury in New York in 1972, based in part on the testimony of both Guillermo Gonzalez, his former associate and long-time employee, and Rafael Richard.[3]

These cases were the most dramatic evidence of growing Panamanian involvement in international narcotics trafficking to the United States. What Washington knew of such Panamanian involvement was publicly revealed in the course of the U.S. Senate's debate on ratification of the Panama Canal Treaties in 1978, when the Senate Select Committee on Intelligence reported to the Foreign Relations Committee and the Senate on U.S. knowledge of Panamanian involvement and its policy consequences.[4] During closed Senate sessions on February 21st and 22nd, Senator Birch Bayh, the Chairman of the Senate Select Committee on Intelligence, described the traffic as "voluminous in narcotics through Panama and, indeed, the intelligence information was voluminous."[5] Early in the debate, Bayh said of Manuel Antonio Noriega, "we do not tread lightly on Colonel Noriega."[6]

The Committee's report stated that a Bureau of Narcotics and Dangerous Drugs' (BNDD)[7] informant named Noriega as having "overall operational control" but Bayh cast doubt on the report, saying that the informant was a "political opponent of the Torrijos regime who had been exiled for participating in an unsuccessful coup d'etat attempt against Torrijos," and later that "...as Panama's intelligence chief, Colonel Noriega has sometimes cooperated with and sometimes frustrated U.S. [drug] enforcement efforts."[8] The informant was reportedly Colonel Amado Sanjur, who, as a high-ranking Panamanian National Guard officer, was in a position to know the truth about Noriega.[9]

Panamanian involvement in drug trafficking became a major issue in the U.S.-Panamanian relationship through a series of diplomatic incidents and near-incidents, caused by the Him Gonzales and Moises Torrijos cases. Gonzalez had been lured into the Canal Zone where U.S. BNDD agents arrested him. Following his arrest, he called General Torrijos and Panamanian Foreign Minister Juan Antonio Tack, asking them to free him. Torrijos subsequently appeared on Panamanian television and accused the United States of kidnapping a Panamanian citizen, implying that if Gonzalez were not freed, Panamanian forces would enter the Canal Zone and free him.[10]

In Washington, where the use of the Panama Canal Zone to effect the arrest of a senior Panamanian official had not been previously approved by the White House or State Department, the arrest immediately became a foreign policy issue. The Army and State departments wanted the Justice Department to release Him Gonzalez. Justice, however, stood by the BNDD and Him Gonzalez was flown to the United States, and was subsequently convicted and sentenced to five years in prison. Torrijos did not act on his threat. The incident, however, caused the United States to take notice of events in Panama and consider a solution to the problem. On July 28, 1971, a BNDD operations officer issued a memorandum listing intelligence reports concerning fifteen prominent Panamanians who were involved in drug trafficking. It was presented to a group of National Security Council (NSC) and Central Intelligence Agency (CIA) officials and apparently had a substantial impact on U.S. foreign policy toward Panama.[11]

BNDD Director John Ingersoll presented a second report to the House Committee on the Panama Canal. It concluded that:

> ...it is clear that the Republic of Panama has not and is not paying sufficient attention to narcotic enforcement activities to achieve noticeable results. This may be due to high level apathy, ignorance and/or collusion. Unless the Republic of Panama is sincerely willing to put forth the necessary effort to combat the traffic, the Republic will continue to serve as a conduit through which vast amounts of illicit drugs are funnelled en route to the United States.[12]

Another serious incident occurred when Ingersoll's

testimony was leaked to Jack Anderson and was published in one of his March 1972 columns. It included questionable narcotics trafficking charges against Panamanian Foreign Minister Juan Tack, arising from his signature on Raphael Richard's diplomatic passport. The Panamanian government reacted to this column by expelling all BNDD personnel from Panama. Different BNDD officers, however, were allowed to replace them.[13]

Indicating that U.S. policy was changing, the State Department approved trips by Ingersoll to Panama to discuss U.S. concerns about Panama's drug trafficking role. He met with General Torrijos and received an encouraging response. However, the United States had continued to receive disturbing intelligence about Panama's prominence as a drug transit nation, and did not respond favorably to Torrijos' request that all information about Panamanian officials' involvement in drug trafficking be turned over to him for action, because the United States did not trust him to use it against the traffickers. This was because of Noriega's key position as head of Panamanian military intelligence, known as G-2, and information, including the Sanjur allegations that had been collected indicating Noriega was central to the Panamanian drug trafficking problem.[14]

On January 10, 1972, Ingersoll had an options paper prepared. It was described by Senator Bayh as a "...memorandum of alternatives prepared for BNDD Director Ingersoll as to how effectively to remove a high [Panamanian] National Guard official from the scene."[15] Those familiar with it indicate that "remove" included assassination as an option, and that the high official was Noriega. Apparently the assassination option was discarded early in the decision-making process, but other options were pursued.[16]

Ingersoll made a fourth visit to Panama and informed General Torrijos that a U.S. arrest warrant had been issued for his brother, Moises, for narcotics violations, pursuant to a sealed New York federal grand jury indictment. Such information is ordinarily a closely held secret to aid in the arrest of the suspect. However, the United States had solid evidence that Torrijos sought to create an incident that would portray Washington as infringing on Panamanian sovereignty and the arrest of the General's brother would have been such an incident. The State Department apparently wanted Torrijos to know that it knew what he was planning, so that his brother would not enter U.S. jurisdiction in the Canal Zone. After learning of U.S. intentions, Moises Torrijos debarked from a cruise ship before it called at the Canal Zone, thereby avoiding the trap that U.S. Customs Service agents had set for him. A month later, BNDD agents actually met with him and briefed him on his indictment. It appears that both General Torrijos and Noriega understood that the limits of U.S. tolerance for Panamanian involvement in drug trafficking had been reached. In his discussion of Moises Torrijos, Senator Bayh described the results as follows:[17]

Intelligence on Moises Torrijos continued to come
during 1973. After that, however, with the arrest
of some major traffickers and an increase in U.S.-
Panamanian cooperation--this is the last part of
1973, now--on narcotics control, Panama became less
important as a narcotics transshipment point. By
the beginning of 1976, the CIA had de-emphasized
narcotics as an intelligence priority for Panama.
The Committee has been unable to find any narcotics
intelligence on Moises Torrijos in recent years.[18]

With reference to the plans to remove Noriega, Bayh said:
"[t]he Panamanians may also have known of BNDD efforts to
neutralize the high National Guard officer. Panama responded
both with anger and, eventually, as it turned out, with better
cooperation on narcotics enforcement."[19]

While Panama's--and Noriega's--involvement with drugs was
deemphasized temporarily, Noriega could not stay out of
trouble. He, an allegedly paid "asset" of U.S. intelligence,
became involved in smuggling guns to Nicaraguan Sandinistas
who were struggling against the Somoza dictatorship. U.S. law
enforcement agencies tracked guns purchased in the United
States as they were smuggled into Panama with Noriega's
assistance and wanted to use this as grounds for indicting
him. However, Noriega allegedly reported these shipments to
U.S. intelligence authorities who allegedly intervened with
the Justice Department to forestall his indictment. Noriega's
gun-running scheme involved two pilots, Floyd Carlton and
Cesar Rodriguez, who flew "planes provided by Noriega from
those confiscated from drug traffickers," to smuggle arms in
1978 and 1979.[20]

Meanwhile, Noriega was praised by top U.S. drug
enforcement officials for his cooperation. In a December 14,
1978 letter from Peter B. Bensinger, President Jimmy Carter's
Drug Enforcement Administration (DEA) Administrator, Bensinger
stated that the DEA "...very much appreciates all of the
support and cooperation which you have extended to our agency
during the last year," and extended to Noriega his "...very
best regards for a very happy and successful new year." Such
good relations continued for many years, with the last known
DEA letter to Noriega written by Administrator John C. Lawn
on May 27, 1987, thanking him for his cooperation in Operation
Pisces, a DEA money-laundering enforcement operation. Lawn's
predecessor, Francis M. "Bud" Mullen, Jr., expressed his
gratitude for an autographed Noriega photograph in a March 16,
1984 letter to Noriega, saying that "I have it framed and it
is proudly displayed in my office."[21]

While Noriega had mended his relations with a U.S. agency
that had allegedly once considered assassinating him, he was
presiding over Panama's re-emergence as a Mecca for drug
traffickers and a center for drug money-laundering. A
convicted Medellin Cartel drug money-launderer testified that
he had used Panama as a safe-haven for drug profits generated
by Florida marijuana traffickers from 1976 to 1979, and that

the officers of the Panamanian National Guard knew of the laundering operation and protected it. He also testified that he was recruited in 1979 to handle the profits of what was to become the Medellin Cartel and that in order to do so, he met with Noriega personally and made an agreement in which: the Panamanian National Guard would provide security for the cash shipments and make good any losses if the security failed; the traffickers would receive immediate credit for cash deposited in Panamanian banks; and Noriega would provide the major traffickers with access to Panamanian assets, including diplomatic facilities, pouches, credentials, contacts, and information on U.S. DEA, Customs, and Coast Guard counternarcotics operations.[22]

This deal was apparently the first major indirect contact between the future Medellin Cartel and Noriega. The second, and perhaps the first direct contact, occurred after the November 12, 1981 kidnapping of Marta Nieves Ochoa, the youngest sister of Jorge Ochoa, one of the future cartel's leaders, by M-19, a Colombian left-wing guerrilla group. This abduction caused the cartel's formal creation and produced its first formal act--the formation of a vigilante group called "Muerte a Secuestradores (MAS)," or "Death to Kidnappers," to attack M-19. The MAS was so successful in assaulting M-19 that the guerrilla group sued for peace. Noriega was chosen as the mediator and Panama became the site for talks between M-19 and the Cartel which resulted in peace and the unharmed release of Marta Nieves Ochoa.[23]

Noriega was now firmly in the Cartel's good graces. The events that were to produce his indictment on cocaine smuggling by a federal grand jury in the Southern District of Florida and on marijuana smuggling by another federal grand jury in the Middle District of Florida, both unsealed on February 5, 1988,[24] began to unfold. In June or July 1982, a Medellin Cartel representative contacted Floyd Carlton, offered to introduce him to some very powerful people in Colombia, and asked him to participate in a business deal. Carlton described this critical meeting as follows:

> When I asked him what the business, what the deal was, they said--or they asked me what the individual who had approached me in Panama had offered, and I said, rather, that it was to take the money from the United States to Panama. And they said, "No, that the deal involved carrying cocaine from Colombia to Panama".
> I then told them that I was not interested in that line of business, that I could not do that, and they would have to consult--I would have to consult, rather, with Noriega. And they said, "Go ahead, ask Noriega."[25]

Carlton asked Noriega and received permission to proceed. Noriega allegedly told him:

...well, find out what the deal really consists of and then you can talk to me about it and see if we can go ahead with it, but as usual, I don't know anything about it. Don't use Panamanian aircraft. We don't want to have a case like the case that happened in El Salvador [when Carlton and Rodriguez crashed a Panamanian Air Force-registered plane while flying guns to the guerrillas].[26]

The terms were set and the operation was put into motion. Carlton showed Colombian pilots the Panamanian military airstrips where they were to land when bringing in drugs, and then, flying with them, made four flights, smuggling in more than 400 kilograms of drugs on each flight. He said that the payments to Noriega were $100,000 for the first flight, $150,000 for the second, and $200,000 for the third. Carlton received $400 per kilogram on the basis of 400 kilograms per flight.[27]

Noriega's indictment also described how he facilitated the purchase of a Lear jet for Pablo Escobar's use in flying drug profits from the United States to Panama, supplied Escobar and Gustavo Gaviria with 500 drums of acetone and ether (chemicals that are used in refining cocaine) in early-1984 for $250,000, and facilitated the smuggling of over 322 kilograms of cocaine into the United States aboard the vessel "Krill" in early-1986.[28]

On September 22, 1983, Steven Michael Kalish flew to Panama with approximately $2.5 million to arrange money-laundering services to support his marijuana smuggling into the United States. He met Cesar Rodriguez (Carlton's partner and, in the past, an arms smuggling pilot for Noriega) and Enrique Pretelt, purchased shell corporations and set up bank accounts, and was told that Noriega was their partner in the operation.[29] Kalish described his dealing with Noriega as follows:

The next day, I was taken to General Noriega's private home. I had been instructed to bring a gift for the General--large enough to show how serious I was about doing business in Panama. I placed $300,000 in cash in my briefcase. During a casual conversation with the General that lasted approximately 30 minutes, I discussed my desire to live in Panama and to invest my moneys there. I made it clear at that time that it was my intention to bring extremely large sums of cash to Panama. As the meeting broke up, I left the briefcase in his office and began to exit the room. General Noriega called me back and told me that I had left my briefcase. I told him that it was for him and he smiled.
That night I was invited to a party with the General at the Panama Canal offices. He was extremely friendly, and he told me to continue to deal with

Rodriguez and Pretel [sic] and that he would do whatever he could do to assist me. He also thanked me for the briefcase.[30]

As a result of that relationship, Kalish made Panama his base of operations and grew so close to Noriega that he described him as a "full-scale conspirator in my drug operations."[31] Kalish even played a pivotal role in resolving a crisis in Noriega's relationship with the Medellin Cartel. On May 19, 1984, Panamanian Defense Forces raided a major cocaine factory in Darien Province that would have begun production as soon as it received its "feed stock," the cocaine base. It had been built by the Medellin Cartel, who believed that it was under Panamanian protection, and when it was seized, they were furious.[32] Kalish described the situation as follows:

> General Noriega asked me to contact my sources in Colombia and find out what was going on. I learned from my sources in the Medellin Cartel that a $5 million bribe had been paid to Panamanian officials to protect their operations in Panama. A high-ranking Panamanian official, Colonel Melo, had been bribed. Melo was behind the cocaine lab and ether shipments; he was intending to assassinate Noriega while he was in Europe and seize control of Panama. I passed word of this to Noriega, and Melo, his associates, and the Colombians were arrested immediately. These arrests angered the Colombians and I was caught in the middle.
> I arranged for the release of these Colombians and established my ability to facilitate their business in Panama. The Cartel was looking for a way to continue to launder $50 to $100 million a month produced from its west coast U.S. cocaine operations. My links to Panama made laundering of this volume of money possible. The General embraced the scheme for his percentage, and I began to negotiate with the Medellin Cartel to ship and launder vast amounts of cocaine profits. After these events, Noriega dealt directly with me and asked that I cut out Pretel [sic] and Rodriguez.[33]

Noriega also advanced in the world of Panamanian politics during the early 1980s. General Torrijos died in an airplane crash in Panama on July 30, 1981, and on August 12, 1983, Noriega became the commander of the Panamanian National Guard and de facto ruler of Panama. On of his earliest official acts was to reorganize the Guard and rename it the Panamanian Defense Forces.[34]

However, while Noriega's power waxed in Panama and he returned to past patterns of exploiting illegal activities for personal gain, the world was changing. The growing power of the Medellin Cartel that was bringing him new wealth was based

on profits from the sale of cocaine in the United States. As
U.S. use of cocaine mushroomed, drug purity climbed, the price
declined, and the number of cocaine-related hospital
emergencies soared. Cocaine became the second most popular
drug of choice among criminals, both in terms of drug
dependency and being under the influence of a drug when
committing a crime. These developments had a major affect on
U.S. public opinion and politics. A Gallup Poll noted that
2% of the Americans polled in January 1985 listed drug abuse
as the most important problem facing the nation. This figure
rose to 6% in May 1985, to 8% in July 1986, and to 11% in
August 1987.[35] Concern rose to the point that a Los Angeles
Times poll taken on election day and released on November 8,
1988 had asked the question, "Which issues--if any--were most
important to you in deciding how you would vote today?"
Fourteen percent of the respondents had replied, "drugs."
Concern continued to increase: a Gallup poll released on
November 13, 1989 listed drugs/drug abuse as the choice of 38%
of the respondents for "the most important problem facing this
country today," leading the second place concern,
poverty/hunger/homelessness, by 28%.[36]

It was against this political background that the story
of Noriega's most recent involvement in international drug
trafficking began to unfold in 1985. A reporter for the
Hearst Newspapers, Knut Royce, wrote a series of articles that
appeared in the San Antonio Light and other Hearst papers,
beginning with a piece entitled "Panama a Haven for
Traffickers," published on June 10, 1985.

Then Hugo Spadafora was murdered. A medical doctor, he
was also something of a revolutionary. He had served with
Eden Pastora's (Comandante Zero's) guerrilla unit in the
Nicaraguan revolution, was a friend of Omar Torrijos (who made
him Panama's deputy minister of health), and was an idealist.
He made a fatal mistake when he decided to publicly accuse
Noriega of drug trafficking and claimed that he had proof of
his allegations. Spadafora was kidnapped, tortured horribly,
and beheaded. His headless body was found stuffed in a U.S.
mail sack near the Costa Rican border on September 14, 1985.[37]

Noriega was accused of ordering the Spadafora kidnapping
and murder. There was organized public opposition and the
independent Panamanian newspaper La Prensa published damning
details of the events leading up to the murder. Noriega's
handpicked president, Nicolas Ardito Barletta, felt the
pressure and made ambiguous statements about establishing an
independent commission to investigate Spadafora's murder. On
September 27, 1985, Noriega deposed Barletta and appointed
Eric Arturo Delvalle to replace him.[38]

Entangled in the Barletta ouster was a struggle for power
within the PDF between Noriega and his chief of staff, Colonel
Diaz Herrera. Diaz Herrera planned a "putsch" against
Noriega, who was out of the country when the Spadafora killing
was news. He put his plan in motion, but failed to win the
allegiance of the PDF. Noriega outmaneuvered him, and he
attempted to disguise his coup-related activities as domestic

security measures needed to respond to the unrest over the Spadafora killing. Noriega knew the truth, but took his time responding.[39]

Meanwhile, Leon Kellner in Miami and Robert Merkle in Tampa were building cases against Noriega, interviewing Floyd Carlton and Steven Kalish, both of whom were in federal custody for drug crimes.[40]

On March 10, 1986, the Subcommittee on Western Hemisphere Affairs of the Senate Committee on Foreign Relations held a hearing entitled "The Situation in Panama." During the proceedings, Norman A. Bailey, a former Special Assistant to President Reagan for National Security Affairs testified on Panamanian drug trafficking.[41] He said, "...there is a great deal of information, ranging from very hard to rather soft, concerning the use of Panama as a transhipment place for both illegal drugs as well as arms to various guerrilla movements, both in Central America as well as Colombia and Peru. Much of this...is classified information."[42]

Section 481 of the Foreign Assistance Act of 1961, as amended, requires the President to certify annually that each major illegal drug producing or drug-transit nation cooperated fully with the United States during the prior year or took adequate measures on its own with regard to illegal drug production, trafficking, and money laundering. Section 2005 of the Anti-Drug Abuse Act of 1986 requires that certain types of U.S. foreign assistance be withheld from major drug producing and transit nations pending annual presidential certification.[43] On March 1, 1987, President Reagan certified to Congress that Panama was "fully cooperating." Obliquely addressing press reports of Panamanian official complicity in drug trafficking, the State Department's March 1987 International Narcotics Control Strategy Report (INCSR) stated that "...as in many countries, a certain amount of corruption exists in the public, as well as private, sector. There is no convincing evidence, however, that Panamanian authorities support drug trafficking as a matter of institutional policy." [emphasis added][44]

The Senate responded with a joint resolution disapproving the President's certification of Panama. S.J.Res. 91 was adopted by the Senate on a voice vote on April 3, 1987. Senate report 100-25 to accompany the resolution contained the following additional views of Senators Jesse Helms and John Kerry explaining why the resolution of disapproval was necessary:

> Even casual observers know that the Panama Defense
> Forces (PDF) control the levers of power in Panama.
> Dozens of press accounts over the past year have
> pointed out the role of the PDF and General Noriega
> in drug trafficking and in money laundering.
> Panama--is a major transhipment point for cocaine
> from South America into the United States....
> There are any number of glaring cases which reflect
> corruption at the highest levels of the Panamanian

government and involvement in drug trafficking.
Last year, one of General Noriega's personal pilots
was killed allegedly over a drug deal gone sour.
Two more of his personal pilots are currently in
U.S. jails serving time for involvement in drug
trafficking.[45]

The Senate report continued, listing the cases of Colonel
Julian Melo and Sebastian Gonzales, and the Spadafora killing.
It also referred to a New York Times story by Alan Riding
published two weeks before "...point[ing] out that the top
Colombian drug mafia members meet clandestinely in Panama.
This could only occur with the knowledge and protection of the
Panama Defense Forces."[46] After passing the Senate, S.J.Res.
91 and a companion House measure, H.J.Res. 211, were referred
to the House Committee on Foreign Affairs, from which they
were not reported.
    Senator John Kerry of Massachusetts, abandoning a
fruitless attempt to link the Nicaraguan Contras to drug
trafficking, turned his Subcommittee on Terrorism, Narcotics,
and International Communications of the Senate Foreign
Relations Committee toward the question of Panamanian drug
trafficking, starting a series of hearings in May 1987. These
hearings included testimony from Floyd Carlton and Noriega's
former chief of political intelligence and Panamanian Counsel
General in New York, Jose I. Blandon.[47]
    In June 1987, Noriega's plotting against his chief of
staff, Colonel Diaz Herrera, was in its final phase and became
public. Herrera had been slowly isolated from remaining PDF
support, while Noriega created a ruse of graceful retirement
for Herrera but apparently intended to dishonorably discharge
him from the PDF. Herrera, learning of this, struck back in
the media, giving a television interview and then launching
into a series of interviews and press conferences in which he
charged Noriega with a variety of misdeeds.[48] Herrera

    ...stated that he collaborated with General Noriega
    in engineering the outcome of the 1984 presidential
    elections; that he had evidence demonstrating that
    Noriega directed the...slaying of...Spadafora; that
    Noriega planned the 1981 death of...Omar Torrijos;
    that members of the PDF are involved in
    international drug trafficking, and in the illegal
    sale of visas to Cubans.[49]

The popular opposition to Noriega exploded into the
streets in massive demonstrations that Noriega's security
forces put down with tear gas, beatings, and birdshot. The
U.S. news media, fresh from covering the "People Power"
revolution in the Philippines, rushed to Panama where the
opposition Civic Crusade promised another peaceful revolution.
The living rooms of America saw surging crowds of protesters
waving white cloths and banging on pots and pans rally against
Noriega's continued control over Panama. But they also saw

the PDF's efficient and dangerous use of riot gas, shotguns, and clubs to clear the streets, and they learned about thugs called "Dobermans" and the so-called Dignity Battalions.[50]

The U.S. Senate responded on June 26th by passing Senate Resolution 239 by a vote of 84 to 2, calling for Noriega and other Panamanian officials to step down pending the outcome of an investigation into Herrera's charges of election fraud, criminal activity, and official corruption. Reacting to this, Noriega turned his thugs loose to attack the U.S. Embassy and the U.S. Information Service, doing much damage. In response, U.S. Ambassador Arthur Davis suspended all aid to Panama.[51]

As Panamanian opposition to Noriega continued, the U.S. Senate kept the pressure on the general. On September 24th, by a vote of 97 to 0, the Senate approved an amendment by Senator Dodd to the Department of Defense Authorization Act expressing the sense of the Senate that within 45 days the government of Panama should take the following steps or all U.S. aid would end and Panama's sugar quota would be terminated: (1) return of the PDF to effective civilian control; (2) initiation of an independent investigation into certain illegal acts by the PDF; (3) a civilian transition government not dominated by the military; and (4) restoration of all rights guaranteed in the Panamanian constitution.[52]

On October 22nd, the Senate Foreign Relations Committee held a hearing on S. 1614, a bill introduced on August 6th to prohibit U.S. assistance to Panama unless four conditions very similar to those listed in the Dodd amendment were met. The bill was favorably reported on November 19th, and placed on the Senate calendar.[53] No action was taken on this measure, because the Senate amended the Omnibus Continuing Appropriations Resolution to ban almost all aid to Panama, including funds for joint military exercises. The resolution also directed the United States to vote against Panamanian loan requests before multilateral development banks and prohibited importation of Panamanian sugar. This bar to aid could only be lifted by a Presidential certification that democracy had been restored in Panama. The resolution was signed into law as Public Law 100-102 on December 22, 1987.

On January 28, 1988, the Senate's Permanent Select Committee on Investigations of the Committee on Governmental Affairs held a hearing on "Drugs and Money Laundering in Panama." At the meeting, Steven Michael Kalish told his story of Noriega's involvement in marijuana smuggling, money laundering, and his relationship with the Medellin Cartel. On February 5th, the marijuana- and cocaine-trafficking indictments against Noriega were unsealed in Florida. While the news of the indictments was still current, Senator Kerry's Foreign Relations Subcommittee on Terrorism, Narcotics and International Communications held four days of hearings at which Carlton and Blandon testified.[54]

After the 1987 battle over Presidential certification that Panama was cooperating in U.S. counternarcotics efforts, word reached the Senate that the State Department had again recommended that the President certify Panamanian cooperation in the 1988 report.   Senator Alfonse D'Amato took the Senate floor

> ...to share with my colleagues my total astonishment
> about published reports that indicate that the
> Bureau of Internal Narcotics Matters [of the
> Department of State] has issued a preliminary report
> requesting Panama be certified as having been "fully
> cooperative" with the United States drug
> interdiction efforts.[55]

D'Amato blasted the proposed certification and recited Noriega's drug links. On March 1st, because of two federal indictments of Noriega and the mass of information on the public record concerning high-level Panamanian involvement in drug trafficking, the President did not certify to Congress that Panama was fully cooperating with U.S. counternarcotics efforts.[56] This noncertification was well received by the Senate.

Following President Devalle's February 25th failed attempt to fire Noriega as the PDF Commander and Noriega's replacement of Delvalle with Manuel Solis Palma, the U.S. State Department certified that Delvalle was still recognized by the United States as the legitimate president of Panama. The Panamanian opposition then used this certification in U.S. federal courts to prevent Noriega's government from gaining access to Panamanian assets held by U.S. commercial banks.[57] On March 11th, the White House announced a package of economic sanctions against Panama, suspending trade preferences granted under a Generalized System of Preferences and the Caribbean Basin Initiative, and placing all U.S. payments due to Panama into an escrow account to which President Devalle had access.[58]

At this point, the United States tried to convince Noriega to step down from power and to leave Panama. A negotiating team meet with him, offering him asylum in Spain and a promise of non-extradition.. Noriega became concerned about the drug indictments and wanted them withdrawn before he would accept an agreement. The talks broke down over this issue.[59]

On March 25th, the Senate passed by a vote of 92 to 0 a sense of the Senate resolution, S.Con.Res. 108, that provided that the "United States should act immediately to impose additional diplomatic, political, and economic pressure on General Noriega and should obtain his extradition from Panama."[60] On April 8, 1988, President Reagan issued Executive Order No. 12635, declaring a national emergency with respect to Panama and invoking his authority under the International Emergency Powers Act. Under this order, the Treasury Department issued regulations blocking all property and interests of the Panamanian government under U.S. jurisdiction and prohibiting payments or transfers of currency to Panama. These Panamanian Transaction Regulations were strengthened further on June 3, 1988.[61]

U.S. negotiations with Noriega resumed, this time with

the offer of withdrawing the drug indictments against him. The decision to make this offer was reportedly made by President Reagan. On May 11th, Noriega approved a provisional plan under which he would leave power on August 12th, in return for withdrawing the drug indictments and other inducements. Word of this agreement was leaked, igniting a firestorm of opposition in the Congress and from the prosecutors. Senator D'Amato said "...what you have here is an administration that has set its hair on fire and is trying to put it out with a hammer."[62]

Noriega, however, finally refused to go along with the agreement. He complained that the news leaks had turned his junior officers against him and made it impossible to sell the deal to his supporters in Panama. He may have believed that negotiations would be reopened at a later date, but the Noriega problem had become an issue in the 1988 presidential race and posed a threat to then-Vice President Bush's electoral hopes. Bush saw the threat from renewed negotiations with Noriega involving withdrawing the drug indictments as so severe that he made his position against withdrawing the Noriega indictments the cause of his first public break with President Reagan.[63]

On September 29th, President Reagan signed the Department of Defense Authorization Act, Fiscal Year 1989, making it Public Law 100-456. It contained provisions restricting U.S. aid to the Panamanian Defense Force and expressing the sense of Congress that the United States should not reach any agreement with Noriega involving dropping the drug indictments against him. On October 1st, Reagan signed the Foreign Operations, Export Financing, and Related Programs Appropriations Act, 1989, which became Public Law 100-461, and continued the economic sanctions previously in place against Panama.

In December 1988, the Senate Committee on Foreign Relations' Subcommittee on Terrorism, Narcotics, and International Operations issued a report entitled "Drugs, Law Enforcement and Foreign Policy," which contained extensive material on Panama's involvement in the drug trade. This report was based in part on testimony given at the Subcommittee's previous hearings. It asserted that "Noriega had turned Panama's political system into what one witness termed a 'narcokleptocracy,' a political system in which [the] Panamanian government became controlled by personal loyalties to Noriega, cemented by graft and corruption, and substantially funded with narcotics money."[64]

On March 1, 1989, President Bush followed President Reagan's lead and refused to certify that Panama was "cooperating fully" with U.S. anti-drug efforts, and on April 6th, Bush renewed the economic sanctions that Reagan had imposed the year before.[65]

On November 21st, the Departments of Commerce, Justice, State, the Judiciary, and Related Agencies Appropriations Act, 1990, was signed into law, becoming Public Law 101-162. It contained a sense of Congress provision to the effect that the international drug summit's agenda should include consideration of how to remove Noriega from power and another provision calling upon the United States to intensify its efforts against Noriega. On the same day, President Bush signed into law the Foreign Operations, Export Financing, and Related Programs Appropriations Act, 1990, which became Public Law 100-167, and which continued the economic sanctions against Panama for another year.[66]

It was finally clear to everyone that Noriega would leave power only at the point of a bayonet. The U.S. will to use that bayonet--Operation Just Cause--was fostered and hardened by Noriega's involvement in drug trafficking. The U.S. political environment was so anti-drug that no acceptable political option existed for dealing with the issues raised by the indictments, while any retreat from them would have damaged the person ordering the retreat.[67] In the end, Noriega had finally overreached himself in his grab for absolute power in Panama. The United States could not tolerate a "drug dealing dictator" who, if left alone, would become responsible for the defense and operation of the Panama Canal.

NOTES

1.   Richard M. Nixon, "Special Message to Congress on Control of Narcotics and Dangerous Drugs, July 14, 1969," in Public Papers of the Presidents of the United States: Containing the Public Messages, Speeches, and Statements of the President, 1969 (Washington, DC: GPO, 1971), pp. 513-518.

2.   John Dinges, Our Man in Panama: How General Noriega Used the United States--and Made Millions in Drugs and Arms (New York: Random House, 1990), pp. 4-5.

3.   Ibid., and Congressional Record, March 3, 1978, pp. S2875-S2876.

4.   Congressional Record, March 3, 1978, p. S2874.

5.   Ibid., p. S2875.

6.   Ibid., p. S2879.

7.   The BNDD was the lineal predecessor of the Drug Enforcement Administration, the current federal drug law enforcement agency.

8.   Congressional Record, March 3, 1978, p. S2880.

9.   Seymour M. Hersh, "Our Man in Panama," Life, vol. XIII (March 1990): 87.

10.   Dinges, pp. 54-55.

11. Ibid., pp. 57-58, 60-61.

12. Ibid., p. 61.

13. Congressional Record, March 3, 1978, p. S2881.

14. Dinges, p. 62; Frederick Kempe, Divorcing the Dictator: America's Bungled Affair with Noriega (New York: G.P. Putnam's Sons, 1990), p. 70.

15. Ibid., p. S2910.

16. Dinges, pp. 63-66.

17. Ibid., p. 67, 72; and Congressional Record, March 3, 1978, pp. S2881-S2882.

18. Congressional Record, March 3, 1978, p. S2882.

19. Ibid.

20. Kempe, pp. 47-54, 95-101; and Dinges, pp. 106-110, 112-113.

21. Drugs, Part 2, p. 393.

22. Ibid., pp. 227-232.   Note that the credibility of this witness is disputed.   See Part 4 of these hearings, pp. 169-170 and 404-412.

23. Dinges, pp. 130-131; and Kempe, p. 192.

24. News Release dated February 5, 1988, by the Office of the U.S. Attorney for the Southern District of Florida.   United States v. Noriega, no. 88-0079CR (S.D. Fla., filed February 4, 1988); and News Release dated February 5, 1988, by the Office of the U.S. Attorney for the Middle District of Florida.   United States v. Noriega, no. 88-0079CR (S.D. Fla., filed February 4, 1988).

25. Drugs, Part 2, pp. 186-187.

26. Ibid., p. 188.   The El Salvador incident is described on p. 194.

27. Ibid., p. 190.

28. Southern District News Release, with an attached copy of Noriega indictment, pp. 17-18; and Laurence Zuckerman, "Wanted: Noriega," Time Magazine (February 15, 1988): 16-17, 20, 22.

29. Drugs and Money Laundering in Panama (hereafter referred to as Money), U.S. Senate Permanent Subcommittee on

44

Investigations, Senate Hearing 100-654, p. 7.

30. Ibid.

31. Ibid., p. 8.

32. Dinges, pp. 1-27.

33. Money, pp. 8-9.

34. Dinges, pp. 121-122, 150-154; and Kempe, p. 119.

35. "Controlling Drug Abuse: A Status Report," General Accounting Office, GAO/GGD-88-39 (Washington, DC: General Accounting Office, 1988), pp. 3, 7-8; and "Drugs and Crime Facts, 1988," U.S. Department of Justice, Office of Justice Programs, Bureau of Justice Statistics, NCJ-118312, September 1989 (Washington, DC: Department of Justice, 1989), pp. 4, 11.

36. Congressional Research Service on-line data base on public opinion polling.

37. Kempe, pp. 132-142; and Dinges, pp. 216-219. See also: Georgie Anne Geyer, "Death in Panama," Washington Times, September 30, 1985.

38. Dinges, pp. 218-228; and Kempe, p. 138.

39. Dinges, pp. 223-225.

40. Carlton was arrested in Costa Rica on July 30, 1986, and extradited to the United States. Kalish was arrested in Florida on July 26, 1984. Dinges, pp. 185, 250, 270-274.

41. S. Hrg. 99-832.

42. Ibid., pp. 33-34.

43. 22 U.S.C. 2291; and Public Law 99-570, 100 Stat. 3207.

44. INCSR, March 1987, p. 168.

45. U.S. Congress, Senate, Committee of Foreign Relations, Resolution Pertaining to the Presidential Certification that Panama has Fully Cooperated with the United States Anti-Drug Efforts, March 27, 1987, S.Rpt. 100-25, pp. 6-7.

46. Ibid.

47. Drugs, parts 1 through 4.

48. Dinges, pp. 259-265.

49. S. Congress, Senate, Committee on Foreign Relations, Restricting United States Assistance to Panama, S.Rpt. 100-257, p. 2.

50. Guillermo Sanchez Borbon, "Panama Fallen Among Thieves: Of General Noriega and a Country Convulsed," Harper's Magazine (December 1987): 62-65; Kempe, pp. 213-214, 357-358; Borbon, p. 62; and Dinges, pp. 264-267.

51. S.Rpt. 100-257, p. 3; and Kempe, p. 269.

52. S.Rpt. 100-257, p. 3.

53. S.Rpt. 100-257.

54. Money; United States v. Noriega, No. 88-0079CR (S.D. Fla. filed February 4, 1988); and Drugs, Part 2.

55. Congressional Record, February 22, 1988, pp. S1068-S1069.

56. U.S. Department of State, International Narcotics Control Strategy Report, March 1, 1988 (Washington, DC: Department of State, 1988), pp. 146-149.

57. Kempe, pp. 265-270. Republic of Panama v. Citizens and Southern International Bank, et. al., 682 F.Supp. 1544 (S.D. Fla. 1988); and Republic of Panama v. Citizens and Republic National Bank of New York, et. al., 681 F.Supp. 1066 (S.D. N.Y. 1988).

58. Kempe. p. 270.

59. Ibid., pp. 318-320.

60. Congressional Record, March 25, 1988, p. S3083. The text appears in Congressional Record, March 24, 1988, p. S3045.

61. 53 Federal Register 12134 (April 12, 1988); and 53 Federal Register 20566 (June 3, 1988). See also: 50 U.S.C. 1701, note.

62. Kempe, pp. 309-316, 322-323.

63. Ibid., pp. 328-329, 332-339. An example of hostile reporting on this issue is Jefferson Morley's article, "Bush's Drug Problem--and Ours," The Nation (August 27/September 3, 1988): 1, 165-169.

64. S.Rpt. 100-165, p. 83.

65. United States Department of State, Bureau of Narcotics Matters, International Narcotics Control Strategy Report, March 1989 (Washington, DC: U.S. Department of State, 1989),

p. 23; and 54 FR 14197, April 7, 1989.

66. See section 613, 103 Stat. 1039-1040, and sections 561 and 562, 103 Stat. 1239-1241.

67. Linda Robinson, "Dwindling Options in Panama," _Foreign Affairs_ (Winter 1989-1990): 192; and Kempe, pp. 332-339.

PART II

The Prelude

4   Indications and Warning Factors

INTRODUCTION

The indications and warning (I&W) factors prior to Operation <u>Just Cause</u> did not represent the typical application of that intelligence discipline.[1] In this case, analysts could trace the indications back over a long period of time and there were less concrete military indications than one might have expected to suggest increasing violence or an armed intervention. Instead, there were open policy statements, harsh rhetoric, economic castigation, battles of will, and tense public military standoffs. Nevertheless, I&W in this setting provided valuable insight and bore significance for U.S. decision-makers. First, it allowed intelligence analysts to evaluate the potential for growing hostility between Panama and the United States and to foresee the wave of sanctioned violence against U.S. citizens. Subsequently, analysts were able to advise military planners and policy-makers who then developed appropriate responses.

In another sense, I&W could have been critical for Noriega, enabling him to anticipate and prepare for U.S. military action. The U.S. government sent clear signals, which, if evaluated correctly, could have provided warning of a U.S. attack.

There were indications of both heightened violence directed by the Noriega regime against U.S. citizens and a U.S. military operation to oust the dictator. In fact, the crisis in Panamanian relations that culminated in the invasion had reached an acute level several times over the previous two and a half years. The lengthy duration of the conflict may seem to have diluted the value of I&W intelligence in Panama, but despite the longstanding and seemingly endless crisis in bilateral relations, several events or acts indicated a culmination was forthcoming.

A HISTORY OF PANAMANIAN-U.S. RELATIONS

Panamanian nationalism, offended by U.S. control of the Panama Canal and a sizeable U.S. presence, erupted into anti-American riots in 1964. The resulting violence and instability led President Carter to negotiate with Panama's then <u>de facto</u> ruler, General Omar Torrijos. The two leaders ultimately reached agreement and, notwithstanding considerable domestic opposition, Carter gained Congressional ratification of the Panama Canal Treaties in 1978. Under the treaties, control of the canal would be transferred gradually, leading to complete Panamanian sovereignty at the end of 1999. The treaties became effective on October 1, 1979. Congressional ratification was conditioned on the presumption that Torrijos would oversee a transition to democratic government before the United States would relinquish operational control of the canal.[2]

Torrijos' sudden death in a 1981 airplane crash and the 1983 ascension of his intelligence chief, Manuel Antonio Noriega, to Commander of the National Guard precluded a successful democratic transition. Instead, Noriega created the Panama Defense Forces (PDF) and placed all military, police, and immigration functions under its control. He then consolidated his power, bringing under his purview not only security but also, business, financial, governmental, and canal operations. In addition, he pursued other, less official interests, ranging from service as a paid agent of the U.S. Central Intelligence Agency to active involvement in the illicit arms and drug trade. His countenance of illegal activities became exceedingly intolerable and their public airing produced a condemning U.S. response that evolved into a firm policy to force Noriega from power.[3]

On June 6, 1987, PDF Deputy Commander Colonel Roberto Diaz Herrera exposed Noriega's involvement in illicit activities, accusing him of fraud in the 1984 presidential elections, drug trafficking, money laundering, and complicity with political assassinations. Widespread public demonstrations in Panama ensued and they were met with a state of emergency and violent repression.

U.S. policy became one of unreserved opposition to Noriega. On June 26, 1987, the Senate approved a resolution calling for democracy in Panama and threatened to cut off U.S. aid. Washington discontinued military assistance in July 1987. U.S. policy became increasingly steadfast after February 1988 when two Florida grand juries returned criminal indictments against Noriega. The formal charges included: protecting cocaine shipments; laundering drug money, and providing safe haven to Medellin Cartel drug traffickers in exchange for a bribe of $4.6 million; allowing the Cartel to shift its drug operations to Panama after the crackdown in Colombia; protecting a drug laboratory; providing a safe haven in Panama for international narcotics traffickers; arranging the shipment of chemicals for cocaine processing; attempting to smuggle over 1.4 million pounds of marajuana into the United States; buying a jet plane that was used to transport illegal drug revenues to Panama from the United States; and accepting a $1 million bribe from drug traffickers in exchange for their use of Panama for money-laundering and drug transhipment.[4]

Amid widespread condemnation of Noriega in Panama and U.S. opposition to his de facto leadership, President Eric

Delvalle attempted to dismiss him as Commander of the PDF. But Delvalle's chosen replacement, PDF Commander Colonel Marcos Justines, refused to accept the position, declaring his loyalty to General Noriega. Noriega quickly arranged for the National Assembly, which he controlled, to oust Delvalle and replace him with less assertive Education Minister Manuel Solis Palma. The United States proclaimed its support for Delvalle and the Latin American governments comprising the Group of Eight revoked Panama's membership. The Reagan administration imposed economic sanctions against the Noriega regime and lawyers for Delvalle succeeded in obtaining a U.S. court order to freeze $7 million in canal revenues and $40 million in Panamanian assets held by U.S. banks.[5]

Mounting domestic opposition to Noriega led to a coup attempt on March 16, 1988. Less than a week prior to the rebellion, State Department officials, testifying in Congressional hearings, said that they hoped the PDF would oust Noriega. The coup's leader, Police Chief Colonel Leonides Macia, was arrested after his defiant adventure was easily crushed. Massive street protests and power blackouts followed, bringing Panama City to a near standstill.[6] Noriega dismissed twelve of 54 majors in the PDF officer corps, attempting to ensure the future loyalty of this pivotal, all important military force.

The anti-Noriega protests following the aborted coup were unprecedented. The opposition staged massive demonstrations and a general strike, hoping it could force Noriega from power, but the dictator called in combat troops and broke up the strike. In response to Noriega's successive acts of tyranny, the Reagan administration tightened economic sanctions against Panama and sent in 1,300 troops between April 5th and April 9th to enhance security on U.S. bases.[7]

Economic sanctions and military scare tactics were used by the Reagan administration in an effort to force Noriega's removal. In addition, the United States negotiated with him from mid-March to May 1988, attempting to persuade the dictator to relinquish power. These talks ended when he rejected a U.S. offer to drop the drug charges in exchange for his departure from power. Secretary of State George Schulz declared, "all offers are withdrawn from the table."[8]

The United States was clearly exhausting its options; nevertheless, it seemed disinclined to resort to military action. The Chairman of the Joint Chiefs of Staff voiced the Reagan administration's unstated policy that it would not purse a military solution that would jeopardize U.S. lives "unless the stakes clearly justified it."[9] The stakes in Panama apparently had not grown that high.

Washington then resorted to covert actions. Reagan signed an intelligence finding authorizing the Central Intelligence Agency to work with former PDF Colonel Eduardo Herrera Hassan to foment a PDF uprising and overthrow Noriega. The Senate Intelligence Committee blocked the action, fearing it would lead to Noriega's murder and amount to U.S. complicity in the assassination of a foreign leader.[10]

The Reagan administration left office having failed to achieve what it effectively identified as a major foreign policy objective. The government's policy and the enormous press coverage it received magnified Noriega's significance to the United States and hardened his will to defy Washington.

ANALYSIS OF THE EARLY INDICATIONS

Indications that were evident prior to January 1989 might have suggested that a collapse in bilateral relations was forthcoming. The U.S.-Panamanian relationship became decidedly strained in the mid-sixties, improved in the late seventies, and then deteriorated in 1987. Clearly, the principal source of tension was the perceived U.S. infringement of Panamanian sovereignty through its dominion over the Panama Canal and the Canal Zone.

Indicators of deteriorating bilateral ties sufficient to prompt open violence did not appear until late-1989 but there was some earlier evidence of increasing hostility and perhaps even preparation for military activity. Indications of hostile intent on the U.S. side were limited to incremental economic sanctions, troop reinforcements, and harsh statements. In contrast, signs emanating from Panama reflected a policy of violence but not one specifically targeted against Washington or U.S. citizens. Noriega responded to popular demonstrations after the aborted coup with repression. The fierce PDF tactics were not used against U.S. citizens selectively but rather, they were directed against the Panamanian population; however, numerous offenses were committed against U.S. service members and employees of the Panama Canal Commission.

Between February 1988 and May 1989, there were over 600 reported incidents of treaty violations involving mistreatment of U.S. citizens, usually by the PDF. Examples include illegal detention, severe beatings, armed intrusions into U.S. military installations, and unchecked harassment. In addition, there were several illegal PDF searches of U.S. service personnel at gunpoint. On June 16, 1988, a private and his eighteen-year old wife were assaulted by a probable PDF member. The private was beaten and locked in the trunk of his car while his wife was raped and battered by the assailant. These incidents were reported to the Panamanian government as formal treaty violations but there was no evidence that serious investigations were ever conducted.[11] These acts and Noriega's failure to adequately respond to U.S. protests demonstrated Noriega's willingness, if not his intent, to unleash violence on U.S. citizens and threaten U.S. interests.

The United States responded to the heightened threat by sending 1,300 troops to Panama, an act that could be interpreted as a warning of hostile U.S. intent; however, Washington was negotiating with Noriega during this time, sending him a signal that it was still not prepared to resort to military force. Once the negotiations failed and it appeared that U.S. options were running out, Noriega might have seen that the United States would continue to seek a resolution. But the passage of time coupled with U.S. inaction probably reduced this perceived threat. Besides, the United States was preoccupied with the 1988 presidential election.

THE YEAR THAT PROMPTED OPERATION JUST CAUSE

When Bush assumed office in January, Panama was receiving minor attention in the press but disputes over the canal and economic issues continued. For example, in accordance with U.S. economic sanctions against Panama, the Canal Commission employees' taxes were not transferred to the Panamanian government. In response, in February 1989, Noriega enacted legislation authorizing the government to seize canal employees' automobiles and property for nonpayment of taxes. Panamanians were prohibited from leaving the country without proof that their taxes had been paid.[12] The PDF continued to commit treaty violations and hostile rhetoric was heard from both sides; but it was the May elections that returned Panama to the front page in the United States.

Prior to the elections, U.S. officials were considering their policy options. The non-military measures included imposing a total trade embargo, suspending U.S. visas to all Panamanian citizens, requiring all U.S. military and civilian employees to move onto U.S. bases, fomenting a rebellion, and abducting Noriega. These officials reportedly assumed that blatantly fraudulent Panamanian elections would prompt Congress to endorse a stronger U.S. policy. An administration statement that, subsequent to fraudulent elections, it would consider new "diplomatic, intelligence, and military" options was the first suggestion of an armed intervention by the Bush administration.[13]

The elections were held on May 7th. Notwithstanding extensive pre-election day fraud, Noriega's candidate, Carlos Duque, was easily defeated by Guillermo Endara. Nevertheless, Duque claimed victory and the following day government troops fired on thousands of opposition demonstrators and raided ballot counting centers. International observers and President Bush denounced the elections and Noriega responded on May 10th by charging foreign interference and annulling the vote. Meanwhile, Noriega's Dignity Battalions attacked and seriously injured Endara and the vice presidential candidate, Guillermo Ford.[14]

On May 11th, President Bush held a press conference and announced a seven-point plan on Panama. Washington pledged to support the initiative of other Organization of American States (OAS) governments and international groups. In addition, Bush withdrew his ambassador, reduced the embassy staff, ordered U.S. employees and their dependents to safe housing, and sent another 2,000 troops to Panama.[15]

The United States then moved to the background as the principal external force in Panama became the OAS. In his May

11th press conference, Bush said, "The United States strongly supports, and will cooperate with, initiatives taken by governments in this hemisphere to address this crisis through regional diplomacy and action in the Organization of American States." However, several months of OAS mediation efforts were fruitless; and negotiations ended in failure on September 1st, when Noriega named a relatively unknown government bureaucrat, Francisco Rodriguez, as the country's new puppet president.[16] Noriega was impervious to a consolidated regional opposition, and another U.S. policy option was squandered.

The Bush administration refused to recognize Rodriguez as president, tightened the economic sanctions, and gave Noriega his first concrete warning that implementation of the canal treaties was in jeopardy. In June 1989, the Senate passed a non-binding resolution that it would not approve a canal administrator nominated by Noriega even if he were endorsed by the White House.[17]

In August, the frequency ·and intensity of hostile encounters between Panamanian and U.S. forces escalated. According to the U.S. Southern Command (SOUTHCOM), on August 8th, U.S. troops detained nine PDF soldiers and eleven other Panamanians for trying to impede maneuvers on U.S.-controlled territory. On August 9th, SOUTHCOM deployed tanks to block the entrance to Fort Amador while helicopters overflew the southern end of the canal, and in an exercise on August 10th, U.S. forces stormed a PDF gate and disarmed its guard. SOUTHCOM reported that the action was taken in response to the PDF's detention of two U.S. soldiers which, in turn, had been in retaliation for the brief detention of 29 Panamanians. On August 17th, SOUTHCOM conducted joint maneuvers at eleven canal installations. While the United States said it was enforcing its rights under the 1977 Treaties, Panama claimed it was violating them.[18] SOUTHCOM reported that the exercise was designed to train U.S. forces "to respond swiftly and decisively in defense of the Panama Canal and protection of U.S. lives and property."

The next critical milestone in the period leading up to Operation Just Cause was the aborted coup of October 3rd. After the OAS initiative had failed and another U.S. policy option was exhausted, the Bush administration encouraged PDF members to rise up against Noriega. Bush emphasized repeatedly that the United States did not have a problem with the PDF but rather, would be willing to work closely with it, under different leadership, toward the reconstruction of a democratic Panama. In addition, immediately following the May elections and the opposition crackdown, Bush implored "the [Panamanian] people...to do everything they can to get Mr. Noriega out of there."[19]

In the early hours of October 3rd, the Chief of Security at PDF headquarters, the Commandancia, led a revolt to oust Noriega. The plan lacked effective coordination and organization; and the attempt was hampered by inadequate command and control. The planners failed to define an objective, hoping to force Noriega's resignation rather than his exile or execution.[20] While leaders of the uprising were negotiating with him, forces loyal to Noriega succeeded in freeing him and defeating rebel troops.

The widely held perception prior to the attempt was that the United States had virtually pledged its support to any effort to dethrone Noriega. But Washington was caught by surprise. U.S. intelligence failed to provide policy makers with an accurate assessment of a coup's likelihood or its chance of success. Bush order limited assistance and once the revolt appeared to be failing, did nothing to resurrect it. This contribution was assessed as half-hearted by the U.S. Congress, Panamanians, and many Americans; and the political backlash was one of the most difficult moments of Bush's presidency. The flurry of news items and editorials that followed the aborted coup harped on the absence of effective U.S. leadership and a coherent policy in Panama, the hypocrisy of the administration's war on drugs, the emerging limits of U.S. power, and the diminishing will of the United States to confront its enemies.[21]

Noriega responded to the uprising with a severe crackdown. His opponents were jailed, tortured, or executed, public employees of questionable loyalty were fired, a pay freeze was imposed, Christmas bonuses were suspended, untrustworthy PDF officers were removed, and some military units were reorganized and disbanded. Noriega reportedly laid off twenty percent of the public work force.[22]

Noriega's determination to remain in power, defying both the U.S. government and the will of the Panamanian people, was hardened by the attempt to overthrow him. His confidence in the loyalty of his subordinates may have been reduced but his expectation that the United States would refrain from direct military action was reinforced. The United States began reviewing its legal options and the Bush administration reportedly began to establish new guidelines for U.S. involvement in further coup attempts. The new rules, in place by the time the invasion was conducted, enabled U.S. intelligence agents to provide support in a coup.[23]

The atmosphere in Panama clearly reflected the hardened policies of both Bush and Noriega. Bilateral tensions ran high during the three months prior to Operation Just Cause and, at times, seemed explosive. Both the U.S. military and the PDF engaged in provocative combat training maneuvers. Several bomb threats were made against U.S. military installations, prompting SOUTHCOM to heighten security at U.S. bases. Reports of PDF Treaty violations continued. On October 31st, U.S. forces held maneuvers along the canal and obstructed highways in a show of force that included tanks and aircraft. On November 20-21st, SOUTHCOM used tanks to impede access to the Health Ministry, arguing that PDF tanks were blocking the U.S. Gorgas Hospital. These forces remained in a standoff for two days.[24]

In early December, the Bush administration banned Panamanian-registered ships from U.S. ports. Also in December, the PDF was ordered to arrest General Maxwell

Thurman, the SOUTHCOM commander, and Major General Marc
Cisneros, Commander of U.S. Army South, for failing to respond
to summonses to appear in court on charges of disturbing the
peace. The charges alleged that military maneuvers conducted
by the officers' subordinate units were a constant harassment
to the citizens of Panama. Washington dismissed the
accusation, explaining that all of its activities were within
the limits of the Panama Canal Treaties. SOUTHCOM said that
it would consider any attempt to arrest the officers an act
of terrorism.[25] This warning was clear.

It was a series of incidents the weekend prior to
December 20th that prompted the invasion. On Friday December
15th, the Panamanian National Assembly, its members appointed
by Noriega, passed a resolution naming him "chief of the
government" and the "maximum leader of national liberation."
The resolution formalized his already sweeping powers in
response to what it termed U.S. aggression. Additionally, the
decree stated, "the Republic of Panama is declared to be in
a state of war while the aggression lasts." The declaration
allowed Noriega to legally override the authority of civilian
President Francisco Rodriguez. This virtual proclamation of
war was initially met with little concern in Washington. The
Defense Department did not report a change in the alert status
of U.S. forces in Panama and President Bush, who had left the
Oval Office early that day, was not even notified by White
House officials until the next morning.[26]

Also on the 15th, ten PDF soldiers armed with .50 caliber
machine guns stopped a U.S. Military Police (MP) patrol car.
One soldier aimed his weapon at an MP, but the arrival of the
MP's commander prompted the PDF to release the Americans.

On Saturday, December 16th, four U.S. servicemen in
civilian clothes were stopped at a PDF checkpoint. The men
drove off after PDF guards aimed loaded AK-47s at them and
forty bystanders swarmed the car shouting anti-American
epithets. The guards then fired at the Americans, hitting 1st
Lieutenant Robert Paz, U.S. Marine Corps. He died shortly
after arriving at Gorgas Hospital. A U.S. naval officer and
his wife, who had been stopped earlier at the same roadblock,
witnessed the shooting and were subsequently detained by
Panamanian soldiers. They were blindfolded and driven to
another location for interrogation. The naval officer was
severely beaten and threatened with death while his wife was
harassed and "sexually threatened." The shooting of Paz was
the most violent confrontation between Panama and the United
States since January 9, 1964, when Panamanian rioters and U.S.
military police clashed in the Panama Canal Zone. In response
to these incidents, U.S. military personnel in Panama were
confined to U.S. bases and routes of travel were restricted.
Also, U.S. troops were placed on maximum alert.[27]

In another incident on December 16th, a PDF policeman
accosted eight U.S. servicemen, aimed his assault rifle at
them, and ordered them to leave the area. The Americans left,
but returned with three MP units who arrested the policeman.
They held him for ninety minutes before releasing him. Also

on Saturday, a U.S. soldier was stopped at a PDF checkpoint and arrested. He was taken to a PDF facility where Panamanian soldiers verbally abused him. The U.S. troop was released when a friend in the PDF intervened on his behalf.[28]

President Bush reportedly reached the decision to send U.S. forces into Panama on Sunday, December 17th. On the 18th, he said he did not rule out military action in response to Panama's provocations. On the 19th, NBC News reported that U.S. military transport planes were flying into Panama every ten minutes. The news program also broadcast C-141 transport aircraft landing in Panama that afternoon. Ten transport aircraft--an unusually high number--and twice the routine number of helicopters were reported at Howard Air Force Base in Panama. Earlier on the 19th, C-141s were seen over Fort Bragg, North Carolina, home of the 82nd Airborne Division; and soldiers of the 7th Infantry Division at Fort Ord, CA were mobilized. U.S. Army spokesmen attributed these activities to readiness training but they did not go unnoticed by the government of Panama. The latter accused the United States of violating its air space and alleged that the U.S. Armed Forces were preparing for military action.[29]

ANALYSIS OF THE INDICATIONS

The U.S. View

Clearly Noriega's provocations began long before his December 1989 declaration of war. Over a period of two years, the actions of General Noriega became increasingly hostile and antagonistic. The policies pursued by his regime and acts committed in the execution of those policies constitute intelligence indicators of hostile intentions; these indications grew in clarity and became more foreboding, leading ultimately to the U.S. government's decision to invade Panama in December 1989. In fact, the United States justified the operation by claiming that U.S. interests, and specifically American citizens, were endangered by Noriega's policies and the violent practices of his military and police forces. The murder of Lieutenant Paz just prior to the operation supported this claim. Moreover, there was no evidence that Noriega was not condoning, and even encouraging, the violent harassment of U.S. citizens. After all, PDF members that were accused of committing treaty violations were never prosecuted or punished.

Early indications suggested that Noriega would continue to provoke the U.S. government and Armed Forces and would govern Panama in a manner antagonistic to U.S. interests. Armed intrusions into U.S. installations, treaty violations, incessant anti-U.S. rhetoric, and support of narcotics trafficking into the United States are examples of Noriega's hostile behavior toward the United States and, as they increased in frequency and impact, should have served as indications of his future intentions.

Yet, these measures clearly did not, by themselves,

provoke the U.S. military response that was Operation <u>Just Cause</u>. Instead, they prompted two successive U.S. administrations to launch policies aimed solely, pointedly, and intensely at the removal of Noriega from power. Once these policies were initiated, Noriega hardened his opposition to the United States and continued to persistently antagonize both Presidents. His willingness to heighten the animosity was, in itself, an indication of his intention to threaten U.S. lives directly. But there were also more specific signals.

Noriega's anti-U.S. rhetoric alone was not an indication of hostile intentions; however, his words were generally well-supported by his actions. Armed intrusions of U.S. military facilities reflected his policy of badgering the United States, and treaty violations, including the harassment of U.S. servicemen and their spouses were sanctioned, indicating that General Noriega meant what he said.

While Noriega's actions in the early months of 1989 were only antagonistic, they soon began to reflect his ruthlessness and determination to maintain absolute control over Panama. His brutal response to opposition protests after the May 7th elections was perhaps the first blatant indication of Noriega's propensity for violence. It reflected his determination to remain in power and plainly explained his refusal to negotiate his departure with the United States. When he presided over the unrestrained, armed attack on opposition protesters, Noriega clearly indicated that he would not bow to international pressure. The vigorous crackdown he launched after the unsuccessful coup in October confirmed that he was guided by this resolve.

Perhaps the most obvious indicator of Noriega's intentions was his National Assembly's declaration of war with the United States. But the General's harsh rhetoric had become commonplace and the White House shrugged it off as more propaganda. The declaration was probably more significant for I&W intelligence analysts than the reaction of senior policy-makers suggests. While it may not have reflected a change in the specific intentions of the Government of Panama vis-a-vis the United States as U.S. officials correctly ascertained, it may have served as a license for PDF members to engage in violent acts against U.S. military personnel without fear of reprisal. This possibility was clearly revealed when Lieutenant Paz was killed. Administration officials said they considered the incident "part of a steady escalation in the harassment of Americans in Panama over the past two years."[30]

These White House officials accurately identified the significance of both the declaration of war and Paz's murder; and this realization enabled them to recognize the threat posed by Noriega and to acknowledge the potential consequences of his policies. The unprecedented nature of the shooting underlined its gravity to U.S. analysts and policy makers trying to discern Noriega's intentions. He had given no indication that he would restrain his forces. In fact, he provided no security guarantees to the United States and seemed to promote violence against its citizens. Noriega's defiance of Washington and his steadfast refusal to bend to U.S. pressure suggested that he would stop at nothing to remain in power. Once this tenacity was understood, any hostile act he committed could be perceived as threatening to U.S. interests. Therefore, the United States launched Operation Just Cause, thus implementing a strategy which recognized that Noriega could only be forced from power.

The Panamanian View

During 1989, there were many indications that the United States might invade Panama. First, Bush ordered 2,000 additional troops to Panama after the May elections. This move certainly could have been construed as a warning. Yet, Noriega may have interpreted it as another U.S. attempt to bully Panama. In fact, while the removal of Ambassador Arthur Davis following the annulled elections was just short of severing diplomatic relations, Bush's response to the violence and brutality in Panama was considered moderate.

The U.S. response to the failed coup of October 3rd was perhaps the most critical influence on U.S. signal in its effect on Noriega's assessment of U.S. behavior and the intentions reflected therein. Clearly, U.S. policy over the previous two years could have been interpreted as one which reflected the absence of resolve. Additionally, Noriega's psychological disposition is characterized perhaps most notably by a sense of invincibility. Nevertheless, during the coup attempt, the U.S. sent the signal to Noriega that it was not willing to commit U.S. troops to a military conflict in Panama where U.S. lives would be at risk. The failure of the United States to lend more substantial and more direct support to the dissident PDF members explains, in part, Noriega's underestimation of the military threat posed by the United States.

Noriega should have studied the political reaction to U.S. non-involvement. The ramifications were severe, ensuring that this incident would be one of Bush's worst moments as President. The backlash was a catalyst for revising and updating the plan to invade Panama, and it must have hardened Bush's determination to oust the infuriating dictator.

There were other indications and warnings that could have been perceived by Noriega as either signs that the United States intended to launch a military operation into Panama or yet another half-hearted attempt to force Noriega's removal indirectly. The level, frequency and visibility of U.S. maneuvers increased markedly in the months prior to Operation Just Cause and were exceptionally bold in mid-August. Moreover, they were described by SOUTHCOM as training for "U.S. forces to respond...in defense of the Panama Canal and protection of U.S. lives and property."[31] In one exercise, U.S. forces launched an amphibious operation in which they landed on an island where Noriega had a home. This display could be interpreted as either a reflection of hostile U.S.

intentions or as a demonstration of force unsupported by the will to use it.

Yet, the simultaneous deployment of troops, equipment, transport planes, and helicopters coupled with the maximum alert status in force at U.S. bases in Panama immediately before H-hour, would be difficult to dismiss as a coincidence.

Additional indications for Noriega were statements made by U.S. officials over the weekend; they clearly reflected the gravity with which the Bush administration viewed the PDF's actions and the overall situation in Panama. Secretary of Defense Cheney said Noriega had "created an atmosphere in which Panamanian Defense Forces feel free to fire on unarmed Americans." Also, a State Department spokesperson said, "We are extremely concerned that a climate of aggression has developed that puts American lives at risk."[32]

Noriega should have seen the direction he was forcing U.S. policy to take. Washington had defined a policy objective, but rather than define adequate means to achieve this end, it pursued cursory and ultimately ineffective measures and it failed to clearly demonstrate a willingness to raise the stakes in order to achieve its defined goal. As the gap between the U.S. policy objective and the means to achieve that objective widened, the continued declaration of the goal--forcing Noriega from power--in itself, became a warning indicator. As one former National Security Council member said, "Whatever else may be said about the American invasion of Panama, it cannot be said to be a surprise." He added, "...it has only been a matter of time--and occasion."[33]

In fact, a plan for the invasion existed when Richard Cheney assumed the office of Defense Secretary and it was discussed in one of the first briefings he received. The plan was modified after the failed coup in October; and several journalists observed that, having been criticized for inaction during the coup, Bush was almost waiting for an excuse to invade. Indeed the President was decisive when he ordered the operation in Panama; he was reported to have declared "enough is enough."[34]

Thus, Noriega should have realized that Washington had identified his ouster as a policy objective and had exhausted all alternative options short of military intervention to achieve that goal. He also should have recognized the discontent and even wrath of his own countrymen. The May elections clearly demonstrated the absence of meaningful popular support for Noriega. The Panamanian dictator had antagonized his own people and had outraged the United States.

Until December 16th the only acts of provocation remaining that Noriega had not committed were attacks on Americans and threats to the canal. He exceeded this unspoken limit when he allowed, if not sanctioned and implicitly encouraged, the shooting of Lieutenant Paz.[35] Thus, the military operation in Panama was indeed the final option; it was the last resort.

CONCLUSIONS

The lessons of indications and warning during the crisis between Panama and the United States demonstrate that indicators manifest themselves in a variety of forms, only one of which is military activity. In Panama, Noriega prodded the United States incessantly for over two years. Notwithstanding tense military standoffs and tough rhetoric, he avoided a direct confrontation with U.S. forces and did not unleash the PDF or Dignity Battalions on U.S. citizens. Yet he consistently demonstrated that he would not bend to pressure from Washington, Latin America, or his own countrymen. And perhaps without accurately interpreting warnings from the United States as indications, he pushed the Bush administration too far and made it clear that he would not only remain in spite of U.S. admonitions but he would allow the killing of U.S. citizens by members of his defense forces. Indications conveyed by the United States were admittedly somewhat ambiguous. The United States seemed to pursue every conceivable option short of direct military action. This strategy apparently led Noriega to conclude that its warnings were virtually meaningless and the United States would continue to refrain from an armed confrontation with Panama; hence his defiance of Washington steadily escalated. Noriega failed to recognize that the ultimate consequence of his actions would be U.S. retribution. The warning not to endanger U.S. forces was real.

NOTES

1.   Indications and warning intelligence is information that alerts a nation of an impending action detrimental to its interests. An indication is a specific action that has been observed or can be inferred and may portend the preparation for or rejection of hostile activity. It bears on an enemy's intention to adopt or reject a particular course of action. It is a general, specific, or theoretical action a foreign power might be expected to take if the enemy intended to launch an aggressive act.
     When two or more nations are exhibiting increasingly hostile behavior toward each other, observers should look for these nations' intentions in order to predict more consequential, perhaps even lethal, action and to develop appropriate responses that could deter or prevent the feared actions. Such indicators are not only military but also, can be political, economic, diplomatic, or domestic.

2.   Robinson, Foreign Affairs 1989/1990.

3.   Ibid.; and The New York Times, December 21, 1989.

4.   The Reuter Library Report, "Basic Facts About Panama," December 20, 1989; and "What He Is Accused Of," Time, January

62

15, 1990, p. 24.

5.   <u>Los Angeles Times</u>, December 21, 1989; and "Chronology of a Crisis," <u>Los Angeles Times</u>, December 21, 1989.

6.   "Combat in Panama; Chronology of a Crisis: 1978-1989," <u>Los Angeles Times</u>, December 21, 1989.

7.   "Chronology 1988," <u>Foreign Affairs 1989/America and the World</u>, p. 247.

8.   Cited in Robinson, "Dwindling Operations in Panama," <u>Foreign Affairs 1989/1990 America and the World</u>.

9.   Admiral William J. Crowe, Jr., Letter to the <u>New York Times</u> article by Elliott Abrams, October 5, 1989.

10. William Scott Malone, "How Not to Depose a Dictator," <u>Washington Post Weekly</u> (May 1-7, 1989): 23; <u>Keesing's Record of World Events</u>, vol. 35, no. 5 (May 1989); <u>U.S. News and World Report</u>, May 1, 1989; and "Who Lost Noriega," <u>Time</u>, October 23, 1989; and Robinson.

11. U.S. Southern Command and Treaty Affairs, <u>Fact Sheet</u>, September 18, 1989; <u>Keesing's</u>; and U.S. Southern Command Treaty Affairs, <u>Fact Sheet</u>.

12. <u>U.S. News and World Report</u> (February 20, 1989).

13. <u>U.S. News and World Report</u> (May 1, 1989); and <u>Time</u> (May 8, 1989).

14. "Pamana--Chronology of a Crisis," <u>Reuters</u> (December 20, 1989).

15. <u>Keesing's</u>, p. 36645.

16. "Dwindling Options in Panama, 1989/1990 America and the World," <u>Foreign Affairs</u>; and <u>Reuters</u>.

17. The assumption by a Panamanian of the Canal administrator position is the first major step in the Canal's gradual transfer to Panama.

18. "US and Panamanian Soldiers Have Had Several Confrontations," <u>Associated Press</u>, December 19, 1989; "U.S. Forces Storm Through Guard Gate in Exercise," <u>Reuters</u>, August 10, 1989; "Panama Seizes then Frees Two GIs After Standoff," <u>Associated Press</u>, August 10, 1989; and "US and Panamanian Soldiers Have Had Several Confrontations," <u>Associated Press</u>, December 19, 1989.

19. <u>Time</u>, "Lead-Pipe Politics," (May 22, 1989).

20. "Coup Leader Barred Giving US Noriega," Washington Post, October 10, 1989.

21. "US Foreign Policy Hurt by Weak Intelligence Gathering," Reuters, October 9, 1989; "Congress-Panama," Associated Press, October 4, 1989; "Bush Defends Stance in Failed Panama Coup," Los Angeles Times, October 7, 1989; "Senate Dissatisfied with US Action in Coup," Los Angeles Times, October 6, 1989; "Bush's Failure in Panama," Washington Post, October 6, 1989; Wall Street Journal, October 6, 1989, pp. 1-4; "Americans Angered at Coup Role," Washington Post, October 16, 1989, "Coup Attempt Against General Noriega," Letters Desk, Los Angeles Times, October 14, 1989, "On Panama: Luck and Incompetence," The New York Times, October 8, 1989, and "Force Never Ruled Out in Panama," Los Angeles Times, October 5, 1989.

22. "The World," The Christian Science Monitor, October 5, 1989, "Panama Opposition Figures Seized in Crackdown," The New York Times, October 6, 1989, "3 Top Officers, 35 Others Arrested in Panama Plot," Los Angeles Times, October 5, 1989; and "Panama: On the Waterfront," The Economist, October 14, 1989.

23. "US Officer, Wife Beaten in Panama," Los Angeles Times, December 18, 1989; and "Bush Orders Troops to Seize Panama's Noriega," Washington Post, December 20, 1989.

24. "Panama: Chronology of a Crisis," Reuters, December 20, 1989; and Associated Press, December 19, 1989.

25. "Pamana Names Noriega Maximum Leader," Washington Post, December 16, 1989.

26. "Noriega Appointed 'Maximum Leader'," Washington Post, December 16, 1989; and "Panama Assembly Names Noriega Government Chief," Los Angeles Times, December 16, 1989.

27. "U.S. Officer, Wife Beaten in Panama," Los Angeles Times December 18, 1989; and "Fighting in Panama: Six Days Leading to the Attack," New York Times, December 21, 1989.

28. "U.S. Officer Shoots, Wounds Panamanian Policeman," Washington Post, December 19, 1989.

29. "U.S. Officer Shoots"; "Fighting in Panama;" "Panama: Chronology of a Crisis," Reuters, December 20, 1989; and "Maneuvers Increase, Panama Accuses United States of Violations," Associated Press, December 20, 1989.

30. Los Angeles Times, December 18, 1989.

31. "U.S. Forces Stage Exercise to Defend Panama Bases," Reuters, August 17, 2989.

64

32. "U.S. Officer, Wife Beaten."

33. <u>Los Angeles Times</u>, December 21, 1989, Op-Ed.

34. "Showing Muscle," <u>Time</u> (January 1, 1990); and <u>Los Angeles Times</u>, December 21, 1989. The bold decision taken by Bush helped boost his approval rating to 79% in U.S. polls. This was higher than that of any president in his first term since World War II. A survey conducted after the October coup found his popularity at only 66%, 10% lower than the previous month. Eighty percent of those polled said they supported his decision to send troops to Panama to depose Noriega. ("Support for Bush, Republicans," <u>Washington Post</u>, January 18, 1990.)

35. <u>U.S. News and World Report</u>, May 22, 1989.

PART III

The Operation

5   The Anatomy of *Just Cause:* The Forces Involved, the Adequacy of Intelligence, and Its Success as a Joint Operation

INTRODUCTION

On December 20, 1989, the U.S. intervened militarily in Panama to depose General Manuel Antonio Noriega. By December 24, 1989, when Noriega sought asylum in the Papal Nunciature, the large-scale operational military action of <u>Just Cause</u> was over. This pre-planned and rehearsed operation, like all U.S. military operations since World War II, was limited and unique.

Because of the long-standing U.S. military presence to defend the canal and, by extension, all of Panama from foreign invasion, U.S. forces were the only troops in Panama organized and equipped to fight other armed forces. The Panamanian Defense Force (PDF) was organized and equipped only for domestic security missions. Thus while <u>Just Cause</u> was nominally the invasion of a sovereign nation and has been correctly described as a <u>coup de main</u>,[1] it also had elements of a <u>coup d'etat</u> in that the military forces responsible for the defense of a state from foreign invasion replaced the government by force.

U.S. forces had uncontested air superiority over Panama permitting the Military Airlift Command (MAC) to air lift and drop troops where U.S. commanders desired, permitting both the U.S. Air Force and Army Aviation to provide close air support as needed. This uncontested air superiority also permitted U.S. ground forces to operate without fear of enemy air attack, just as they have in every U.S. military operation since the Korean War.

Preparing a narrative analysis of such an operation without access to classified material is hazardous at best. For instance while this analysis was being written, Secretary of Defense Richard Cheney ordered an inquiry into a report that one F-117A stealth fighter had "...missed its target by more than 300 yards due to pilot error." Air Force spokespersons and Lieutenant General Carl W. Stiner, the field commander, had stoutly defended the use of the stealth fighter because of its bombing accuracy without mentioning the mishap.[2] Much of what must be known to write a definitive analysis of <u>Just Cause</u> is classified and will remain so for many years.

Therefore this analysis, of necessity, is based on public

sources: official and semi-official accounts as well as
printed news stories and analyses. By looking at reports
about <u>Just Cause</u> and studying interviews with key decision-
makers and field leaders afterwards, one can develop a basic
outline of the plan.
     This analysis is divided into two parts: the planning
and the execution of <u>Just Cause</u>. What did the commander want
to happen? What actually happened?

<u>PLANNING</u>

     Like all modern military forces, the U.S. military
maintains plans for foreseeable contingencies. One of the
military's roles in any government is to be able to present
coherent plans of action if the executive asks for the
military options in a given international situation. The
intervention in Panama was such a contingency for which the
Department of Defense had done extensive planning. <u>Secretary</u>
<u>of Defense Cheney, in his December 20, 1989 news briefing at</u>
<u>the outset of Just Cause,</u> stated that the plan "...had been
<u>in existence for some time.</u>" General Maxwell R. Thurman the
<u>Southern Command Commander explained that the plan used in</u>
<u>Just Cause was his updated version of one in existence when</u>
<u>he took command on October 1, 1989.</u> President Bush, Secretary
Cheney, and General Colin Powell, Chairman of the Joint
Chiefs, had all approved the plan used in December 1989 "by
November...."[3]   A U.S. military intervention in Panama had
been a very real possibility for some time and had therefore
been planned well in advance.
     According to Bernard Trainor in <u>The New York Times</u>, there
were three military options available to President Bush in
Panama. The option the President selected was to use so much
force at the outset that Noriega and his supporters would be
convinced that they had no realistic chance of survival. The
second option was to stage a raid by special forces to seize
Noriega with support from troops stationed in Panama. The
last was to have troops stationed in Panama attack and seize
the Panama Defense Forces' Headquarters.[4] The last two
options might have led to a quicker capture of Noriega but
entailed a risk of prolonged conflict with Panamanian units
either loyal to Noriega or simply following a nationalist
impulse to resist a foreign invader. A prolonged conflict
would have opened Bush to both domestic and international
criticism and pressure as the campaign dragged on. The
operation selected was the most complex and thus had the
greatest chance for difficulties or failure. If the plan was
executed successfully, however, it provided the opportunity
for the president to present domestic and international
critics with a fait accompli.
     The elements of the plan for <u>Just Cause</u> most clearly
evident from an analysis of the reported action were: the
objective; hostile forces; friendly forces, including both
ground and air forces; intelligence and deception; rules of
engagement; and projected casualties and medical evacuation

arrangements. What is not included here is the logistics planning. The operational elements presented here are analogous to the visible tip of an iceberg supported by the submerged and unseen body of logistics.

OBJECTIVE

The planning process ideally starts with a clear political objective that is militarily achievable. The publicly announced U.S. political objective in Just Cause had four parts: (1) to protect American lives; (2) to protect American interests and rights under the Panama Canal Treaty; (3) to restore Panamanian democracy; and (4) to apprehend Noriega.[5] These politically palatable words could be boiled down to the removal of the Noriega regime and its replacement with a government more acceptable to the Bush administration. Thus merely capturing Noriega would not have accomplished the objective. The military achievement of this objective was, of course, merely the first step in the political process of achieving it permanently.

Given the political objective, planners had to translate it into operational military objectives. In Just Cause the initial operational military objectives fell into three categories: (1) destroying the combat capability of Panama Defense Force (PDF) units and seizing the lines of communication (roads, bridges, and airfields) over which they could be reinforced; (2) seizing facilities essential to the operation of the Panama Canal; and (3) apprehending Noriega and rescuing prisoners held by him.

Success in destroying the combat capability of the PDF was essential to achieving the other operational objectives and all parts of the political objective. Defense Secretary Cheney and Lieutenant General T.W. Kelly, Director of Operations for the Joint Staff, both made this point during their December 20, 1989 news briefings. General Maxwell Thurman, U.S. Southern Command Commander, and Lieutenant General Carl Stiner who commanded Joint Task Force South that executed the plan also emphasized this point in separate interviews with the press after Just Cause was completed.[6] To accomplish this primary objective, the plan called for every major Panamanian force along the Panama City to Colon north-south axis and along the Fort Cimarron to Rio Hato east-west axis to be either hit directly or blocked from moving into Panama City at H-hour.

Once these initial operational objectives were accomplished U.S. military forces could simultaneously both attack or, hopefully, merely round-up the smaller PDF units around the country and deploy to establish order among the civilians. General Thurman referred to this follow-up action as "Stage Two" while Lieutenant General Kelly spoke of the plan as "phased."[7] The timing of this follow-up action and the forces to be used depended entirely upon the success or failure of each part of the opening actions at H-hour. This dependence on previous actions made planning specific

objectives and timing impossible. What the planners did do
was to gather intelligence on the outlying PDF posts and to
make a move on David, the capital of Chiriqui Province, a high
priority.

HOSTILE FORCES

The PDF consisted of approximately 19,600 personnel
including 6,000 in the formal army organized into three
battalions, eight infantry companies, one special force
company, and one engineer company. Police and paramilitary
units including the so-called Dignity Battalions, had another
12,300 personnel. Neither the regular PDF forces nor the
paramilitary forces were armed to defeat an invasion force.
The air force, with only 400 personnel, had no combat aircraft
or armed helicopters. Their largest guns were 60mm mortars.
They had 29 armored cars but no tanks. The PDF naval forces
included two coast guard cutter-type craft, four patrol boats
under 100 tons, four mechanized landing craft (LCM), and one
medium landing ship, all manned by 900 naval personnel.[8] The
PDF wās an internal security force; security from a foreign
invasion was the responsibility of Panama's allies.

The PDF installations that the U.S. plan gave first
priority to lay on two axes: along the canal between Colon
and Panama City and on the Pacific Coast from Rio Hato to Fort
Cimarron. These installations included the airfield and
barracks at Rio Hato on the Pacific coast about 25 miles west
of the canal, Fort Cimarron about 20 miles east of
Torrijos/Tocumen Airport, the Torrijos/Tocumen Airport itself,
the Comandancia (PDF Headquarters), and Fort Amador at the
Pacific mouth of the canal.

The best known of the paramilitary forces, whose name was
applied to about 24 such units, was the Dignity Battalion.
The name comes from its claim to be defending Panamanian
dignity against Yankee imperialism. Actually their role had
been to bully Noriega's domestic opposition. They were
composed of men and women from working class and poor
neighborhoods and were provided arms but little formal
military training. Professor Richard Millett of Southern
Illinois University has pointed out that they were analogous
to the Ton Ton Macoutes of Haiti. General Thurman estimated
the Dignity Battalions as including about 1,800 people in as
many as six battalions of 300 each.[9] Their threat to the U.S.
forces was of harassment during the U.S. attack on the regular
PDF units and as the nucleus for a guerrilla force after the
end of formal combat.

Once President Bush decided to attack with overwhelming
force, the PDF had no hope of winning the conventional battle.
Noriega's one hope of remaining in power was a popular rising
and a guerrilla campaign. The U.S. plan was designed to
defeat the PDF so decisively that those loyal to Noriega would
be thoroughly demoralized and unable to organize a guerrilla
campaign before the Endara government could be established and
to convince the Panamanians that their future lay in

cooperation with the United States, not in resistance.

FRIENDLY FORCES

Given the objective and the numbers and capabilities of the hostile forces, U.S. planners must select which forces to use. This selection is not as simple as it might seem, each military unit has different capabilities and requirements. Some Army units are trained and equipped to deploy by parachute drop. Deploying a heavy armored division clearly requires more sealift and airlift than does a light infantry division. Units expend ammunition at different rates. Enemy air defenses and the type of targets anticipated largely determine which air units to employ, and the most appropriate air unit might come from Army Aviation, the Navy, the Marines, or even the Air Force.

After selecting the appropriate units, the planners must organize the forces selected into a task force. Only rarely will the forces for a major operation all come from the same service, and thus the task force will usually be labeled as "joint." Joint Task Force South executed the plan for Operation Just Cause in Panama. Lieutenant General Carl Stiner, U.S. Army, commander of XVIII Airborne Corps stationed at Fort Bragg, North Carolina, commanded Joint Task Force South. He reported to General Thurman, Commander of U.S. Southern Command, who, in turn, reported directly to the Chairman of the Joint Chiefs of Staff. The Chairman, of course, reported to the Secretary of Defense. General Stiner was selected early enough to participate in the planning and to have the units involved practice assaulting their targets during a series of training exercises.[10]

Friendly Forces: Ground

Joint Task Force South included approximately 13,000 military personnel permanently stationed in Panama or deployed in advance, and approximately 9,500 additional troops flown from the United States during the operation.[11] The planners divided the ground combat forces into six task forces for the initial phase of the plan: Black, Red, Bayonet, Semper Fi, Pacific, and Atlantic. The task forces were organized according to units (Marines, 82nd Airborne, special operations, and so forth), geographic area of operations, type of fighting expected (urban or rural), or whether physically in Panama at H-hour or being deployed from the United States. The planners also provided follow-on forces to reinforce and replace as required and to accomplish the later phases of the plan.

Supporting the ground forces were air units including both the transports to bring the troops from the United States and tactical aircraft (helicopters, fighters, and C-130 gunships) to support them in combat. An Air Operations Center on the ground and an Airborne Command and Control Center (ABCCC), a C-130 with a communication and command capsule in the cargo area, controlled air activities over the combat area.[12]

Most early accounts of <u>Just Cause</u> omit reference to Task Force Black, composed of U.S. Army Special Forces units including Delta Force. General Colin Powell, in his morning briefing on December 20th, described to the press the operations of the other five task forces by name but covered the activities of Task Force Black less forthrightly,

> ...I might add that throughout the area of operations, the special forces group elements belonging to Southern Command have been performing reconnaissance and surveillance, and some of those reconnaissance and surveillance efforts cut out to the Pacora River Bridge early and blocked that.[13]

When <u>Washington Post</u> reporter William Branigin asked why the activities of Delta Force had not been publicized, he was told that "Delta Force 'is a silent weapon.'"[14]

The February 1990 <u>Army</u> article "Operation Just Cause" described "Task Force Black" in some detail. These Special Forces soldiers had the mission of ground reconnaissance including following Noriega before H-hour. At H-hour their job was to capture Noriega, to rescue at least one U.S. citizen held by him, and to provide blocking forces to prevent the movement of PDF forces while larger U.S. forces maneuvered into position. The planners assigned Special Forces teams to monitor and, if directed, assault seven spots frequented by Noriega. One of their most important blocking actions was to seize the Pacora River Bridge on the road between the Torrijos/Tocumen Airport and Fort Cimarron. The Army Special Forces involved were the 3rd Battalion, 7th Special Forces Group (Airborne) stationed in Panama and Company A, 1st Battalion, 7th Special Forces Group deployed from outside Panama. A total of 3,500 special operations personnel including soldiers, airmen, and frogmen participated in <u>Just Cause</u>.[15] Task Force Red was made up of the 1st, 2nd and 3rd Ranger Battalions of the 75th Infantry Regiment (Ranger) (Airborne) and personnel of both the 4th Psychological Operations Group (Airborne) and the 96th Civil Affairs Battalion all of whom belong to the U.S. Army Special Operations Command and were stationed in the United States. Task Force Red's mission was to fly from the United States and jump on the airfield at Rio Hato west of the canal and the Torrijos/Tocumen Airport east of Panama City. Torrijos/Tocumen was a joint military and civilian airfield with a PDF base (Tocumen) on one side and a civilian terminal (Torrijos International Airport) on the other. At Rio Hato, Task Force Red was to defeat the 6th and 7th Rifle Companies of the PDF while at the Torrijos/Tocumen Airport they expected to oppose the 1st Infantry Company and ground crews of the PDF. The plan called for the 1st Ranger Battalion and a company of the 3rd Ranger Battalion to jump into the Tocumen/Torrijos Airport while the rest of the 3rd Battalion and all of the 2nd Battalion jumped into Rio Hato.[16]

Task Force Red thus was made up of U.S. ground troops with the same training and capabilities coming from the United States and attacking similar but geographically separate targets. Between the targets of Task Force Red were targets of both Task Forces Bayonet and Semper Fi, while Task Force Pacific was to follow Task Force Red into the Torrijos/Tocumen Airport.

Task Force Bayonet was composed of U.S. forces in Panama at H-hour, including the 193rd Infantry Brigade (Light) that was permanently assigned to U.S. Army South. Deployed in advance to fill needs identified by the planners were a Sheridan tank platoon with four tanks from the 82nd Airborne Division, the augmented 4th Battalion of the 5th Infantry Division (Mechanized), and Navy SEAL (sea, air, land) teams.

These Task Force Bayonet units were ordered to move into position before H-hour to be ready to attack the Comandancia (PDF Headquarters), the Presidential Palace, Fort Amador, the Patilla Airport, the small PDF fleet, and other PDF facilities in Panama City. The PDF forces at the Comandancia were the First and Second Public Order companies and part of both the 6th and 7th Infantry stationed at Rio Hato. The PDF 5th Infantry Company was in its barracks at Fort Amador. Task force Bayonet was also responsible for protecting such U.S. facilities in Panama City as the Southern Command Headquarters, the housing area at Fort Amador, the embassy, and Fort Clayton. The plan also called for a small force, primarily military police, to cooperate with Task Force Semper Fi to secure the Bridge of the Americas across the canal, and then both were to join U.S. Air Force personnel to protect Howard Air Force Base.[17]

Task Force Semper Fi, as its name implies, was the Marine Corps' contingent in Just Cause. K Company of the 3rd Battalion of the 6th Marine Regiment and D Company of the 2nd Light Armored Infantry Battalion with amphibious vehicles, a detachment of the Brigade Service Support Group from Camp Lejeune, and the Marine Corps' First Fleet Antiterrorism Security Team deployed to Panama for the operation. These units were combined with the Marine Corps Security Force Company permanently stationed in Panama, about 600 men total. In addition to the Bridge of the Americas and the Howard Air Force Base area security, this task force was responsible for the Arraijan Tank Farm about five miles west of the city. The Marines had deployed to Panama before H-hour.[18]

Task Force Pacific, on the other hand, was composed of forces in the United States before the operation. 82nd Airborne Division units comprised most of this task force. These units included the 1st Brigade of the 504th Parachute Infantry Regiment (PIR), Company A of the 3rd Battalion of the 505th PIR, the 4th Battalion of the 325th Airborne Infantry Regiment, 1st and 2nd Battalions of the 82nd Aviation Brigade, 3rd Battalion of the 319th Field Artillery Brigade, part of the 82nd Signal Brigade, part of the 307th Engineer Battalion, part of the 313th Military Intelligence Battalion, part of the

3rd Battalion of the 73rd Armor Regiment (Airborne) with more Sheridan tanks, Company B of the 307th Medical Battalion, Company A of the 407th Supply and Transportation Battalion, A Company of the 782nd Maintenance Battalion, and part of Battery A of the 3rd Battalion of the 4th Air Defense Artillery Battalion. Joining these 82nd Airborne Division units in Task Force Pacific were part of its corps headquarters, the XVIII Airborne Corps, General Stiner's command. These included the 1st Support Command, 16th Military Police Brigade (Airborne), part of the 525th Military Intelligence Brigade, and the 35th Signal Brigade.

Task Force Pacific was not to jump at H-hour but after the Rangers had secured the Torrijos/Tocumen Airport. The planners scheduled the drop of most of Task Force Pacific to start approximately one hour after H-hour at Torrijos/Tocumen Airport. Once on the ground, Task Force Pacific's mission was to relieve the Rangers and the nearby special operations elements of Task Forces Black and Bayonet. The plan called for Task Force Pacific to move out from the airport and deal with any PDF resistance including relieving the Rangers at the Pacora River Bridge and moving further eastward to combat PDF Battalion 2000 at Fort Cimarron. The planners also assigned Task Force Pacific responsibility for the PDF unit at Panama Viejo and the PDF 1st Infantry Company at Tinajitas. Planners designated a small element of Task Force Pacific to jump near Madden Dam and reinforce troops from Task Force Atlantic at that vital facility.[19] The plan called for Task Force Pacific to perform specific assigned missions and to provide the Joint Task Force South Commander with an operational reserve force in the vicinity of Panama City.

Task Force Atlantic operated from about ten miles north of Panama City to Colon. It included the 2nd Battalion of the 27th Infantry of the 7th Infantry Division and the 3rd Battalion of the 504th Infantry of the 82nd Airborne Division which had been training in the Jungle Operations Training Center in Panama. The plan called for Task Force Atlantic to secure the electric distribution center at Cerro Tigre, the prison at Gamboa, Madden Dam, and the Colon area. While securing these facilities and areas, Task Force Atlantic was to neutralize the PDF 8th Infantry Company near Colon and a PDF naval infantry company near Coco Solo.[20]

The plan called for these six task forces to be deployed and in action at H-hour or within a few hours thereafter. The only exceptions were a few headquarters elements identified as part of Task Force Pacific. This massive and immediate application of combat power was designed to overwhelm the PDF and accomplish the objective of destroying its combat capability at the outset of the operation. This objective also contributed to the desirability of hitting late at night when most of the PDF would be in their barracks.

For planners the most obvious drawback to committing so many troops at once was that they all would become exhausted at about the same time. At the end of the first day of combat, many of the troops would not have slept soundly for three days as a consequence of being alerted for deployment, reporting for duty, boarding aircraft, flying south in combat gear, jumping, and fighting. Relief forces had to be provided. The plan called for bringing in the 2nd Brigade of the 7th Infantry and the 16th Military Police Brigade Headquarters with two companies late on the first day of action.[21]

Once Joint Task Force South defeated the PDF, it could turn to other tasks. The initial operational objectives were in the vicinity of Panama City and the canal where the bulk of the population lived and most of the PDF forces were stationed. Once that area was secured, the second phase of the plan called for U.S. forces to spread out into the rest of the country, reduce PDF outposts, and establish the authority of the Endara government. At the same time U.S. forces would begin policing the streets of Panama City and organizing a new Panamanian security force for the Endara government.[22]

Friendly Forces: Air

The planners dealing with the air side of Just Cause had to provide transport for the ground forces and, once they were engaged in battle, firepower and observation to support them. The transport to Panama came from Military Airlift Command (MAC) C-130s, C-141s, and C-5s supported by Strategic Air Command (SAC) tankers. Helicopters from both Army Aviation and the Air Force provided transportation and observation within the combat zone. The planners selected Air Force C-130 gunships and Army helicopters both backed up by Air Force fighters to provide firepower to support the troops. The gunships and fighters also provided observation. Because the planners had selected ground units without much artillery assigned to the unit, this decision reduced the air transport needs but made the availability of airborne firepower critical. To keep losses to a minimum while using transports to deliver the ground forces directly to the targets and while using the relatively slow C-130s and helicopters for firepower, two things were necessary: complete air superiority and night operation.

U.S. forces operated with complete air superiority; the PDF had no aircraft to contest command of the air. Planners had to deal with the possibility of hostile aircraft from a third country--the most likely of which was Cuba. Transports from Fort Bragg and Fort Polk using the most expeditious route in international airspace would pass near Cuba. The possibility of aircraft from Nicaragua appearing over Panama, no matter how far fetched, also could not be ignored. Major General William A. Roosma, Deputy Commander of XVIII Airborne Corps, has stated that during Just Cause the Navy defended "...the skies in which U.S. forces flew...."[23] Planners no doubt called for carrier based fighter aircraft to escort the transports and to patrol over Panama during the fighting. The numbers and types of aircraft and ships involved remains

76

unpublicized.

The other element of the plan designed to hold down air losses and, in the case of the transports, ground force losses was setting H-hour at 1 a.m. The ready availability of hand held, visually aimed, heat-seeking, anti-aircraft missiles such as the Soviet SA-7 and the U.S. Stinger provides a real threat to aircraft operating in daylight. This threat added to the advantage of catching the PDF in its barracks led the planners to select night operations.

Ever since the disastrous 1980 attempt to rescue the hostages in Teheran, if not before, the U.S. Armed Forces have pursued the capacity to fly and fight in the dark, and they have achieved that ability. Planners were able to call for aircrew members in this operation to be provided night-vision devices (primarily the ANIS-6s). Ground forces wore arm patches and tapes on their uniforms that made them readily distinguishable from the PDF and civilians when viewed through the night-vision devices. The equipment was available and the people were able to use it effectively to fly in and out of restricted landing zones and to fly in close proximity to one another safely.[24]

It was a complex problem to plan air drops of 1700 Rangers at 500 feet above the ground over two landing zones (the airfield at Rio Hato and Torrijos/Tocumen Airport) held by hostile forces. Add the fatigue factor of flying over 3,500 miles from Fort Lewis, and a few errors could lead to disaster. The Rangers were to be followed about an hour later by a second jump of about 2,000 Airborne troops into Torrijos/Tocumen Airport with Sheridan tanks and other heavy equipment.[25] The planners assumedly selected jump deployment of follow-on forces to avoid congesting the limited parking space at the airfields and, in case the Rangers had not completed securing the airport, to limit the time the transports were exposed to hostile fire.

Planners called on 27 active duty and reserve Military Airlift Command units stationed at 21 bases to provide 22 C-130s, 77 C-141s, and 12 C-5s. They scheduled 19 C-130s, 63 C-141s, and 2 C-5s to fly jump missions the first night while the remainder landed to unload at U.S. bases or the airfields seized by the Rangers. Because the C-130s cannot air refuel, planners had to make provisions to refuel them in Panama. The primary plan was to land at Howard Air Force Base and refuel before returning to the United States. In case the runway there was obstructed by a wreck or was under attack, an alternate plan was to land at Torrijos/Tocumen Airport and refuel the C-130s from a C-5 on the ground. This alternate refueling plan required that Task Force Pacific jump into the grass near the runway and taxiway so that their Sheridan tanks or other heavy equipment would not obstruct the runway if the equipment was damaged when it landed. Some of the C-141s were also scheduled to land in Panama to evacuate wounded to Kelly Air Force Base, San Antonio, Texas. The C-141s and C-5s that were not required to carry loads back were simply scheduled to fly home empty. En route they would meet Strategic Air

Command (SAC) KC-135 and KC-10 tankers for refueling. SAC provided tankers from 26 squadrons at 14 bases in the United States to support the operation.[26] Many of the transports coming from the U.S. west coast would also need refueling on the way to Panama.

In addition to these transports, planners used 167 Army and nine Air Force helicopters to perform transportation, firepower, and observation roles. The planners incorporated Army UH-60s, CH-47s, UH-1s, AH-1s, AH-64s, AH/MH-6s, and OH-58s as well as Air Force HH-53s and MH-60s.[27] In many instances, the plan called for troops on the ground to move to their operational objectives in Army and Air Force helicopters. These troops included some of those in Panama before H-hour and some who were brought in by MAC airlift. The AH-1 Cobra and AH-64 Apache gunships flew in support of the troops, no matter when they arrived or how they traveled, and were available on call. Most of their missions could not be planned in advance because they had to respond when the ground forces hit particularly stiff resistance and called for support.

The plan called for UH-1 Huey, Ch-47 Chinook, and UH-60 Blackhawk helicopters to move troops in all directions. The helicopters were to lift troops from Task Force Bayonet to Fort Amador and other targets in the Panama City area. Two UH-1s were to land troops from Task Force Atlantic inside the El Renacer Prison near Gamboa, while one AH-1 strafed the guards barracks. Helicopters were scheduled to pick-up Task Force Pacific airborne troops when they landed at Torrijos/Tocumen Airport and take them to outlying targets such as the Pacora River Bridge, Panama Viejo, the Patilla Airport, and Fort Cimarron. The timing of these missions depended upon the success of the jumps, assembling the soldiers, and the progress of Task Forces Black and Bayonet. The planners apparently assigned the Air Force MH-53 Pave Lows and MH-60 Pave Hawks to support both the Army Rangers moving forward to Pacora Bridge and the Navy SEALs of Task Force Bayonet during their initial assaults on Patilla Airport.[28]

To have the needed helicopters available at H-hour, planners called for secret deployments in advance of the operation. Late in November six AH-64 Apaches equipped with a 30mm Chain gun in a turret and a combination of Hellfire anti-tank missiles or 2.75- inch rockets arrived. They flew every night but spent their days inside hangers. "A few days before..." H-hour C-5s brought 20 MH-6/AH-6 special operations forces scout/attack helicopters in at night. These helicopters also remained in hangers until the commencement of <u>Just Cause</u>. The Air Force flew HH-53s and MH-60s in under their own power and also hid them in hangers during daylight.[29]

In addition to using helicopters to provide firepower for close air support of ground forces, the planners included fixed wing aircraft. Seven AC-130 Spectre gunships were to patrol the skies during the operation to provide firepower when needed. AC-130s have three weapons which fire out the left side of the aircraft: a 105mm howitzer in the rear of the cabin, a 40mm Bofors cannon in the middle, and two 20mm Vulcan cannons at the front. This aircraft has a laser target designator, low-light TV cameras, infrared target acquisition equipment, and a search light which can only be seen by troops with night vision devices. The 919th Special Operations Squadron deployed two AC-130s well in advance of the operation, and the 16th Operations Squadron sent two just prior to Just Cause.[30]

The slow moving gunships were backed up by A-7s and OA-37s. The plan included A-7 Corsair II fighter-bombers from the Air National Guard 180th Tactical Fighter Group of Toledo, Ohio. Coronet Cove is a program under which National Guard A-7 units regularly rotate to Howard Air Force Base and, at the time of Just Cause, six A-7s were present in Panama.[31] Twenty-one OA-37 Dragonfly observation aircraft capable of delivering bombs were assigned to the 24th Composite Wing stationed at Howard.

For close air support, the slower the aircraft the easier it is for the crew to be highly accurate. Most fighters use speed in and out of the target area to defend the aircraft against hostile ground fire or hostile aircraft. In an operation where a force has complete control of the air and enemy ground forces have at most a small supply of air defense missiles or anti-aircraft artillery, the most effective systems for close air support are the slower helicopters and AC-130 gunships. AC-130s really are, although the Air Force institutionally abhors the label, flying artillery.

General Stiner selected one other aircraft, the F-117A stealth fighter, to provide close air support. He did this because the Air Force advised him that it was the system that could accomplish the mission precisely. He ordered two F-117As to deliver 2,000-pound bombs within 150 meters of the Rio Hato PDF barracks without hitting or collapsing them. The intent was to terrify PDF personnel while the Rangers of Task Force Red were jumping. The plan included four other F-117As. Two were in position to support special operations personnel searching for Noriega, and the other two were in position to back-up the first four. All six used multiple air refuelings to fly from their base at Tonapah, Nevada, and return without landing.[32]

Planners had to arrange servicing for the aircraft operating in Just Cause. The gunships and fighters apparently operated out of Howard Air Force Base to use pre-positioned supplies of fuel and ordinance. Three refueling points to service the helicopters were set up: one at Fort Sherman on the north Panamanian coast, one southwest of Howard, and one a few miles north of Panama City on the canal. The helicopters would also be able to refuel from the C-5 positioned on the Torrijos/Tocumen Airport if the C-130s that dropped the troops did not need it.[33]

The approximately 20 by 20 mile air space over Panama City and its vicinity would be crowded on December 20th. The planners had to find space for 111 transports, 7 AC-130 gunships, 173 helicopters, 21 OA-37s, 6 A-7s, and 6 F-117As.

No one has made public the details of the flight plans for the transports and tankers. The numbers involved and the critical timing of the drops at H-hour mean that planners had to create a very complex and detailed package of altitudes and ground tracks well in advance. They had to designate assembly and holding points for the transports outside the combat area. Some control agency had to keep track of which aircraft had arrived and when, clear them in on the ingress routes to the drop zones, and check them out. The ground Air Operations Center could have provided this command and control for the transports, but the center's personnel usually deal with aircraft providing close air support to ground forces and therefore would be occupied. The Air Operations Center certainly knew the preplanned routes and altitudes for the transports, but the planners more likely assigned this responsibility for checking the transports in and out to the ABCCC.[34] Another likely possibility is that they used one or more Airborne Warning and Control (AWACs) aircraft orbiting off either coast of Panama. No one, however, has reported the involvement of AWACs in the operation. Whatever the control agency, the risk of a midair collision was very high.

INTELLIGENCE AND DECEPTION

Planners for Joint Task Force South had a number of sources of intelligence and deception in Panama. The performance of the PDF units in the failed coup of October 3, 1989, provided them with basic intelligence. The presence of U.S. forces and installations in Panama provided planners and troops with both excellent operational intelligence and the opportunity to deceive the PDF as H-hour drew near. In preparing for Just Cause, U.S. Southern Command conducted a series of exercises that permitted scouting target areas, rehearsing maneuvers, and masking increased activities. Special operations forces were sent into the field in advance of H-hour to observe specific targets, including the activities of General Noriega. Intelligence was also available from satellites and CIA sources.

The planners' analysis of the October coup attempt identified priority targets. The PDF units most loyal to Noriega in October were the 6th and 7th Companies at Rio Hato and Battalion 2000 at Fort Cimarron. In October the 7th Company flew to Panama City to come to Noriega's aid while Battalion 2000 arrived by truck. In light of this information, the planners made seizing the airports at Rio Hato and Panama City, disabling the Panamanian aircraft, and seizing the bridges high priority targets. In fact, the Rio Hato airport and PDF barracks were not even H-hour targets until after the October coup.[35]

To familiarize the troops involved with their targets and operations, joint exercises, code named Purple Storms, and single unit exercises, code named Sand Fleas, were held weekly for several months prior to Just Cause. In July a sequence of joint exercises rehearsing parts of the Just Cause plan began. After the operation was complete, General Stiner reported that "We practiced every target." The troops that were not in Panama or brought in for exercises practiced on mock-ups at Fort Bragg. Significantly the junior ranking personnel never realized that they were practicing a real plan.[36]

Many participants in Just Cause had local knowledge of Panama that provided valuable operational intelligence. Second Lieutenant John Shaw of the 193rd Infantry Brigade stationed in Panama, participated in the attack on the Comandancia and said afterwards that the officers in his company had been meeting on weekends to discuss the operation. They had devised exercises to practice moving platoons through buildings. Sergeant Hans Denger of the same company said that their local knowledge of the roads and ability to scout the Comandancia from high ground was very helpful. He also reported that Americans who had friends in the PDF were able to take advantage of these friendships to reconnoiter PDF installations.[37] Such intimate knowledge and the exercises produced invaluable operational intelligence.

By plan, the same exercises that allowed U.S. forces to gain their operational intelligence provided deception about U.S. intentions. U.S. training at all hours of the day and night with various sized units lulled the Panamanians into a sense of complacency. When U.S. forces established the forward refueling points for use by helicopters in Just Cause, the Panamanians accepted it as just another training activity.[38] In a November exercise, Marines drove their armored vehicles across the Bridge of the Americas, control of which was a primary objective for them as Task Force Semper Fi.[39] Planners hoped that the intensity of these exercises would ensure that an increase in activity just prior to H-hour in Just Cause would not provide a warning to Noriega.

Finally the planners worked to obtain intelligence about Noriega's habits and movements. Working directly for General Thurman, a National Security Agency detachment with a CIA liaison officer tracked him by monitoring his communications and movements. The trackers were aware that he routinely moved from place to place as often as five times a night and sent false radio messages to mask his movements. Special forces teams were watching some of his known residences and operating locations, and in advance of H-hour, they staked-out seven of those spots. The U.S. Southern Command could identify Noriega's location for 75 to 80 percent of the time. The planners had also identified his possible means of escape by sea or air.[40]

RULES OF ENGAGEMENT

The long term U.S. goal of good relations with Panama required that U.S. Armed Forces accomplish their operational objectives with as little destruction and as few casualties as possible. Combat, however, is inherently destructive and the friction of war ensures that there will always be damage and civilian deaths. The easiest way to hold U.S. casualties to a minimum, a practice that U.S. soldiers have been criticized for relying on too heavily since at least the French and Indian War, is the liberal application of firepower. Full application of all available U.S. firepower while holding down U.S. casualties and destroying the PDF would also create large numbers of Panamanian casualties and resultant bitter feelings against the United States. It would also exacerbate the Endara government's legitimacy problems created by its birth at the point of U.S. bayonets. Thus, holding both U.S. casualties and Panamanian death and destruction to a minimum while destroying the PDF's combat capability required great care. A balance had to be planned and maintained.

As a consequence the commanders and planners of Just Cause laid down strict rules of engagement (ROE); General Thurman, the U.S. Southern Command Commander, ordered "'the minimum use of power required'" to achieve battlefield victories. He required that an officer of lieutenant colonel or above order the use of indirect fire weapons such as artillery or mortars and the use of aerial strafing or bombing. Lieutenant General Stiner, the Joint Task Force South Commander, further restricted the use of artillery and aerial bombing in the city by requiring the approval of a major general for artillery fire and of himself for bombing. These stringent restrictions did not apply to the use of highly accurate gunship cannon and rocket fire. The ROE prohibited helicopter door gunners from returning small arm fire which was expected to be received from individuals hiding in city houses and crowds.[41]

Each infantry company attacking a PDF barracks was accompanied by a psychological operations team. Once a barracks was surrounded, U.S. forces played a recording on a loud speaker announcing that they were there to liberate Panama and did not want to harm anyone, and appealing to the PDF to surrender within fifteen minutes. If the PDF did not surrender, U.S. forces would call in a helicopter or AC-130 for a "... 'measured application of fire.'" After the gunship fired a short burst or a 105mm round, U.S. forces were to play the tape again and set a new time limit for a surrender.[42] If resistance continued, the U.S. ground commander could call for more firepower with the approval of senior commanders.

These ROE were designed to reduce Panamanian casualties without significantly raising U.S. losses. The same idea lay behind the decision to have the F-117As drop their bombs near but not on the PDF barracks at Rio Hato. A tradeoff there was the decision to jump at 500 feet above the ground rather than at the training height of 800 feet. The lower altitude meant less time in the air thus reducing the exposure to small arms fire of airborne troops hanging in their parachutes. Lower jumps, however, could result in increased landing injuries because the paratroopers had less time to prepare for the landing and did not use a reserve parachute.[43] The small arms fire could have been reduced by bombing the PDF barracks which, of course, would have substantially increased Panamanian casualties.

PROJECTED CASUALTIES AND MEDICAL EVACUATION (MEDEVAC)

For U.S. planners any casualties are too many by definition, but no one could expect to execute an operation such as Just Cause with no casualties. The planners expected injuries from two causes; enemy action and accidents. They anticipated that the single largest cause of accidents would be the 500-foot paratroop jumps onto the runways. In peacetime training the U.S. Army normally suffers a six percent casualty rate on jumps that are made at 800 feet. The plan included an estimate of 70 U.S. personnel killed and "several hundred" wounded.[44] No estimate of Panamanian casualties has been made public.

Planners had to make provisions for the several hundred U.S. wounded to receive immediate attention. They had to arrange for the seriously wounded to be stabilized and then moved to a hospital for treatment. The Army Community Hospital at Quarry Heights and other U.S. facilities in Panama would treat as many as they could, but it obviously would be overwhelmed even though a team would come from Fitzsimons Army Medical Center in Denver to assist. Planners set-up assessment areas where troops arrived by helicopter and ambulance. One such assessment area was near Howard Air Force Base, and another was in the terminal of the Torrijos/Tocumen Airport. There may have been others, perhaps, near Colon and Rio Hato. At Howard, an Army Forward Surgery Team—Airborne (FST-A) worked under canvas. Plans called for the 1st Air Medical Evacuation Squadron from Pope Air Force Base to work in tents next to the FST-A tending patients ready and waiting for flights to the United States.[45]

Plans also called for regular and reserve Air Force C-141s to make the flights to the United States. Their destination was Kelly Air Force Base where doctors would check the patients on board the aircraft and determine which would go into the Air Force's Wilford Hall Medical Center at Kelly and which would be transported 20 minutes by ambulance or eight minutes by helicopter to Brooke Army Medical Center. The most severely wounded would go immediately into Wilford Hall for emergency treatment. Most orthopedic injuries sustained jumping into Panama would also go into Wilford Hall because it had more capacity for orthopedic injuries than Brooke.[46]

Planners assumed that Panamanian medical facilities would provide primary care for Panamanian casualties. U.S. medical personnel, however, would also care for Panamanians, who would be accepted at Gorgas Army Community Hospital and the airport terminal. The air evacuation plans did not include Panamanian casualties.[47]

EXECUTION

On Sunday December 17, 1989, President Bush ordered the execution of Operation <u>Just Cause</u>. He or Secretary of Defense Cheney set H-hour at 1 a.m. on Wednesday, December 20, 1989. Commanders immediately made pre-attack notifications, putting troops and aircrews on alert and using an exercise as the cover story. MAC had to assemble transports from their usual peacetime missions and position them at their departure airfields. It also had to notify its crews and put them into "crewrest" status for twenty-four hours in advance of their operations. The preparation reached down to the level of ordering Army helicopter crew members in Panama not to have any alcoholic drinks without telling them the reason for such abstinence.[48]

U.S. activity increased as H-hour approached. General Stiner arrived in Panama the evening before to make last minute adjustments with his commanders, as C-141s shuttled in and out of Howard Air Force Base with troops and supplies. Task Force Black's teams conducted reconnaissance and moved out to positions near their targets to strike at H-hour or earlier, while Task Forces Bayonet, Atlantic, and Semper Fi units moved into staging areas. Task Force Red troops had been airborne for hours, while Task Force Pacific troops were loading their aircraft except where weather interfered. One item of preparation not essential for operational readiness but part of the effort to protect American lives was a December 19th notice to U.S. civilians to restrict their movements. All this preparation allowed Joint Task Force South to hit 27 targets simultaneously at H-hour, which General Stiner advanced fifteen minutes for fear of security leaks.[49]

This increased activity and some espionage appear to have prevented a complete surprise. A Reuters despatch on Tuesday, December 19th, reported that President Bush had met with key advisors that afternoon but said it was about the war on drugs. Reuters also reported that NBC television had broadcast footage of C-141s landing every ten minutes in Panama while CBS reported the departure of transports from Fort Bragg, North Carolina. The same report included a statement by the Defense Department that the 82nd Airborne's 18th Airborne Corps was participating in a readiness exercise.[50] Between 24 and 48 hours before H-hour the National Security Agency intercepted a telephone call to Noriega. The unknown caller told him that a source in the U.S. State Department had said U.S. military intervention was imminent. Someone in the State Department reportedly placed a call to a member of the Canal Commission, warning him to keep his children home that night, and he supposedly warned his friends. At 10 p.m. on December 19th Panamanians supposedly overheard two U.S. soldiers discussing H-hour. The result of these compromises were warnings on Panamanian radio that the U.S. was attacking at 1 a.m. and that PDF units should report, draw arms, and prepare to fight. Noriega appears to have

believed that something was about to occur without knowing
precisely what or when. He increased his movements but did
not put the PDF on alert, although some units did increase
their readiness on their own initiative.[51] Thus, the massive
U.S. exercise activities in the month before Just Cause
apparently provided sufficient uncertainty for Noriega and
other Panamanian leaders that they did not recognize the real
operation until too late.

Task Force Black at H-hour

Before H-hour the special operations teams of Task Force
Black moved into position and started to strike. The first
into action was the Delta Force team assaulting the Carcel
Modelo (Model Jail) to free Kurt Frederick Muse. In April
the Noriega regime had arrested Muse, an American who had
grown up in Panama, for running a clandestine anti-Noriega
radio station. He claimed to be working for the State
Department but was accused of working for the CIA. Prison
authorities had told Muse he would die if the United States
pursued Noriega. The Delta Force team arrived shortly after
midnight in several armored personnel carriers and in a
helicopter that landed on the roof. They struck so suddenly
that the guards never used their weapons, but nearby PDF
troops opened fire and killed a gunner in the first armored
personnel carrier. The Delta Force team rescued Muse and took
him to the helicopter. The PDF poured heavy small arms fire
into the helicopter, which went down, breaking the pilot's leg
and giving Muse a fracture. An armored personnel carrier then
rescued Muse and drove off at about 12:45 a.m., six minutes
after Delta Force had begun attacking the prison.[52]

Delta Force, Army Special Forces, and other special
operations personnel had been following Noriega and were in
position to strike seven of the places he was known to
frequent. On December 19th Noriega had gone to Colon but
returned to Panama City that afternoon by car instead of on
an airplane that the National Security Agency tracking team
expected him to use. His mistress later said that he went to
a hotel next to the Torrijos/Tocumen Airport to visit a
prostitute, and fled as U.S. Rangers hit the airport. The
Task Force Black teams raided four of the sites they had under
surveillance but failed to capture Noriega. For the next five
days they chased Noriega from place to place until he sought
refuge in the Papal Nunciature.[53] Capturing Noriega might have
helped reduce PDF and Dignity Battalion resistance. His
escape and flight for five days was not a critical operational
failure, however, because the U.S. plan foresaw this
possibility and ensured that Noriega had no way to leave
Panama. While he was fleeing, he did, however, cause the Bush
administration some embarrassment; and if he had escaped to
Cuba or another sanctuary he could have become a rallying
point for opposition to the Endara government, which could
have been a disaster.

At H-hour, meanwhile, a Task Force Black Army Special

Forces team emerged from cover and seized control of the
Pacora River Bridge, the choke point on the route from Fort
Cimarron to Panama City and the Torrijos/Tocumen Airport.
Battalion 2000 at Fort Cimarron, which was being observed by
a Task Force Black team, could have been a real threat if it
attacked the Rangers jumping on the airport. The plan called
for Rangers to move up and relieve the Special Forces at the
Pacora River Bridge, but the Rangers were not yet in place
when Battalion 2000 started down the road in a convoy. The
Special Forces called in an AC-130 gunship that destroyed the
first nine vehicles in the convoy, and the remainder fled back
to Fort Cimarron. Battalion 2000 disappeared into the jungle
and played no further role in opposing Just Cause.[54]

Task Force Bayonet at H-hour

On the night of December 19th, Task Force Bayonet
deployed to three jumping-off points: Albrook Air Force Base,
the Southern Command Headquarters compound at Quarry Heights
on Ancon Hill, and Fort Clayton. During this deployment, the
augmented 4th Battalion of the 5th Infantry Division
(Mechanized) assigned to the 193 Brigade moved in its M-113
armored personnel carriers from Camp Gator near Howard Air
Force Base to Albrook Air Force Base. They had to divert to
a secondary bridge when reconnaissance patrols reported PDF
forces on the Bridge of the Americas and the placing of large-
caliber weapons at the National Department of Investigations.
They reached Albrook without incident.[55] From these jumping-
off points Task Force Bayonet simultaneously hit the
Commandancia (PDF Headquarters), Fort Amador, the National
Department of Investigations and the Department of National
Transportation buildings, Patilla Airport, and other targets.
Some of the most intense combat in Panama City occurred
at the Commandancia, which was inside a walled PDF compound
in the poor El Chorillo neighborhood just below Ancon Hill.
The Commandancia building was a forty year-old reinforced
concrete structure with two-foot thick walls. Members of the
Dignity Battalions (1st and 2nd Public Order Companies) and
elements of the regular PDF 6th and 7th Companies from Rio
Hato armed with small arms as well as anti-tank and anti-
aircraft weapons defended the Commandancia.[56]
At about 12:30 a.m. three infantry companies of the 193rd
Brigade in trucks and M-113s moved toward the Commandancia
from Albrook Air Force Base while the 82nd Airborne Sheridan
platoon advanced from Fort Clayton. The infantry came under
sniper fire and had to break through road blocks as they moved
down the hill. Meanwhile AC-130s and helicopter gunships
fired on the Commandancia for ten minutes. The infantry
dismounted about two blocks from the Commandancia and rushed
forward, while the M-113s and Sheridans breached the compound
walls. The thick walls of the Commandancia were impervious
to 50 calibre fire but the Sheridans effectively fired into
windows where snipers appeared. In Spanish and English, U.S.
forces repeatedly called on the PDF to surrender. While the

infantry was attacking the Commandancia, the M-113s established a defensive perimeter to guard against a counter-attack by PDF. During the fighting that night, two special operations force's helicopters, assumedly, MH/AH-6s, were shot down.[57]

In the face of stiff resistance and unwilling to accept the casualties of an infantry rush, the 193rd Brigade commander Lieutenant Colonel Mike Snell, called for support from AC-130s. On their first run against the Commandancia, they had strafed it without using their 105mm guns, had destroyed anti-aircraft batteries, and had set fire to a number of vehicles including two water cannon. This time the AC-130s obliterated the third floor of the Commandancia with 105mm shells.[58]

The infantry waited until dawn to enter the Commandancia. The PDF had retreated from it during the night but remained in other buildings in the compound and in the surrounding civilian buildings. The infantry cleared those buildings room-by-room and floor-by-floor where, in addition to their normal weapons, each squad leader carried a shotgun to blow doors open and clear rooms. To minimize the civilian casualties, U.S. forces did not use tanks or gunships against snipers in the civilian buildings, but relied on counter-sniping or hunting the snipers in the buildings. The process was very slow and hazardous.[59]

By the time Task Force Bayonet had eliminated the organized resistance at the Commandancia on the afternoon of December 20th, much of the El Chorillo neighborhood had burned. After the operation, a number of Panamanians appeared on television and said the Dignity Battalions had set the fires, and accused the Battalions of setting fire to gasoline stations in order to threaten U.S. soldiers from the rear. Some of the fires, however, were certainly started by tracer rounds from U.S. weapons.[60]

At the same time as Task Force Bayonet attacked the Commandancia, Black Hawk helicopters of the 1st Battalion, 228th Aviation Brigade, carried another part of the 193rd Brigade into Fort Amador, the quarters for both the PDF 5th Company and for U.S. military families. Between the two was a golf course where the Black Hawks landed. During this assault an OH-58 scout helicopter, the only conventional force's helicopter lost during the first night's action, went down.[61]

The PDF barracks at Fort Amador faced the golf course with the Gulf of Panama behind it. When U.S. troops attacked, many PDF personnel immediately fled and swam for their lives. A Boston Globe report credits the Navy with picking up 500 men. The U.S assault force commander, Lieutenant Colonel Billy Rae Fitzgerald, explained to the Washington Post that they called on the PDF to surrender for over an hour before attacking. To encourage the Panamanians, Fitzgerald's troops shelled an empty building with their 105mm howitzer. In the actual attack on the barracks, U.S. forces killed six PDF troops and wounded three, while the PDF inflicted no casualties on U.S. troops. Most of the PDF casualties occurred before the attack on the barracks, when U.S. forces fired on a bus load of about 21 men trying to escape. Fitzgerald's troops also captured 99 prisoners.[62]

The plan called for Company C of 5th Battalion of the 87th Infantry assigned to the 193rd Brigade to secure the National Department of Investigations and National Department of Transportation buildings. The Armed Forces Journal reported that an AC-130 destroyed the National Department of Investigations building after PDF troops there refused to surrender. The accompanying photograph dramatically showed a number of undamaged buildings with one in the middle demolished. An Army magazine article about C Company's combat provides a first hand account of two squads taking positions in front and behind an unidentified building. When the PDF in the building pinned down the squad in front, the Americans called in a weapons platoon with a M-60 machine gun and a 90mm recoilless rifle. The weapons platoon drove the PDF out the rear of the building into the waiting squad's ambush. The AC-130 does not appear in the Army story.[63] If both accounts are correct, the Army story deals only with the National Department of Transportation building. Both accounts describe effective and discriminate use of superior firepower.

Forty-eight Navy SEALs assigned to Task Force Bayonet attacked the Patilla Airport at H-hour. Their objective was to control the airfield and to disable Noriega's airplane so that he could not use it to escape from Panama. Just before they attacked, the SEALs were ordered to wreck the landing gear of the airplane rather than destroy the entire aircraft in order to prevent the collateral damage that would occur if Noriega's aircraft exploded and started fires in other planes or nearby civilian buildings. This required the SEALs to go right up to the aircraft rather than fire on it from a distance.

The PDF defense of the Patilla Airport was much stronger than expected. U.S. intelligence had reported only lightly armed civilian security police there, but the SEALs ran into some of Noriega's best troops who were heavily armed and were ready to fight. The combination of a last minute change in plans and inaccurate intelligence was fatal. Advancing across the open airfield, the SEALs took heavy fire. Four died and three suffered severe wounds. The problems continued as some of the wounded were not evacuated by helicopter for hours. The SEALs finally fired an AT-4 round into the cockpit of the aircraft, destroying it, the airport hanger, and at least two other aircraft. Eventually 82nd Airborne troops of Task Force Pacific relieved them.[64]

Task Force Bayonet also hit other targets at H-hour without experiencing as much combat. SEALs boarded and disabled patrol boats in the harbor to preclude Noriega's escape by sea. An element made up primarily of military police moved to the Bridge of the Americas and met Marines in Task Force Semper Fi. The task force also seized the Presidential Palace and provided protection for Fort Clayton, the U.S. Southern Command Headquarters, and the U.S. Embassy during the opening phases of Just Cause.[65]

Some controversy emerged about Task Force Bayonet's protection of the U.S. Embassy. The Panamanians had fired rocket propelled grenades at the embassy at 1:22 a.m. No U.S. troops beyond the usual Marine Corps guards appeared until 4:20 a.m., and these troops were about to move on when the embassy called Washington and the Department of Defense ordered them to remain. A senior embassy official told the Washington Post that no extra forces were moved to the embassy on Tuesday to avoid telegraphing to Noriega that the increased activity was more than an exercise. Some embassy employees complained bitterly about their exposure to danger.[66]

Apparently the Joint Task Force South Commander and the U.S. Southern Command Commander felt that the embassy would be best defended, as were the rest of the Americans in Panama, by having Task Force South destroy the combat capability of the PDF. Their thinking seems to have been that if the PDF was totally on the defensive and unable to launch any offensive actions in the early hours of December 20th, the embassy's Marine guards would be able to handle any small party looking for hostages. Some embassy personnel did not feel adequately protected, but the reality was that although everybody in Panama City faced greater risk, the embassy was sufficiently secure. Additional security could only have been provided by reducing combat power in places where there was either active combat or a higher risk of combat.

One of the first objectives of Task Force Bayonet, to seize the Panamanian television station, was accomplished as planned. Not included in the plan was immediately capturing the Panamanian radio station, and Noriega used it to broadcast a call for resistance during the first day of Just Cause. It was shut down the next night when a U.S. helicopter fired rockets into the building and the station went off the air.[67] No one has reported any attempt by infantrymen to occupy the building; the U.S. simply blew the station apart to silence it.

Task Force Atlantic at H-hour

At Colon, Task Force Atlantic quickly defeated the 8th PDF Company, which did not offer great resistance. The Task Force Atlantic battalion, including troops from the 82nd Airborne Division and the 7th Infantry Division then moved to Coco Solo where they came up against a determined PDF Naval Infantry unit that fought well. During the Colon fighting, the PDF shot down an MH/AH-6 SOF helicopter, killing the pilot. By the afternoon of the 20th, however, PDF resistance was reduced to sporadic firing.[68]

At H-hour, Hueys carried Task Force Atlantic troops into El Renacer Prison near Gamboa, while a Cobra helicopter gunship attacked the PDF barracks. This assault was launched without warning for fear that the guards would kill the prisoners or use them as hostages. Forty-eight Panamanian prisoners were rescued, while five U.S. soldiers were wounded, including three injured by their own satchel charges. Five PDF troops were killed and fifteen were captured. The paratroopers then moved to protect a housing area at Gamboa.[69]

Troops from this same battalion secured two other vital objectives. They seized the electrical distribution center at Cerra Tigre and the Madden Dam that provided the water to operate the canal locks. If saboteurs had been able to blow-up the dam, the canal could have been disabled for a year or more.[70]

Task Force Semper Fi in Action

Task Force Semper Fi, the smallest of the task forces, was composed of conventional but elite forces. The approximately 600 Marines secured an area of about six square miles southwest of Panama City. This area included U.S. Naval Station Panama (Rodman), Howard Air Force Base, the Arraijan Tank Farm, and the Bridge of the Americas. In securing the bases, the Marines deployed into the areas around the bases beyond the positions of the normal perimeter security forces.

The Marines moved on the Bridge of the Americas from the west where they joined the military police unit from Task Force Bayonet. They secured the bridge without resistance and set up road blocks there and on the Inter-American Highway.[71]

They met resistance while securing the Arraijan Tank Farm, a fuel depot essential to supporting aircraft at Howard Air Force Base upon which much of Just Cause depended. The 1st Fleet Anti-Terrorist Security Team attacked a PDF compound near the tank farm and dispersed the PDF troops there. The Marines then moved by light armored vehicles (LAVs) to assault another PDF compound at the town of Arraijan. Near the town they found a roadblock and a platoon of PDF. The Marines scouted the roadblock, attacked the PDF, and seized the compound, suffering one killed and two wounded in the process.[72]

Task Force Red at H-hour

Rangers from Fort Lewis, Washington, Fort Benning, Georgia, and Hunter Army Airfield, Georgia, boarded MAC transports before sunset on December 19, 1990, and jumped at H-hour into the airfield at Rio Hato, home of the 6th and 7th PDF Companies, and Tocumen/Torrijos Airport.

At Rio Hato, the action had opened with two F-117As dropping 2,000 pound bombs near the PDF barracks to stun and disorient the defenders. Because of pilot error, the bomb reportedly landed more than 300 yards off the intended point. Still the effectiveness of this action was supposedly demonstrated by reports of PDF troops "'running around in their underwear.'"[73]

Despite the F-117A's mission, the PDF had been alerted, was partially prepared, and began firing when the transports were about 1000 meters from the drop zone. The first U.S.

combat casualty was a Ranger shot in the head by groundfire as his transport approached the drop zone.[74] Given this warning and the firing by the PDF, the decision to jump from 500 feet instead of 800 no doubt saved U.S. lives.

Once on the ground the Rangers secured the airfield, and then moved on the PDF barracks with AC-130 support. The 6th and 7th PDF Companies fired on the Rangers as they advanced but usually evacuated a building from the rear as the Rangers entered the front. As the Rangers charged out the rear of a building, they drew fire. After engaging the first few Rangers, the PDF routinely fled into the next building or into the bushes. When PDF forces regrouped and tried to counter-attack, they met not only the Rangers but also the fire of the AC-130s.[75]

Special operations personnel with the Rangers continually called on PDF troops to surrender and were often successful. Another reason to surrender was the stream of C-130s with 7th Division light infantry men assigned to Task Force Pacific that began landing within two hours of the first jump and before the fighting had ended.

An incident at Rio Hato reflects the restraint and discipline of U.S. forces. During the fighting to clear the PDF barracks, a Ranger captain burst into a large room ready to fire at any hostile sign. He found 180 PDF unarmed trainees backed into a corner. Neither the captain nor the Rangers rushing in right behind him fired, but less disciplined, less alert personnel could have, with disastrous effects.[76]

Numerous sources describe the fighting at Rio Hato as among the hardest in Just Cause. While U.S. losses were significant, they could easily have been much worse. Task Force Red suffered four killed and 44 wounded at Rio Hato, 41 of whom were injured in their parachute jumps. The possibility of much higher losses was due to the arms captured there. If the four ZPU-4 anti-aircraft guns (manually operated four barrel weapons that were very effective against helicopters in Vietnam) had been properly positioned, manned, and serviced, they could have played havoc with the U.S. transports. The 48 rocket-propelled grenades, 55 machine guns, eight 81mm mortars, and 16 armored cars could have decimated the Rangers in the air and on the ground had not Task Force Red achieved an effective tactical surprise.[77]

Task Force Red achieved an equally effective surprise in its jump at the Tocumen/Torrijos Airport. Noriega appears to have been either at a hotel or the officers' club at the airport and to have fled as approximately 700 Rangers (all of the 1st Ranger Battalion and one company of the 3rd Battalion) jumped from the sky. AC-130 gunships had softened up this objective prior to the jump at H-hour. The Rangers met half-hearted and disorganized resistance from the PDF. Once the Rangers had surrounded the civilian terminal, psychological operations personnel called on the PDF to surrender. The injuries in this operation were almost all jump-related and included about two percent of U.S. personnel. By dawn, U.S.

forces had control of the airfield and had sent patrols out
to the east, including patrols to reinforce Task Force Black
special forces at the Pacora River bridge.   The Rangers
effectively blocked both any possible surface move by
Battalion 2000 on the capital and any possible flight into the
Tocumen/Torrijos Airport by PDF forces.[78]

Task Force Pacific at H-hour

At 1:55 a.m. Task Force Pacific, built around the 82nd
Airborne Division, started jumping into the Tocumen/Torrijos
Airport and near the Madden Dam to reinforce the troops
already at those objectives. The bulk of the paratroopers at
Tocumen/Torrijos Airport were simply jumping there,
assembling, and moving out by truck or helicopter to seize
other objectives.   Half of the 20 C-141s carrying
approximately 2000 paratroopers from Fort Bragg were delayed
three hours at Pope Air Force Base by an ice storm. The base
had only enough de-icing equipment to handle six of the
aircraft at a time.   The troops were loaded on schedule and
sat there wet and cold waiting to launch.   They finally
reached the drop-zone at 5:15 a.m.   While en route some of
these C-141s were intercepted by Cuban MiG-21s as they flew
between Cuba and the Yucatan Peninsula.   One C-141 reported
that a MiG-21 appeared to fire a warning shot from its
cannon.[79] Thus, the provision of naval aviation to secure the
skies was not an idle precaution.
Unlike that of Task Force Red at the Tocumen/Torrijos
Airport, the drop of Task Force Pacific was offset from the
runway. Here paratroopers were supposed to land on the grass
so as not to block runways and taxiways with their Sheridan
tanks or other heavy equipment that might be damaged in the
drop. Before the operation, the landing zone was scouted from
the air, but without someone landing and walking on it, U.S.
forces could not tell that some of the grass was head high and
that some places were poorly drained.   Thus, when the heavy
equipment landed some of it was instantly stuck in the mud,
and some of the troops had trouble seeing each other and
joining their units. This led to news reports of the drop
missing the landing zone and hitting a swamp while MAC
reported that the drop was right on target.[80]
The late arrival of half of Task Force Pacific at
Tocumen/Torrijos Airport meant moving in daylight. Most of
the 45 Army helicopters hit by hostile fire during Just Cause
were hit during daylight operations the first day. These came
largely from small arms, and only one of the battle-damaged
Army helicopters remained out of service after twenty-four
hours.[81]
Helicopters and surface transport moving the 82nd
Airborne paratroopers to their targets were opposed by a PDF
company at Tiajitas and a cavalry squadron at Panama Viejo.
They relieved the SEALs at Paitilla Airport and moved up the
road to Fort Cimarron, relieving the Rangers at the Pacorra
River bridge while en route. When Task Force Pacific reach

Fort Cimarron, Battalion 2000 had disappeared.[82]

Follow-up Action

The follow-up action, involving troops of Joint Task South and the arrival of reinforcements from the United States, included some additional combat and a great deal of effort to establish order. Combat included action in Panama City and moving out into the country both to reduce small PDF outposts and to establish the Endara government's authority. Establishing order included police duties, primarily in Panama City. Hunting Noriega played a role in both operations.

In the 4:40 p.m. Pentagon news briefing on December 20th, Lieutenant General Kelly reviewed the actions and objectives of each task force in Panama. He announced that organized resistance had ended but that the Dignity Battalions were still operating in Panama City. In response to reporters' questions, he asserted that troops would be working to restore order in the city and to apprehend Noriega. While Kelly was announcing that organized resistance was over, he was anxious to get the follow-on forces into Panama.[83]

The follow-on forces included the 2nd Brigade of the 7th Infantry Division from Fort Ord, California, and two companies of the 16th Military Police with their Brigade Headquarters from Fort Bragg, North Carolina. Some of the 7th Infantry Brigade ran into fog in California trying to move by convoy to Travis Air Force Base to load onto transports. Eventually the transports flew to Monterey Airport, picked up the troops, and unloaded them at airfields in Panama.[84]

These forces joined the troops already in place to secure lower priority objectives in Panama City. One was the relief of the Marriott Hotel where news media people had been during the operation. When the 82nd Airborne paratroopers traveling in HUMVs reached the Marriott, they found 29 American civilians and 35 individuals from other countries. When an unidentified armored personnel carrier (APC) approached, the U.S. troops in the hotel opened fire. The APC, which turned out to be American, returned the fire. In this unfortunate but almost inevitable incident reflecting the friction of war, an English and a Spanish photographer died in the crossfire. The survivors were taken to the Tocumen/Torrijos Airport.[85]

U.S. troops moved to secure Panamanian government offices and cut off Noriega's diplomatic escape routes. Among other objectives secured were the Foreign Ministry, Health Ministry, and Finance Ministry and Central Bank. To prevent his seeking political asylum, U.S. troops surrounded the Cuban, Nicaraguan, and Libyan embassies. One patrol investigating a reported arms cache searched the Nicaraguan Ambassador's house over his vehement objections.[86] Lieutenant General Kelly announced the end of "organized resistance" on December 20th, but on December 22nd, General Thurman said that his troops were fighting a "real war" against organized resistance. The apparent discrepancy lay in the definition of "organized resistance" and "real war." In fact the regular PDF forces had been destroyed as cohesive military organizations within seven hours of the U.S. attack. There were no longer PDF units manning fixed positions and resisting U.S. forces, which was apparently what Kelly meant by "organized resistance."[87] There were, however, armed individuals and groups moving about Panama City and firing at U.S. forces--urban guerrilla Noriega loyalists who had to be subdued, which was apparently what Thurman meant by "real war."

On December 21st, infantry squads patrolled the streets on foot and in vehicles, searching for PDF members and weapons. Staff Sergeant Edward McCrane of C Company of the 87th Infantry's 5th Battalion led one such patrol in a five ton truck. Their mode of operation was simple. They would stop at intersections, and he would display an AK-47. In Spanish Sergeant McCrane would explain that this was a PDF weapon and ask the people to surrender any weapons as well as any PDF members. At one point a brown Toyota sedan with a white flag on the radio antenna started closely following McCrane's truck, and he tried to wave it off. When the Toyota remained, he ordered his driver to turn and his troops to point their weapons in the Toyota's direction. It quickly ducked down a side street. Later another group of troops questioning civilians at another intersection heard gunfire down the street. The civilians ran as the troops pressed against the buildings for cover. Over the radio came the message, "It was a drive-by shooting. Be on the lookout for a brown Toyota with a white flag tied to its antenna."[88] Operations in Panama City remained dangerous and nerve racking regardless of what was said in Washington.

On December 23rd, the guerrillas launched their most dramatic attack when, at 11:30 a.m., Noriega loyalists attacked the police headquarters near the Southern Command Headquarters at Quarry Heights. The police headquarters was controlled by police who had joined the Endara government. The Noriega loyalists attacked with mortars, machine guns, and automatic rifles. The attack lasted "at least ten minutes" and wounded "several." The closeness of the attack to Quarry Heights and the sound of U.S. troops firing a 105mm howitzer at the warehouse from which the mortars appeared to be firing led to false reports that the attack was on the Southern Command Headquarters itself.[89]

This small counterattack did not constitute massive resistance and did not threaten to drive Joint Task Force South from Panama. It did, however, threaten the lives of individual U.S. military personnel and was sufficient cause for concern about continued low level resistance.

U.S. patrols moved systematically across Panama City. On December 22nd, the U.S. Southern Command assigned police duties to about 3,000 U.S. troops. On the 23rd, the 82nd Airborne swept the city from the northeast to the southwest while the 193rd Brigade and part of the 6th Military Police Company swept in the opposite direction.[90] Panama City was suffering from the after effects of a battle that had eliminated the police force but not yet replaced it. The PDF had melted into the civilian population, and looting and arson were widespread. As long as Noriega remained at large there was reason to fear that he could provide leadership and direction to the guerrillas and that the PDF personnel who had fled and the Dignity Battalions who were not conducting "organized resistance" against the U.S. forces could conduct a "real war."

On the 24th, the streets of Panama City appeared to be calm for the first time. General Thurman told reporters of his belief that life would soon be normal in Panama City. U.S. troops concentrated on looters and occasional snipers and former PDF members participated in joint patrols with U.S. troops. About 1,000 of the former PDF members responded to a call to join a new Panamanian security force commanded by Colonel Roberto Armijo. That afternoon as resistance wound down, Noriega ended the possibility of his leading a guerrilla movement by walking into the Papal Nunciature and requesting asylum.[91] The operational side of Just Cause in Panama City was over.

Follow-up Action Outside of Panama City

While U.S. forces established order in Panama City and chased Noriega, they also fanned out into the rural areas of Panama in order to capture PDF outposts and prevent a long-term rural guerrilla campaign. As long as Noriega was free, there was a possibility that he would flee to the mountains where he had served as a military commander and had popular support.[92]

U.S. troops only fired three shots while moving westward toward the Costa Rican Border. In David, the second largest city in Panama and reported Noriega stronghold, Major Kevin Higgins, commander of the Special Forces company moving against the PDF installation called the PDF commander on the telephone from a public school. They arranged a surrender while AC-130s circled overhead and Rangers were landed by helicopter at the airport. Once the PDF surrendered, Higgins told the PDF commander to tell smaller PDF units to surrender. The announcements were made and surrenders were arranged. Key to this success was the action of Army Special Forces trained in Spanish, knowledgeable of the area, and acquainted with the PDF commanders. Their influence was strongly enhanced by the highly visible presence of ground forces and AC-130s.[93]

Some interesting developments occurred in the David area. By December 28th, the Special Forces had confiscated 38,875 weapons, including assault rifles, mines, machine guns, mortars, timers, and other bomb components. One important anti-Noriega guerrilla force was the unit known as the Hugo Spadafora Armed Liberation Group (Flash) led by Jose Manuel Echevers Martinez. When Just Cause began, it had seized control of a Costa Rican border crossing and had broadcast calls for the PDF to rise against Noriega. U.S. forces in David and Flash worked together in the border area. The U.S. commander at David, Colonel Lin Burney, explained that this cooperation was a matter of convenience that was established when they found Flash in place and Martinez professed loyalty to the Endara government.[94]

CASUALTIES AND MEDICAL EVACUATION (MEDEVAC)

As expected, Just Cause produced casualties on both sides. The twenty-three U.S. fatalities were much lower than the planners' estimate of seventy, and the 324 wounded U.S. servicemen fell within the public estimate of "several hundred." Many of these casualties were accidental and some were the result of friendly fire.

After Just Cause was completed, estimates of actual Panamanian casualties varied widely. The official U.S. estimate was 220 civilians and 324 PDF personnel, with some of those listed as civilians possibly being PDF personnel in civilian clothes. The Southern Command had acknowledged that only 50 PDF bodies were found and as few as 53 may be the correct number of PDF deaths. The Panamanian Institute for Legal Medicine estimated 203 Panamanian civilians killed while the Reverend Jesse Jackson gave an estimate of 1,200 on television.[95] Because of the lack of press attention, the lower estimates seem more believable.

The planned treatment facilities, while working close to capacity, particularly in Panama, worked as planned. Between December 20th and 26th the Gorgas Army Community Hospital treated 67 U.S. service personnel, four service dependents, five U.S. civilians, 43 PDF members, and 194 Panamanian civilians. The hospital staff normally employed 59 civilians, only one of whom came to work. The staff was supplemented by a 32-member team of nurses, anesthetists, and medics from Fitzsimons Army Medical Center in Denver. At one point doctors operated on a Panamanian with a 50 calibre wound in the stomach. When asked what he was doing before he was shot, his answer was, "I was shooting Americans." The wounded came in for treatment for almost two weeks, and no one was turned away.[96]

The low number of U.S. fatalities indicate that the Medevac system worked as planned. There were exceptions, such as the SEALs at Patilla Airport who waited hours for a helicopter, but surgeons at Kelly Air Force Base, Texas, who received the 256 wounded flown there, credited excellent field treatment with saving many lives. The wounded in Panama were funneled to Howard Air Force Base where, if they needed surgery or stabilizing, they entered the Army FST--A (Forward Surgical Team--Airborne) deployed from Fort Bragg. Once stable but still needing to be Medevaced to Kelly, they entered one of two Mobile Air Staging Facility tents run by the 1st Air Medical Evacuation Squadron deployed from Pope Air Force Base.[97]

At Kelly the military medical establishment was prepared. Before the first C-141 carrying 43 wounded arrived at noon on December 20th, the hospital staff had canceled all elective surgeries and focused on the incoming wounded. While the C-

141 was still in the air, the aircrew radioed the hospital concerning each patient's injuries, and the hospital staff made the initial decision about who would go to Wilford Hall or Brooke Medical Center, thus proportioning the hospital load. Lieutenant Colonel Robert I. Solenberger, MD, served as the chief triage officer at Kelly. When the aircraft landed he and other physicians went on board and sorted the patients. Their triage divided the patients into those needing immediate surgery, those needing surgery or other intensive treatment but able to wait, and those with relatively minor injuries.[98]

CONCLUSIONS

Just Cause went essentially as planned. The largest operational problems were caused by adverse weather in the United States that delayed the arrival of some Task Force Pacific and follow-on troops. The stronger than expected resistance of the Dignity Battalions created serious concern by December 23rd, that a long, drawn-out guerrilla campaign might be developing, and then it collapsed. The U.S. inability to catch Noriega instantly caused great concern in the press but did not have a significant adverse effect on the operation. Given the possibility of disastrous incidents, ranging from mid-air collisions to a well placed round shooting down a C-141 full of paratroopers, things went well for the United States.

The calculation that hitting all the major PDF units simultaneously with overwhelming force would destroy their combat capability and prompt all concerned to accept the United States' replacement of the Noriega regime with the Endara government was correct. The use of overwhelming numbers was a departure from previous thinking concerning economy of force. The planners in this operation defined economy of force as the number of troops necessary to accomplish the mission expeditiously but without either running the risk of having inadequate forces or so many forces that they interfered with one another. Thus, U.S. forces were able to accept loses and meet unexpectedly strong resistance without facing disaster. Soldiers, not bureaucrats, planned this operation. As a result, Just Cause appears to have been an overwhelming success at the operational level. For the U.S. military, this was a joint operation, vice an Army show. True, the ground forces came overwhelmingly from the Army and the few SEALs and Marines probably could have been replaced by Army soldiers. Air Force units, however, played an essential role. The AC-130s supported the infantry with firepower, providing a degree of accuracy combined with mobility and timeliness not available elsewhere. The ability to stop the PDF convoy at the Pecora River bridge was critical for making the jumps into the Tocumen/Torrijos Airport as uneventful as they were. Without the MAC transports, the troops from Forts Lewis, Ord, and Bragg would have been irrelevant. The point is that while the United States establishes and trains individual units as Army, Air Force, Navy, and Marines, they fought in Panama and probably will fight in the future in a joint task force drawing on the capabilities of each service to accomplish the operational objectives.

Perhaps in an individual service's ideal war the Air Force would duel for command of the air, the Army would get down in the trenches in hand to hand combat, the Navy would have a proper fleet engagement contesting command of the sea, and the Marines would assault a beach all by themselves. In the real world, however, the president will probably call on the U.S. Armed Forces to achieve political objectives that will imperfectly translate into operational objectives and will require a different mix of the individual service's capabilities. Just Cause is both a unique historical event whose precise circumstances will never reoccur and a window to the future of the U.S. Armed Forces. As always, however, that window is opaque.

NOTES

1.   Edward N. Luttwak, "Just Cause--a Military Score Sheet," Washington Post, Dec. 31, 1989, p. C4.

2.   Michael R. Gordon, "Inquiry into Stealth Performance in Panama Is Ordered by Cheney," New York Times, April 11, 1990, p. A19; Robert R. Ropelewski, "How Panama Worked: Planning, Precision, and Surprise Led to Panama Successes," Armed Forces Journal International (February 1990): 32; and David F. Bond, "Six F-117As Flown in Panama Invasion: Air Force Broadens Daytime Operations," Aviation Week & Space Technology (March 5, 1990): 30.

3.   U.S. Department of Defense, Office of the Assistant Secretary of Defense (Public Affairs), News Briefing by Secretary of Defense Dick Cheney and General Colin Powell, USA, Chairman, Joint Chiefs of Staff, Pentagon, December 20, 1989, 7:45 a.m.; and George C. Wilson, "SouthCom Commander Rewrote Contingency Plans for Action," Washington Post, January 7, 1989, p. A1.

4.   Bernard E. Trainor, "Gaps in Vital Intelligence Hampered U.S. Troops," New York Times, December 21, 1989, p. A21.

5.   Cheney and Powell.

6.   U.S. Department of Defense, News Briefing by General Kelly, Pentagon, December 20, 1989, 4:40 p.m.; Wilson, p. A1; and "The Architect of 'Just Cause' Lt. Gen. Carl Stiner Explains his Panama Plan," Army Times (March 12, 1990): 14.

7.   Wilson, p. A1; and U.S. Department of Defense, News

Briefing by General Kelly and Admiral Shaefer, Pentagon, December 21, 1989, 12:10 p.m.

8.   The Military Balance, 1988-1989, (London: The International Institute for Strategic Studies, 1988), pp. 201-2.   The numbers reported for the PDF varied greatly.   Peter Koch, "Panamanian Forces Quickly Overwhelmed," Army Times (January 1, 1990):   R8, reported 15,000 personnel total with 3,500 in the formal army.

9.   Sam Fulwood III, "Combat in Panama; Dignity Battalion Still Lurks in the Shadows; Resistance: Many Call the Paramilitary Groups Common Street Toughs;   They Still Roam the Cities,"   Los Angeles Times, December 22, 1989, p. A7, as cited in Mead Data Central Lexis Nexis search; and "Noriega Loyalists Hit Back at U.S. Military as Chaos Grips Streets," Los Angeles Times, December 24, 1989, p. A1, as cited in Mead Data Central Lexis Nexis search.

10.   "The Architect Explains His Plan," p. 14; and Kelly.

11.   Cheney and Powell.

12.   Ropelewski, p. 32;   Margaret Roth, "Panama: An Attack Plan for the Future," Army Times (January 8, 1990):   10.

13.   Cheney and Powell.

14.   William Branigin, "U.S. Agent Rescued from Panama Cell Minutes before Anti-Noriega Offensive," Washington Post, January 1, 1990, p. A12.

15.   Dennis Steele, "Operation Just Cause," Army (February 1990):   40-1; Branigin, p. A12; Patrick E. Tyler and Molly Moore, "U.S. Paratroopers May Have Seen Noriega Escape During Invasion," Washington Post, January 7, 1990, p. A1; and "Task Forces Demonstrate Range of Army Capabilities," Army Times (January 1, 1990):   R34.   Not all of the special operations personnel were included in Task Force Black.   The Navy SEALs who attacked Patilla Airport in Panama City and the PDF fleet are usually listed as part of Task Force Bayonet.

16.   Steele, p. 35; and Cheney and Powell.

17.   Ibid.

18.   Elizabeth P. Donovan,   "Marines Seize Control of Panamanian Military Compounds," Navy Times (January 1, 1990): R3; Steele, p. 35; and "Units Deployed for Operation Just Cause," dated December 22, 1989, provided to the author by U.S. Department of Defense, Office of the Assistant Secretary of Defense (Public Affairs).

19.   Donna Miles, "Operation Just Cause," Soldiers (February

1990): 20-24; Steele, p. 35; and Kelly.

20. Cheney and Powell; Miles, pp. 20-24; and "Units Deployed." December 22, 1989. The 7th Infantry unit in Task Force Atlantic is given in Soldiers as the 4th Battalion of the 17th Infantry while an Assistant Secretary's list of "Units Deployed" gives it as the 2nd Battalion of the 27th Infantry.

21. Kelly.

22. Kelly and Shaefer.

23. Roth, p. 10.

24. Ropelewski, p. 26.

25. David Hughes, "Night Airdrop in Panama Surprises Noriega's Forces," Aviation Week & Space Technology (January 1, 1990): 30; and "The Architect Explains His Plan," p. 14.

26. "The Architect Explains His Plan," p. 14; Hughes, pp. 30-31; "Units Deployed;" and Ropelewski, p. 26.

27. Ropelewski, p. 26.

28. Wilson, p. A1; Ropelewski, p. 26; and Miles, pp. 20-24.

29. Ropelewski, p. 26.

30. Ibid., and Ross Simpson, "Devil in Disguise," Soldier of Fortune (May 1990): 45.

31. John Ginovsky and Davis Fulghum, "A-7s, OA-37s Patrol over Panama," Air Force Times (January 1, 1990): R1. This article reported that at the time of Just Cause the 388th Tactical Fighter Wing from Hill Air Force Base was deployed to Panama, but no one has reported any activity by their F-16s in Just Cause.

32. Bond, p. 30.

33. "The Architect Explains His Plan," pp. 14; and Ropelewski, p. 26.

34. Ropelewski, pp. 28, 32; and Roth, p. 10.

35. Kelly; Melissa Healy, "Combat in Panama: Panamanian Military 'Decapitated' by Coordinated American Strike," Los Angeles Times, December 21, 1989, p. A4, quoted in Mead Data Central Lexis Nexis search; and Douglas Jehl, "Ranger Force Bore Brunt of Panama Toll," Los Angeles Times, January 7, 1990, p. A1.

100

36. "The Architect Explains His Plan," p. 14.

37. Robert K. Brown, "U.S. Warriors Topple Panamanian Thugs: 'We Came, We Saw, We Kicked Ass'--82nd Airborne Graffiti, Balboa, Panama," Soldier of Fortune (April 1990): 57.

38. Ropelewski, p. 26.

39. Donovan, p. R3.

40. Kelly; Patrick E. Tyler and Molly Moore, "Strike Force Struck Out: Special Teams Failed to Find Noriega," Washington Post, December 23, 1989, p. A1; and Tyler and Moore, "U.S. Paratroopers," p. A1.

41. Wilson, p. 1; "The Architect Explains His Plan," p. 14; and Ropelewski, p. 26.

42. "The Architect Explains His Plan," p. 14.

43. Ibid.

44. Ibid; and Bill Gertz, "Noriega Tipped Off by a Spy," Washington Times, January 2, 1990, p. A1.

45. David Maraniss, "A Trooper's 4 Days in Action: from Fort Bragg Cold to a Leg Wound," Washington Post, December 28, 1989, p. A1; Paul Scicchitano, "On Patrol: Panama: Stories of Friends Made, of Friends Lost, of Friends Left Behind," Army Times (January 8, 1990): 6; and Soraya Nelson, "'All of the Blood...'," Army Times (January 22, 1990): 10.

46. Nelson, p. 10.

47. Scicchitano, p. 8; and Nelson, p. 10.

48. Cheney and Powell; and Ropelewski, p. 26.

49. Ellen Rafshoon, "Some U.S. Civilians Caught in the Wrong Place at the Wrong Time," Air Force Times (January 1, 1990): R7; and Patrick E. Tyler, "U.S. Commander Decries Leak on Panama Invasion," Washington Post, February 27, 1990, p. A7, quoted in Mead Data Central Lexis Nexis search.

50. Gene Gibbons, "U.S. Aircraft Reported Landing in Panama," Copyright Reuters, December 19, 1989, a.m. cycle, quoted in Mead Data Central Lexis Nexis search.

51. Tyler and Moore, "U.S. Paratroopers," Washington Post, January 7, 1990, p. A1; Bill Gertz, "Pentagon Investigates Possible Security Leak by Troops in Panama," Washington Times, January 5, 1990, p. A6; Bill Gertz, "NSA Eavesdropping Was Vital in Panama," Washington Times, p. A6; and Tyler, "U.S. Commander Decries Leak," p. A7. On March 6, 1990, Mr. Peter

Williams, Assistant Secretary of Defense (Public Affairs) denied General Stiner's account of security breaches.

52. Branigin, p. A12; and Tyler and Moore, "U.S. Paratroopers," p. A1.

53. Patrick E. Tyler, "No Pre-Invasion Leaks, Pentagon Says," The Raleigh News and Observer, March 14, 1990, p. 2A.

54. Steele, p. 35.

55. Ibid.

56. Ibid.; and Cheney and Powell.

57. Steele, p. 35; Miles, pp. 20-24; Brown, p. 57; and "The Architect Explains His Plan," p. 14.

58. Brown, p. 57; Ropelewski, p. 26; and Simpson, p. 45.

59. Brown, p. 57; and Miles, pp. 20-24.

60. Wilson, p. A1; and Kelly.

61. Ropelewski, p. 26.

62. "'We Will Chase Him,'" p. A1; Steele, p. 35; Wilson, p. A1; and Walter V. Robinson and Philip Bennett, "The Harrowing Tales of an Untidy Invasion," Boston Globe, Dec. 28, 1989, p. 1. The Boston Globe account of the reduction of these barracks reports a much bloodier battle with the PDF troops who did not flee but stood and fought to the death. This account makes much of the physical destruction of the barracks but does not square with the casualty figures given in the Washington Post. The Boston Globe gives no casualty figures.

63. Ropelewski, p. 26; and Steele, p. 35.

64. Bill Gertz, "Assault on Patilla Airport Costs Elite Navy Unit 4 Dead," Washington Times, December 22, 1989, p. A7; and Donnelly, "Precision and Professionalism," p. 11. In some reports the SEAL fatalities have been attributed to the unexpected appearance of PDF armored cars (see: George C. Wilson, "Panamanian Commanders Fled Their Posts, Thurman Says," Washington Post, January 6, 1990, p. A13). The majority of accounts do not place PDF armored cars in combat with the SEALs.

65. Steele, p. 35; and Kelly and Shaefer.

66. William Branigin, "U.S. Embassy Staff Attacks Security," Washington Post, December 31, 1989, p. A20.

67. General John W. Foss, "The Future of the Army," Army

Times (March 5, 1990): 12; and "'We Will Chase Him," p. A1.

68. _Cheney and Powell_; Miles, pp. 20-24; "The Architect Explains His Plan," p. 14; and Jim Tice, "Helicopters, Repairs Get High Marks in Panama Fight," _Army Times_ (January 22, 1990): 14.

69. Wilson, "Commander Rewrote Plans," p. A1; and Miles, "Operation Just Cause," pp. 20-24.

70. _Kelly_.

71. Miles, pp. 20-24; and Elizabeth P. Donovan, "Marines Seize Control of Panamanian Military Compounds," _Navy Times_ (January 1, 1990): R3.

72. Donovan, p. R3.

73. John D. Morrocco, "F-117A Fighter Used in Combat for First Time in Panama," _Aviation Week and Space Technology_ (January 1, 1990): 32; and Michael R. Gordon, "Inquiry into Stealth's Performance in Panama Is Ordered by Cheney," _New York Times_, April 11, 1990, p. A19.

74. "The Architect Explains His Plan," p. 14; Donnelly, p. 11; Jehl, p. A1; and Tyler, p. A7.

75. Donnelly, p. 11; and Simpson, p. 45.

76. Donnelly, p. 11.

77. Ibid.; and Jehl, p. A1.

78. Molly Moore, "U.S. Seeks to Rebuild Structure: Some Units Spread Propaganda," _Washington Post_, December 30, 1989, p. A1; David Maraniss, "A Trooper's 4 Days in Action," p. A1; Jehl, p. A1; DOD, _Cheney and Powell_; Hughes, pp. 30-31; and Tyler and Moore, "U.S. Paratroopers," p. A1.

79. Hughes, pp. 30-31; Ropelewski, p. 26; Maraniss, p. A1; and Bill Gertz and Rowan Scarborough, "Noriega 'Tipped off' to U.S. Strike," _Washington Times_, December 29, 1989, p. A1.

80. "The Architect Explains His Plan," p. 14; and Ropelewski, p. 26.

81. Tice, p. 14.

82. Miles, p. 24; and _Kelly_.

83. _Kelly_.

84. Ibid; and Hughes, pp. 30-31.

85. <u>Kelly and Shaefer</u>; and Eloy O. Aquilar, "U.S. Troops Comb City for Missing," <u>Washington Times</u>, December 22, 1989, P. A1.

86. James Gerstenzang and Marjorie Miller, "Deadly Battles Continue in Panama; Fighting: 2000 Fresh Troops Bolster U.S. Forces. Capital in Near-Anarchy," <u>Los Angeles Times</u>, December 23, 1989, Southland Edition, p. A1, quoted in Mead Data Central Lexis Nexis search; and Wilson, p. A1.

87. Peter Koch, "Panamanian Forces Quickly Overwhelmed," <u>Army Times</u> (January 1, 1990): 1.

88. SSgt Phil Prater, "Combat in the Streets: Securing Panama City Required a Lot of Skill," <u>Soldiers</u> (February 1990): 25-32.

89. Kenneth Freed and Marjorie Miller, "Panama Bands Stage Bloody Attack; Combat: Troops Believed Directed by Noriega Hit Downtown. Continued Resistance Mocks U.S. Claims that Situation Is Under Control," <u>Los Angeles Times</u>, December 23, 1989, Home Edition, p. A1, quoted in Mead Data Central Lexis Nexis search; and Dana Priest and Al Kamen, "U.S. in 'Real War' in Panama, General Says; Anarchy Continues to Rule Streets of Capital," <u>Washington Post</u>, December 23, 1989, p. A1.

90. Andrew Rosenthal, "American Troops Press Hunt for Noriega; Order Breaks Down; Looting Widespread: Curfew is Defied: Bush Urges New Leader to Take Control--Fighting Persists," <u>New York Times</u>, December 22, 1989, p. A1; and Freed and Miller, p. A1.

91. William Branigin and Dana Priest, "U.S., Panama Report Some Success in Restoring Order," <u>Washington Post</u>, December 24, 1989, p. A1; and John M. McClintok, "U.S. Troops Left Embassy Unguarded: Vatican Envoy Consulted U.S. General on Giving Sanctuary to Noriega," <u>Baltimore Sun</u>, December 26, 1989, p. A1.

92. Doyle McManus, "Combat in Panama; U.S. Widens Hunt for Noriega to Mountains of Western Panama; Tactics: the General Is 'Turning Out To Be a Lot Tougher Than We Anticipated,' a U.S. Official Concedes," <u>Los Angeles Times</u>, December 23, 1989, Home Edition, p. A3.

93. Wilson, p. A1.

94. Tom Donnelly, "With So Many Weapons--Can 'Communists' Be Far?" <u>Army Times</u> (January 8, 1990): 7; and Mark A. Uhlig, "The U.S. and Panama: Soldiers of Fortune; an Untold Guerrilla War: Noriega Foes Rule Border," <u>New York Times</u>, January 10, 1990, p. A1; quoted in Mead Data Central Lexis Nexis search.

95. Melissa Healy, "Pentagon Puts Panama Civilian Deaths at 220; Invasion: Estimates Suggest 10 Died for Each U.S. Soldier Who Fell.   Defense Force Losses Put at 314," <u>Los Angeles Times</u>, January 10, 1990, p. A1, quoted by Mead Data Central Lexus Nexis search; Douglas Jehl and John M. Broder, "Truth Was Trampled in Panama Invasion," <u>Raleigh News and Observer</u>, April 25, 1990, p. 2A.

96. Scicchitano, p. 7; and Nelson, p. 10.

97. "Bush Not Likely to Find Many Panama Wounded in San Antonio," Reuters, December 27, 1989, Wednesday, a.m. cycle, quoted in Mead Data Central Lexis Nexis search; and Nelson, p. 10.

98. Nelson, p. 10.

6 Command, Control, Communications, and Intelligence (C³I) Factors

INTRODUCTION

Operation Just Cause was performed almost flawlessly; a vivid contrast to Operation Urgent Fury in Grenada in 1983, the last coup de main conducted by U.S. military forces. Urgent Fury was marred by many problems, including a complex, multi-layered command and control organization, and extremely poor communications between the forces of the various services. By comparison, Just Cause was organized simply, with the command, control and communications (C³) structure contributing to the operation's success. This chapter assesses the planning for and the organization and effectiveness of C³ in Just Cause. It examines how the failed coup of October 3, 1989, the familiarity with the nation, and military rehearsals all helped U.S. planning and preparation for the invasion. Additionally, it shows how the lessons learned from Grenada helped to avoid some of the same problems that plagued that operation.

COMMAND, CONTROL, COMMUNICATIONS AND INTELLIGENCE (C³I) IN OPERATION JUST CAUSE

Planning and the Role of Intelligence

The area of operations for Just Cause was the entire isthmus of Panama, and Panamanian Defense Forces (PDF) were based at several locations across this region. The Panama Canal, being an essential route between the Atlantic and Pacific oceans, was a prime consideration in the planning.

Relations between Panama and the United States deteriorated after the 1988 indictment of General Manuel Noriega on drug-running charges, and all U.S. political and economic measures had been unsuccessful in removing him from office. Until the arrival of General Colin Powell, U.S. Army, as Chairman of the Joint Chiefs of Staff (CJCS) and General Maxwell Thurman, U.S. Army, as Commander-in-Chief, U.S. Southern Command (CINCSOUTH), U.S. contingency plans concerning Panama relied more on political measures. Additionally, the military plans were complex and unwieldy.[1] After the failed coup d'etat led by rebel PDF officers, Thurman and Powell worked together to rewrite the plans. As

Thurman noted, the major change was that the new plan called for a single, overwhelming force that would attack in the middle of the night, would isolate the PDF as Noriega's power base and would then provide "the capability to rebuild the [PDF]"[2] to provide for Panamanian defense needs.

Three contingency plans were drawn up and presented as military options to the President by Secretary of Defense Dick Cheney and General Powell prior to the decision to invade: to use only the troops in Panama (about 12,000) to capture Noriega and the Commandancia; to perform a commando raid with special operations forces to capture Noriega; or to use overwhelming force to convince the PDF that they had no way of winning.[3] The first option might or might not have succeeded in capturing Noriega but certainly would have left troops loyal to him free to resist U.S. forces for an extended period. The second alternative would have left President Guillermo Endara's government facing guerrilla resistance, and the support of the PDF would remain in question. Additionally, both options would have required detailed intelligence on Noriega's whereabouts at all times, something that U.S. intelligence could not provide the night Just Cause was executed. Conversely, a positive factor of both these alternatives was that casualties to civilians and military alike were expected to be low.

One of President Bush's major concerns was to minimize civilian and military casualties in any operation. However, he wanted to bring Noriega to justice quickly. The full-blown invasion plan that became Just Cause was chosen because it gave the "fullest assurance" that the PDF and Noriega would be removed from power as quickly as possible,[4] and its rules of engagement were carefully designed to prevent large civilian casualties.

Target Choices. The targets of the operation were chosen to isolate all PDF forces from Noriega. Here U.S. intelligence targeted every major PDF stronghold to ensure that no major, organized PDF resistance could come to his assistance. Additionally, the plan also ensured that he could not flee the country. For example, the operation at Rio Hato quickly demoralized the elite Battalion 2000, while U.S. operations at Torrijos and other airfields prevented Noriega's escape. Once the military option was chosen by President Bush, the plan maximized U.S. forces in order to minimize both U.S. and Panamanian casualties.

Rehearsals. After the plan was approved by the Joint Chiefs of Staff, it was rehearsed several times by many of the forces that participated in Just Cause. For example, the 2nd Ranger Battalion had finished a rehearsal at Fort Benning, Georgia, and had just returned to Ft. Lewis, Washington, when it received the execute order for Just Cause.[5] Units in Panama had rehearsed some of their operations at the actual locations where they carried them out, an act that ultimately desensitized the Panamanians from expecting an attack.

Organization

The objectives and requirements of Just Cause required a simple and direct C³ structure, allowing for direct control of forces using an uncomplicated chain of command. The C³ organization, shown in Figure 6.1, led from the National Command Authorities (NCA) and General Powell (CJCS) to CINCSOUTH to the forces through the Joint Task Force South (JTF South) commander, Lieutenant General Carl Stiner, U.S. Army. Every group from the platoon to the task force level ultimately worked for JTF South.[6] The overall force was primarily made up of Army units, including units in Panama attached to SOUTHCOM and reinforcements from the United States.

Over 26,000 U.S. military personnel from all services participated in the operation. They were divided into four assault task forces, designated Task Force Atlantic, Task Force Bayonet, Task Force Pacific, and Task Force Semper Fi. A task force of Special Operations forces was also involved in the fighting. There were additional support Task Forces that included Task Force Aviation, a Military Police Task Force, and Navy and Air Force support forces.[7] All were directly responsible to JTF South.

Task Force Atlantic, consisting of forces from the 82nd Airborne Division and the 7th Infantry Division, was assigned an area from the Atlantic coast of Panama to the middle of the isthmus of Panama. It was to secure and protect Americans in Gamboa, engage and subdue the PDF 8th Infantry Company and the PDF Naval Infantry Company, and secure the Madden Dam, vital to the operation of the Panama Canal, and an electrical distribution center at Cierre Tigre.[8]

Task Force Bayonet, consisting of two U.S. Army battalions based in Panama, a battalion from Ft. Polk, an MP battalion from Ft. Meade and an armor platoon from the 82nd Airborne Division, was assigned to protect the central Panama Canal region and secure Panama City, including the Commandancia, Noriega's Headquarters.[9]

Task Force Pacific, consisting of three battalions of the 82nd Airborne Division, was allocated to an area from the Pacific coast of Panama to the middle of the isthmus. Its mission was to contain the PDF 1st Infantry Company and secure an airport where Noriega kept one of his planes.[10]

A Marine rifle company and a light armored infantry company composed Task Force Semper Fi. Its mission was to secure the Bridge of the Americas and prevent a PDF attack on Howard Air Force Base. Task Force Red, part of the special operations task force and made up of Ranger units and other special operations forces, was used to attack Rio Hato barracks where members of the 6th and 7th Rifle Companies of Battalion 2000 were stationed, and secure Torrijos International Airport, which the PDF 7th Infantry had used as a base to overwhelm rebel forces in October.[11]

108

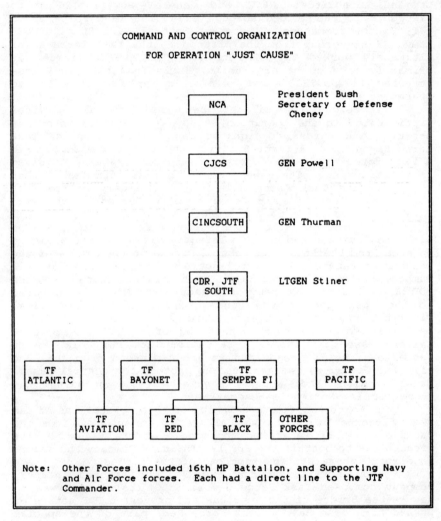

COMMAND AND CONTROL ORGANIZATION

FOR OPERATION "JUST CAUSE"

NCA	President Bush Secretary of Defense Cheney
CJCS	GEN Powell
CINCSOUTH	GEN Thurman
CDR, JTF SOUTH	LTGEN Stiner

TF ATLANTIC   TF BAYONET   TF SEMPER FI   TF PACIFIC

TF AVIATION   TF RED   TF BLACK   OTHER FORCES

Note: Other Forces included 16th MP Battalion, and Supporting Navy and Air Force forces. Each had a direct line to the JTF Commander.

FIGURE 6.1

FACTORS INVOLVED IN THE C³ CHOICE

Goals of Operation Just Cause

President Bush stated the goals to be achieved in Just Cause when he announced the operation to Americans at 7 a.m. on December 20th: to protect the 35,000 Americans in Panama; to ensure the safety and integrity of the Panama Canal; to restore a democratic and freely elected government to Panama; and to bring Noriega to justice in the United States.[12] These goals influenced the choice of the operation and forces. To accomplish them quickly and install the new Panamanian government, a quick, fast, overwhelming strike was the only option that would assure a PDF surrender. The military goal was to have U.S. forces isolate the PDF from Noriega, thereby severing him from his power base. As the President stated in his news conference on December 21st, "...[Our] argument was not with the PDF, but with Noriega, and if they would get rid of him and recognize a democratically elected government, we could have gone back to more normalized relations ... we have no ax to grind with the institution of the PDF."[13] This consideration drove the President's decision to use a large, overpowering force which led to the C³ structure that was developed.

Intelligence

Preparation and Planning. SOUTHCOM Headquarters in Quarry Heights, Panama was ideally located to collect intelligence on Panamanian forces. Detailed knowledge of PDF troop locations and positions was vital to the planning of the operation, and some Americans in Panama who were friendly with the PDF were able to exploit these contacts for information that would assist U.S. forces in preparing for the invasion. Since the location also gave the command full knowledge of the terrain on which the battle would be fought,[14] the units involved in the operation were able to train and rehearse at the sites where the battles would be waged.

The October 3rd coup also gave SOUTHCOM accurate information identifying the units that were most loyal to Noriega. For example, during the coup, forces of the PDF 7th Infantry Company landed at Torrijos International Airport to stop the rebel officers. Battalion 2000, an elite PDF force located at Rio Hato and known to be quite loyal to Noriega, and the Dignity Battalions that conducted pro-Noriega terror over the past few years were also targeted. Thus intelligence was instrumental in determining targets and Panamanian orders of battle.

The Decision to Attack. President Bush's decision came after the situation had deteriorated to the extent that the safety of Americans in Panama was in jeopardy. On December 14th, Noriega declared himself "Maximum Leader" and declared that his nation was "at war" with the United States. A Panamanian warrant for the arrest of General Thurman and

General Mark Cisneros, Commanding General, U.S. Army South, was issued. The charge was "harassment" because of the U.S. military maneuvers that had been held in Panama. On December 17th, 1st Lieutenant Robert Paz, U.S. Marine Corps, was killed by PDF forces at a PDF road block and a Navy officer and his wife who witnessed the murder were brutalized. After reports of these attacks were received, President Bush decided that a military solution was necessary. The President said to his closest advisors "Enough is enough...Let's do it."[15]

Just before the operation commenced, another piece of information confirmed that the safety of U.S. citizens in Panama could no longer be ensured. A PDF informant reported that a 250-man militia had been formed with Cuban help to terrorize U.S. citizens living in Panama City.[16] This reconfirmed that the invasion was justified, as the United States could no longer count on the Panamanians to provide for the safety of U.S. citizens.

Operational Intelligence. While intelligence support for the decision-making and planning processes appears to have been good, there were a few problems concerning human intelligence (HUMINT) that affected the operation. HUMINT resources did not accurately report on the strength of the Dignity Battalions, which fought heavily for several days. Additionally, a lack of a HUMINT capability in Panama resulted in U.S. forces not capturing Noriega at the start of the operation and may have also led the SEAL teams in Task Force Red to expect less resistance than they actually encountered.[17] While these intelligence failures prolonged some aspects of the operation and perhaps allowed for unnecessary U.S. deaths, it did not significantly detract from the operation's success.

Lessons from Grenada

Several lessons from the Grenada operation were applied in Just Cause. Some of the problems with Urgent Fury were: a multi-level, complex C³ structure without a true joint task force (JTF) commander (see Figure 6.2); large gaps in intelligence concerning the island, government, and armed forces order of battle; little time available for planning and preparation; and campaign objectives that were unclear. Additionally, the CINCLANT planners failed to follow their own approved contingency plan for Grenada, which assigned operational control to Commander, U.S. Forces Caribbean (now dismantled), provided for a JTF commander, and designated forces to be involved in the operation. This plan was never even considered or activated.[18]

A comparison of Figures 6.1 and 6.2 shows the simplicity of the Just Cause C³ structure. Its emphasis on use of a majority of single-service forces, while remaining a joint operation, has been noted by several authors as being one of the reasons that Just Cause was so successful.[19]

Another problem that occurred during Urgent Fury was a lack of interoperability in communications equipment. To date, there has been no mention of major communications

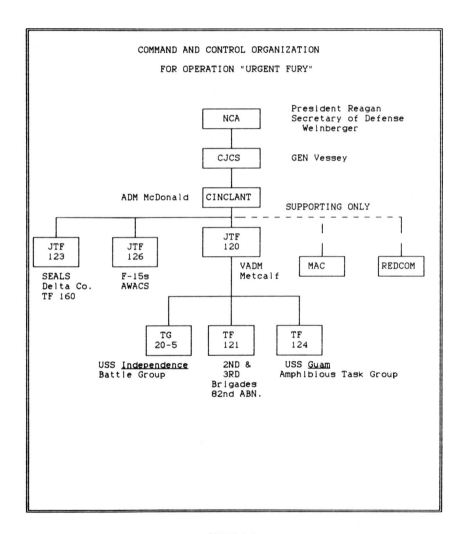

FIGURE 6.2

problems in _Just Cause_ and certainly none of the kind noted
in Grenada. Lieutenant General Kelly stated that, although
there were some human mistakes, no "major glitches" caused by
communications were observed.[20]

RESULTS

The results of _Just Cause_ were that all the goals set by
the President were accomplished. The simple C^3 organization
worked very well. Lieutenant General Kelly declared that
"command and control [in the operations] has been
excellent."[21] Its simplified structure with a direct line
between the NCA to the CJCS to CINCSOUTH to the JTF commander
worked well. A pre-planned contingency operation was used and
executed as written. Communications were effective in
providing for positive control of forces during the operation.
While there were some intelligence failures, none of them
seriously detracted from the decisive success of the
contingency plan.

Just Cause was in almost every aspect an extremely
successful operation that was well planned, controlled, and
executed. The C^3 structure helped the operation achieve its
goals with few casualties and restore Panama to a democratic
society with a free people.

NOTES

1. Michael R. Gordon with Andrew Rosenthal, "U.S. Invasion:
Many Weeks of Rehearsals," _New York Times_, December 24, 1989,
p. 9.

2. George C. Wilson, "Invasion of Panama Reflected GEN
Thurman's Gung-Ho Style," _Washington Post_, January 7, 1990,
p. A22.

3. Bernard E. Trainor, "Gaps in Vital Intelligence Hampered
U.S. Troops," _New York Times_, December 21, 1989, p. A21.

4. Ibid.

5. Gordon, p. 1; and "The Architect of 'Just Cause'," _Army
Times_ (March 12, 1990): 18.

6. Office of the Assistant Secretary of Defense (Public
Affairs), "News Briefing by LTG T. W. Kelly, USA, Director of
Operations, Joint Staff," _News Briefing_ (Washington, D.C.:
Department of Defense, December 20, 1989), p. 3.

7. Donna Miles, "Operation Just Cause," _Soldiers_ (February
1990): 20.

8. Ibid., p. 23; and Office of the Assistant Secretary of
Defense (Public Affairs), "News Briefing by Secretary of

Defense Dick Cheney and General Colin Powell, USA, Chairman, Joint Chiefs of Staff," News Briefing (Washington, D.C.: Department of Defense, December 20, 1989), p. 2.

9. Miles, p. 23; and Cheney and Powell Briefing.

10. Miles, p. 23.

11. Ed Magnuson, "Sowing Dragon's Teeth," Time (January 1, 1990): 26; and "The Panama Blitz," Newsweek, (January 1, 1990): 16-17.

12. George Bush, "Panama: The Decision to Use Force," Vital Speeches of the Day 56, no. 7 (January 15, 1990): 194.

13. "Excerpts from Bush's News Conference on Central America," New York Times, December 22, 1989, p. A16.

14. Robert R. Ropelewski, "Planning, Precision, and Surprise Led to Panama Successes," Armed Forces Journal International (February 1990): 26.

15. Thomas L. Friedman, "Panama Shooting Condemned by U.S.," New York Times, December 18, 1989, p. A9; David Hoffman and Bob Woodward, "President Launched Invasion with Little View to Aftermath," Washington Post, December 24, 1989, p. A1; Russell Watson, "Invasion," Newsweek (January 1, 1990): 20; and George J. Church, "Showing Muscle," Time (January 1, 1990): 23.

16. Watson, p. 21.

17. "The Architect...," p. 18; and Bruce B. Auster, "Military Lessons of the Invasion," U.S. News and World Report (January 8, 1990): 22-23.

18. Mark Adkin, Urgent Fury: The Battle for Grenada (Lexington, MA: D.C. Heath and Co., 1989), pp. 125-144.

19. See Benjamin F. Schemmer, "Panama and Just Cause: The Rebirth of Professional Soldiering," Armed Forces Journal International (February 1990): 5; and Edward Luttwak, "'Operation Just Cause'--What Went Right, Wrong," Navy Times (January 1, 1990): R7.

20. Kelly Briefing, December 20, 1989, p. 6.

21. Ibid., p. 3.

7 Assessing the Role of Air Power

Operation <u>Just Cause</u> has prompted many questions concerning the future use of air power. Does this operation mark the beginning of a new chapter concerning the role of U.S.-based air power in U.S. foreign policy? If the predictions that future conflicts will be oriented more toward "North versus South" than "East versus West" are true, does the use of U.S.-based air power take on added importance? Or is Panama just an anomaly in that future conflict arenas may not have 13,000 U.S. troops and a U.S.-controlled air base ready for action when the operation begins? Only time can answer these questions with any certainty. Nonetheless, there is value in examining the use of U.S. air power during the invasion of Panama.

<u>Just Cause</u> was a success and has been described by military experts as a well executed <u>coup de main</u>. There is widespread consensus that it may not have been as successful, and surely would not have been as well executed without the airlift that provided a rapid buildup of forces in the theater. There is also general agreement that air power's contributions to the operation in Panama were outstanding and significant to the outcome. This chapter will discuss the two relevant types of air power--the air lift and the other air operations--and will assess their relative contributions to the operation.

Airlift support for <u>Just Cause</u> was superb. Troops and equipment from U.S. bases were flown to Panama aboard C-5, C-141, and C-130 aircraft from the Military Airlift Command (MAC), the Air National Guard (ANG), and the Air Force Reserves (AFR) in a well-orchestrated operation. Tactical Air Command units and Air National Guard A-7s provided general operational support, while Strategic Air Command K-10 and KC-135 tankers supported with aerial refueling. Tables 7.1 and 7.2 list the MAC, ANG, and AFR units that participated in <u>Just Cause</u>.

MAC's 21st and 22nd Air Forces provided both strategic and tactical airlift support on C-5s, C-141s, and C-130s, primarily for Army, Air Force, and Marine personnel. Twenty-four active duty MAC units from ten states participated in the operation. In addition to the airlift aircraft and crews, aeromedical evacuation units, special operations units, a weather detachment, an aerial port squadron, maintenance

TABLE 7.1
Active Duty Military Assistance Command (MAC) Units that Supported Operation <u>Just Cause</u>

Unit	Location
60th Military Airlift Wing (MAW)	Travis Air Force Base (AFB), California
62nd MAW	McChord AFB, Washington
63rd MAW	Norton AFB, California
436th MAW	Dover AFB, Delaware
437th MAW	Charleston AFB, South Carolina
438th MAW	McGuire AFB, New Jersey
314th Tactical Airlift Wing (TAW)	Little Rock AFB, Arkansas
317th TAW	Pope AFB, North Carolina
463rd TAW	Dyess AFB, Texas
1st Special Operations Wing	Hurlburt Field, Florida
Detachment 5, 15th Weather Squadron	Dover AFB, Delaware

TABLE 7.2
Air National Guard and Air Force Reserve Units that Supported Operation <u>Just Cause</u>

Unit	Location
349th Military Airlift Wing (TAW)	Travis Air Force Base (AFB), California
445th MAW	Norton AFB, California
446th MAW	McChord AFB, Washington
512th MAW	Dover AFB, Delaware
315th MAW	Charleston AFB, South Carolina
514th MAW	McGuire AFB, New Jersey
433rd MAW	Kelly AFB, Texas
439th MAW	Westover AFB, Massachusetts
459th MAW	Andrews AFB, Maryland
118th Tactical Airlift Wing (TAW)	Nashville, Tennessee
136th TAW	Naval Air Station, Dallas, Texas
139th Tactical Airlift Group (TAG)	St. Joseph, Missouri
145th TAG	Charlotte, North Carolina
146th TAW	Channel Islands, California
165th TAG	Savannah, Georgia
166th TAG	Wilmington, Delaware
172nd Military Airlift Group	Jackson, Mississippi

TABLE 7.3

Special Operations Aircraft that Participated
in Operation Just Cause

Number	Type	Unit
11	AH-64 Apaches	82nd Aviation Brigade
11	AH-6 Gunships	Task Force 160
20	UH-60 Blackhawks	Task Force 160
5	MH-53 Pave Lows	1st Special Operations Wing
4	MH-60 Pave Hawks	1st Special Operations Wing
9	MH-6s	Task Force 160
3	CH-47Ds	Task Force 160
2	MH-47s	Task Force 160
7	AC-130H Gunships	1st Special Operations Wing
2	AC-130A Gunships	1st Special Operations Wing
3	MC-130E Combat Talons	1st Special Operations Wing
2	HC-130 Refuelers	
6	F-117A Stealth Fighters	37th Tactical Air Wing, Tonopah, Nevada

crews, and an airlift control squadron went to Panama.
Reserve support was provided by 18 units, nine from the Air
National Guard and nine from the Air Force Reserves.

MAC deployed a total of 111 aircraft on the night of the
invasion. These consisted of 77 C-141 Starlifters, 12 C-5As,
and 22 C-130s, carrying a total of 10,000 combat troops. Of
these, 6,000 were landed and helicoptered into action, while
the remaining 4,000 parachuted in. All arrived at their
correct destinations at the proper time. The planes flew at
low altitude all the way from the United States in order to
minimize their exposure to Cuban radars. The most aggravating
problems to the pilots were heavy fog in California and icing
and cold temperatures in North Carolina.

Panama was considered a secure area for air operations.
There was no air threat and the ground threat was limited in
its scope and intensity. However, the airlift forces did
incur some damage from ground fire. Of the fourteen MAC
transport aircraft that reported damage during the operation,
thirteen were due to small arms fire, and one, a C-141, had
its tail cone damaged during an airdrop. Damage by small arms
fire was reported by eleven C-130s and two C-141s. Seven of
the damaged C-130s were from the 317th Tactical Air Wing (TAW)
and four were from the 314th TAW. All of the damaged C-141s
were from the 437th Military Airlift Wing (MAW). All of this

118

was considered minor, and two weeks after the invasion, all but two of the damaged aircraft were fully operational.

General Colin L. Powell, Chairman of the Joint Chiefs of Staff, said, "MAC did an absolutely outstanding job supporting the joint cause in Panama."[1] Although some other aspects of air support in Panama are open to more debate, there is also general agreement that special operations air support was the best that has ever been provided by U.S. forces.

For the first time, special operations air forces played the major role for which they were designed and trained. The initial assault was conducted at night and included units from the 1st Special Operations Wing, Hurlburt Field, Florida; Task Force 160, Fort Campbell, Kentucky; and the 82nd Aviation Brigade, Fort Bragg, North Carolina. These units performed exceptionally well. They are well trained since they reportedly fly over 50% of their training flights at night using night vision devices, and they executed their mission in Panama with precision. This is the air support area of Just Cause that warrants the most detailed examination.

The invasion of Panama employed the largest number of special operations aircraft in U.S. history. The 65 helicopters and 20 fixed-wing aircraft are shown in Table 7.3. All of these aircraft actually flew on the night of December 20th. Lieutenant General Carl Stiner, commander of the Panama Joint Task Force was reported to have said that support for the entire operation included 185 fixed-wing aircraft and 170 helicopters.[2]

Four helicopters were shot down, resulting in three deaths. Eighteen of the twenty UH-60 Blackhawk helicopters used to transport troops were hit ten or more times during the fighting. Three AH-64 Apaches were hit by small arms fire, one eight, one fifteen, and one twenty-three times. All were able to return safely to base after being hit.

The F-117s were not generally considered to be special operations aircraft in the past. However, based upon their unique capabilities and the way they were used in Panama, it may be fair to list them as such in the future. Also, it could be argued that they have such superb special operations employment features that they should be used in similar roles in the future. One authority, Jane's Bill Sweetman, has called the F-117A a plane very much designed to support special operations forces.[3]

Use of the Stealth fighter in Just Cause was the most politically sensitive air issue with Congress. There were many other aircraft available, but the F-117A was chosen to shock the Panamanian troops at Rio Hato barracks. Although only two aircraft were used, their choice has been called an overkill due to the absence of an air defense threat. It was reported that the F-117s were used more for their night bombing accuracy than for their stealth, and this appears to have been the case. They dropped their bombs in order to stun Panamanian Defense Force troops while UH-60 Blackhawks landed U.S. Army Rangers to secure the barracks. General Stiner said that many of the Rio Hato defenders began to throw down their weapons and run after ordnance from one Nighthawk landed within 50 yards of their barracks.

Stealth fighters were not the only aircraft to perform well in the darkness. All of the other types of special operations aircraft mentioned earlier made meaningful contributions to the overall success of Just Cause. Special operations AC-130 gunships had attacked Rio Hato, firing with great accuracy in support of an Army Ranger battalion parachute jump that was made into the area before the arrival of the F-117A Stealth fighters. These 130s were then joined by an AH-64 Blackhawk and two AH-6 Little Birds to suppress enemy ground fire as the Rangers jumped from C-130 transports. This close-in fire suppression may have been much more valuable than has been widely recognized. After Rio Hato was secured, U.S. troops discovered ZPU-4 antiaircraft guns and V300 armored personnel carriers. Had these weapons been able to fire at the transport aircraft without threat of retaliation, many more casualties may have resulted.

Both the AH-64 Apaches and the AC-130 Spectres performed superbly. General Stiner said the Apache can fire a Hellfire missile "through a window at five miles away at night." The Spectres use their Infrared Search and Track (IRST) system to employ an impressive array of firepower with extremely high reliability and accuracy. Armed with a 105mm Howitzer, a 40mm cannon, and a 20mm rapid fire gun, each was able to attack specific buildings without damaging the surrounding ones.[4] Despite the strong showing of the Apaches and Spectres, the ground troops' first choice for close fire support may still be the AH-6 Little Bird, with its 2.75 inch rockets and 7.62mm guns.

As in any military operation, much of the success of Just Cause can be traced to those behind the scenes. Because many experts consider Panama to be an unusual case, little has been written about the U.S. electronic warfare efforts there. No attempt was made to jam the Cuban radars that may have been the source of the much publicized "leak" to Noriega, but two EF-111A Ravens from Mountain Home Air Force Base, Idaho reportedly jammed Panamanian surveillance radars as the airborne invasion force neared Panama. This effort was meant to confuse the Panamanians as to the timing of the invasion and the numbers of aircraft that were approaching, even though they may have already known that the attack was occurring.

Another aspect that contributed to the operation, but about which little has been written was aerial refueling. The HC-130 refuelers serviced the MH-53 Pave Low and CH-47D helicopters, and the F-117A Stealth Fighters were said to have been refueled aerially several times while en route from Tonopah to Rio Hato.

An examination of air power in Operation Just Cause would be incomplete without mentioning the night vision goggles (NVGs) or simply "goggles." One of the unchallenged tenets of war is that "he who owns the night owns the war." We relearned this lesson dearly in Vietnam, and since then, the United States has made a concerted effort to improve its nighttime military operating capability. One of the most significant steps in this program has been the NVGs, which allow pilots to see at night by intensifying the available light and images. They have been criticized often because learning to fly safely while wearing them is difficult. However, when used by properly trained pilots, as they were in Panama, they provide a significant advantage over unaided night vision. Many who flew in Just Cause claim that the goggles were instrumental to their success. Colonel Billy Miller, U.S. Army, commander of the 160th said they "enabled us to do a mission we otherwise would not have been able to do...If we had to do the same mission in daylight, I think my losses would have been catastrophic."[5] Miller's unit alone reported over 600 flight hours of "goggle time," including 400 night combat hours in support of the initial assaults.

What, then, were the air "lessons learned" in Panama? In order to answer that, one must first look at the operation in its entirety and relate it to other situations that might require the use of U.S. armed forces. In that context, the value of Just Cause has been overrated, even by those experienced military leaders who should have known better. It has been compared frequently with the Iran hostage rescue attempt and with Operation El Dorado Canyon, the air raid on Libya. From an air perspective, a comparison with the former is farcical. The Iran hostage rescue mission involved a few C-130s and H-53s that attempted a long range covert entry into a hostile nation 10,000 miles from home. Panama was simply a matter of massing aircraft in a nation that already had an existing U.S. command structure, an existing U.S. air base, and 13,000 U.S. troops stationed within a one-leg flight of our border.

It may be possible to make a more meaningful comparison between Panama and Libya, but again, the respective sizes and durations of the two operations makes this difficult. The United States did not do well at night in Iran. We did better in Libya, and better still in Panama. In Panama we were familiar with the terrain, the weather, and many of the people, and control of the skies was not a problem. As in Iran and Libya, there was no enemy aircraft threat, and the ground-to-air threat was actually higher in Libya. Thus it is reasonable to conclude that the most effective air forces for the future, regardless of the scope and intensity of the conflict, will be those that can operate most effectively at night. Panama lends further credence to that opinion.

Just Cause also showed vividly that MAC can be relied upon for support. Discounting those U.S. troops who were already located in Panama and the 6,000 who were landed by aircraft, air-dropping 4,000 paratroopers at the right time and place was significant. In the same vein, the performance of U.S. special operations air units must be recognized, as they accomplished their missions admirably.

It appears that the night fighting capabilities of U.S. air forces has improved, but we must guard against the temptation to regard Panama as a true test. It was not. The deck was just too well stacked in our favor, regardless of the way the operation is analyzed. I have cautioned against overrating Just Cause. We should also take care not to underrate it. Notwithstanding the absence of a serious antiair threat, the United States operated a large number of aircraft in the dark more effectively than it ever had before.

Finally, perhaps the most useful lesson that we relearned in Just Cause was one that can never be overemphasized. The military was permitted to plan and execute the operation without a great deal of civilian interference. History has shown clearly and repeatedly that this tactic almost always results in the most rapid and successful attainment of objectives at the least cost and with the fewest casualties.

NOTES

1.   "Operation Just Cause, 459th Assists in Panama Invasion," Capital Flier (Gaithersburg, MD: Morkap Publishing Co., January 1990).

2.   Caleb Baker, "Army Officials Credit Success in Panama to Planning, Few Bureaucratic Obstacles," Defense News, March 5, 1990.

3.   Peter Almond, "Stealth Steals Some Applause for Panama Debut," Washington Times, January 8, 1990.

4.   David Hughes, "Night Invasion of Panama Required Special Operations Aircraft, Training," Aviation Week and Space Technology, March 5, 1990.

5.   Rowan Scarborough, "Controversial Night Goggles Hailed in Panama," Washington Times, January 15, 1990.

8   The Adequacy of Logistic Support

The success of operation <u>Just Cause</u>, like Operation
<u>Urgent Fury</u> in Grenada in October 1983 and other recent U.S.
military operations, was due in large part to effective
logistics. The airborne, light infantry, and special forces
troops in <u>Just Cause</u> were so effectively supported
logistically that much was taken for granted by those
commentators who discussed the operation. Despite the fact
that some of the participating forces were already based in
Panama, good logistics contributed significantly to the
success of the operation.

On December 17, 1990, when President George Bush ordered
that <u>Just Cause</u> be accomplished, the logistics force began
operations. Military transport aircraft of the Military
Airlift Command (MAC) began flights to Howard Air Force Base
in Panama on December 19th, in preparation for the operation.
The combat forces involved in <u>Just Cause</u> had some significant
logistical advantages not ordinarily possessed by invading
troops. First, about half of the military personnel involved
(13,000 people, including 9,500 Army personnel) were already
positioned in Panama, at bases in and around the Canal Zone
area. The rest were flown in from U.S. bases, including Fort
Bragg, North Carolina, Ft. Lewis, Washington, Hunter Army
Airfield, Georgia, Fort Ord, California, Fort Polk, Louisiana,
Fort Stewart, Georgia, and Fort Benning, Georgia.[1] Second,
U.S. forces had secure logistics installations, including a
major air base in Panama that facilitated speedy airborne
troop introduction and ensured airborne resupply. A third
significant advantage was the extensive U.S. airlift
capability. Finally, there were secure air logistics supply
lines, since the Panamanian Defense Forces (PDF) did not have
the ability to disrupt U.S. flights. Out of a total of 408
flights, only 14 MAC aircraft were damaged, mostly by small
arms fire, and all were repairable. It remains uncertain
whether these aircraft were hit deliberately, since most of
the air logistical activity occurred in a 30-by-30 kilometer
area that included Howard Air Force Base, and it is likely
that the flights in and out of that installation were hit by
stray rounds from nearby combat.[2]

COMMAND AND CONTROL

The Military Airlift Command (MAC) was responsible for the air logistics effort. Most of its 408 flights (55 C-130, 254 C-141, and 99 C-5 flights) between December 20th and January 1st, flew into Howard Air Force Base, Panama. A total of 19,500 personnel and 11,700 tons of materiel were delivered. Concerning personnel transport, a total of 84 parachute drops were made; 2 from C-5, 63 from C-141, and 19 from C-130 aircraft. Twenty-seven other MAC flights, 10 by C-5s, 14 by C-141s, and 3 by C-130s, delivered other troops.[3]

MAC controlled this massive air logistics effort, involving elements of 21 military and tactical airlift wings from 15 U.S. bases, from Scott Air Force Base, Illinois. Other units, including airlift control, aerial port, and aeromedical evacuation units, also participated, with many of the U.S. Air Force units from the reserves.[4]

Route security, especially past Cuba, was ensured by the U.S. Air Force, which supplied fighter escorts and airborne jamming and intelligence assets to the MAC flights. Practically all troop transport and resupply missions flew over the Yucatan Channel and then southward along the Caribbean coast of Central America, approaching Panama from the north. Panamanian command and control was interrupted and PDF air and naval assets were neutralized, insuring that the Panamanian threat to MAC flights was minimal.[5] No in-flight mishaps occurred and no major problems save for winter weather that slightly delayed some of the units, were encountered.[6] The transport flights ranged from six to nine hours, and spanned distances from 1,300 to 3,500 miles. Most of the personnel airlifted to Panama were from the 82nd Airborne Division from Fort Bragg, North Carolina via Pope Air Force Base, the 7th Infantry Division from Fort Ord, California via Travis Air Force Base, and Rangers from Fort Lewis, Washington via McChord Air Force Base.[7]

Following the initial action, airlift aircraft delivered relief items, including medical supplies, food, and temporary housing, to those Panamanians injured or made homeless during the operation. By December 26th, the Department of Defense had coordinated enough U.S. aid to feed 50,000 people for 30 days, and most of this was transported to Panama by MAC.[8]

TACTICAL LOGISTICS

Secure air resupply and significant supplies of stores at U.S. installations in Panama meant that tactical resupply, involving deliveries of goods in and around the former Canal Zone, was the main task for logisticians. In this respect, several factors dominated tactical logistical planning. Because of the limited area of operations in the Panama City area--most action occurred within a 20-kilometer radius of the capital--resupply involved relatively short distances. Thus, fuel and maintenance problems were not a significant factor for logistical vehicles. Supply lines, even in urban areas, once they were secured, could be kept open because of the overwhelming numerical superiority of U.S. forces and the collapse of most resistance shortly after <u>Just Cause</u> was begun.

The air drops were well-executed and battlefield helicopter lift proved to be an invaluable and fairly secure means of troop transport. Few helicopters involved in support operations were hit, even during the heavy combat of the night assault operations on December 20th. This vividly contrasted the 45 of 170 combat helicopters that were hit, four of which were lost. Even captured PDF helicopters were used to transport personnel and equipment in the assault against Tocumen Airport.[9]

With nearby resupply readily available, the main tactical logistics problem was often transporting U.S. troops. This ranged from airmobile operations, such as transporting Task Force Bayonet troops by Black Hawk helicopters in the assault against Fort Amador, to simple ground actions, generally accomplished by a mix of light infantry and mechanized elements. In one case, a platoon of U.S. troops of the 193rd Infantry Brigade was conveyed by bus to attack the Panamanian National Department of Investigations so as to not attract undue attention.[10]

CONCLUSIONS

To some degree, logistical support of <u>Just Cause</u> was a special case. The United States already had bases and forces in Panama, which facilitated the airborne resupply from the United States. Additionally, the operation was planned and executed by the U.S. Army, through U.S. Southern Command (U.S. SOUTHCOM), which was composed mostly of Army elements. This contrasted greatly <u>Urgent Fury</u>, the U.S. intervention in Grenada in October 1983, which suffered from multi-service management and short preparation time. In this context, <u>Just Cause</u> was relevant as an indicator of the existing state of the U.S. logistic and air transport capabilities.

NOTES

1. See <u>Soldiers</u>, February 1990, pp. 20-23, for a list of the U.S. Army units involved, with their home installations.

2. <u>Armed Forces Journal International</u> (February 1990) 26-27.

3. Ibid.

4. <u>Air Force Times</u> (January 1, 1990): R8.

5. <u>Los Angeles Times</u>, December 24, 1989, p. Alf; and <u>New York Times</u>, December 21, 1989, pp. 18f.

6. One transport problem involved 7th Infantry Division troops at Fort Ord, who lacked their own airhead and were transported to Travis Air Force Base in dense fog, causing some difficulties. Poor winter weather conditions at Fort Bragg and Pope Air Force Base also caused some slight delays. Nevertheless, in neither instance did the weather cause more than a slight interruption in plans. (New York Times, December 21, 1989, pp. 18f.)

7. Ibid.

8. Los Angeles Times, December 26, 1989, p. A9.

9. Los Angeles Times, December 24, 1989, pp. A1f; and Armed Forces Journal International (February 1990): 26-27.

10. Army, February 1990, p. 43.

9   Civil Affairs Operations

President George Bush's decision to execute Just Cause on December 19, 1989 climaxed U.S. Southern Command's eighteen-month preparation for implementing Operational Plan Blue Spoon. Among the 27,000 U.S. military men and women who participated in Just Cause were over 200 Reservists from one of the Army's least known branches, Civil Affairs. Some of them were still in Panama months later, helping the nation to recover.

THE OPERATION

Civil Affairs combat involvement began when the Army's only active duty civil affairs unit, the 96th Civil Affairs Battalion, headquartered at Fort Bragg, North Carolina, deployed to Panama with the combat troops. Some of the initial civil affairs teams accompanied airborne units that flew from Pope Air Force Base and jumped into Panama during the first hours of the operation. They quickly began to assess civil affairs needs, especially the need for population control and support, and established a camp for displaced civilians. The homeless were, for the most part, people who lived in the El Chorrillo area that had been burned when the Panamanian Defense Forces (PDF) set fires there as a diversion against U.S. troops. They were soon housed in Balboa High School, a school for U.S. dependents. Quickly establishing and administering this facility was one of the major civil affairs accomplishments in Panama.

Army Reserve civil affairs volunteers were requested and on December 22nd, a twenty-five-person U.S. Army Reserve Civil Affairs Task Force staff was selected from 875 volunteers. They arrived in Panama on the December 26th. Their immediate duties were to assist the Panamanian government and to plan additional civil affairs programs for providing critical support, including assisting the new Panamanian Ministers, augmenting the U.S. Embassy, and restoring critical public services.

A Task Force headquarters was staffed with another 118 Reservists that were selected from over 2,000 volunteers. These came from more than twenty Special Operations Forces Units (Civil Affairs, Psychological Operations, and Special Forces) that were elements of the Army's new Reserve Special

Operations Command, and arrived in Panama on January 1, 1990. They were augmented by nine Reservists from the Individual Ready Reserve (IRR) who lived in Panama.

The Task Force began assisting Panama in reestablishing law and order, restoring the corrections system, distributing food and medical supplies, assessing and restoring basic utilities, and providing health and sanitation services. From the last week in December through the second week of January, it fulfilled more than twenty-five priority missions including: providing direct support to Panama's ministries, helping to develop a twenty-hour civilian police training course for the new police, opening prisons, assisting the 96th Civil Affairs Battalion with the displaced civilian camp at Balboa High School, and re-supplying public health facilities.

Elsewhere, the Task Force conducted general assessments of Panamanian governmental infrastructures in David and Colon and began arranging for food, equipment and personnel for a displaced civilian camp of over 11,000 people, providing doctors and engineers to assess and improve conditions at Coiba prison, furnishing veterinarians to assess livestock health and sanitation problems, and restoring the judicial system and sanitation services to Colon and Panama City. The Task Force included Reservists from many civilian professions, including U.S. marshals, lawyers, doctors, federal, state, and county administrators, budget directors, urban planners, engineers, educators, and economists, who worked with and advised U.S. Embassy and high level U.S. military personnel on civil affairs issues.

Each of the Task Forces's embassy and Panama Ministry representatives was supported by a team of about eight officers, noncommissioned officers, and enlisted personnel, many of whom were proficient in Spanish. The teams' compositions were changed rapidly as issues or problems dictated. For example, a U.S. Navy civilian educator and teacher helped assess Panama's school requirements and buildings, while an engineer was loaned to a public works team to help determine the status of wiring in a damaged apartment building. Urban planners examined needs in the severely damaged El Chorrillo area.

During the second half of January, civil affairs personnel faced new challenges and missions. First, as a U.S. Embassy staff began to arrive, much of the ministerial assessments and assistance were finished and subsequently phased out, although representatives remained in the Ministries of Education, Public Works, and the embassy's office of economics and aviation.

Meanwhile, Task Force civil affairs Reservists supported combat, airmobile, and infantry sweeps and other tactical operations with Army Infantry, Marines, and Special Forces units. For example, civil affairs teams went with the Green Berets to remote areas to assess needs concerning water supply, electrical power, medicine, and sanitation. They provided basic support to tactical troops by acting as the military's liaison with the civilian government, police officials, and the Panamanian public.

The need to transform the former PDF into a civilian police force capable of handling routine law enforcement functions was assigned to the Task Force. Since several of its personnel had law enforcement experience, an ad hoc team was formed on January 17th to conduct an assessment. Initial coordination also was accomplished with representatives of the International Criminal Investigation Training Program (ICITAP) that became the contractor for supporting the PDF's transition to a civilian police force. Developing a twenty-hour police training course for former PDF personnel who would serve in the new Panamanian police force was also accomplished by the Civil Affairs Task Force. Army Reservists who were in law enforcement in civilian life assisted and advised the new Panamanian police.

By late-January, a problem was the lack of continuity and the disruption caused by using "39-day volunteers" who had to return to their civilian jobs. Task Force operational effectiveness and staffing were affected by the turnover of some 79 of 146 civil affairs specialists on January 25th. Even though this provisional Task Force reorganized its personnel properly in order to meet rapidly changing needs, time delays occurred and were compounded by transportation and logistical problems.

Another critical situation was the lack of a dedicated Civic Action Fund of at least $2 million and two contracting officers to assist in immediately initiating coordinated and embassy-approved projects. This fund would have allowed the Task Force to quickly resolve war damage claims and diffuse negative public reaction.

As February began, the Task Force still had a small element advising the U.S. Embassy concerning civil aviation and economics, and had prepared ten major Nation-Building Assessments that were presented to the U.S. Agency for International Development (USAID). The agency accepted seven of these, which, for the most part, concerned the highly populated Panama City--Colon corridor, and consisted of road work, school improvements, water supply, and improving and rebuilding the fire-ravaged El Chorrillo neighborhood of Panama City. The purpose of the assessments was to identify high impact projects that would improve Panama's economic and governmental infrastructures, and allow the largest number of people to return to work.

USAID's limited and constantly rotating staff element made communications difficult, but the Task Force provided the necessary data for developing a U.S. Congressional aid package and served as an extension of its staff in assessing the various support packages. While earlier USAID officials projected the need for the type of civil affairs support it would need in conducting the various programs, a formal request apparently was not levied on the Department of Defense to provide the following support: preparing project profiles and action plans; pre-qualifying construction firms bidding on construction projects; conducting field inspections along with Ministry representatives; monitoring contract compliance; reviewing material requests; creating spare parts and inventory lists for heavy equipment; and identifying small community development projects. The USAID staffing shortages continued into March and eventually delayed the timely transfer of excess Department of Defense Dependent School equipment to Panama in order to improve the reopening of its school system in April.

In mid-February, Company "C" of the 96th Civil Affairs Battalion returned to Fort Bragg, North Carolina, leaving Reserve civil affairs forces responsible for the entire civil affairs effort. More personnel continued to arrive for duty as others returned to their civilian jobs. By February 17th, the Task Force began finalizing a nationwide prioritization list of over 200 civic action projects that were designed to improve the quality of life, and then developed a strategy for coordinating the projects through U.S. military channels, Panamanian provincial governors, and the national government. The Task Force first conducted discussions and assessments with western province governors and mayors, and then the Governor of Panama Province visited several critical proposed rural civic action sites. Meanwhile, Task Force teams at various sites throughout Panama recommended that local proposals be staffed through the country's respective national ministries, thereby encouraging interaction between the provincial governors and their national government.

By March, the Task Force had contributed significantly to establishing and maintaining security against domestic threats and improving basic services. After more than two months of intense planning, assessments, and reporting, the Joint Chiefs of Staff Fuerzas Unidas nation-building exercise was approved. On March 12th, a combined Southern Command, U.S. Army South and Civil Affairs Team met with the Ministry of Public Works national and provincial directors to approve Fuerzas Unidas. For years into the future, U.S. Reserve and National Guard units are expected to complete projects that include critical farm-to-market road-building and improvement, and work on clinics, schools, and other public facility structures.

ASSESSING CIVIL AFFAIRS

The civil affairs effort was very successful. Nonetheless, as in any operation, some aspects went better than others, and it is of value to consider the operation's strengths and weaknesses. First, in the operational arena, successes were enjoyed in almost every task to which assets were assigned because Panama had experienced such severe economic degradation under Noriega and the U.S. economic sanctions that any positive action resulted in an improved situation. Second, concerning Joint Chiefs of Staff strategic planning, coordinating civil-military operations with the State Department and USAID did not occur early enough to ensure the most effective use of civil affairs personnel.

Third, the mobilization of Army Reserve civil affairs units designated for specific theater areas of operations should be executed and selectively implemented through strategic and tactical civil affairs packages. The mobilization of these special operations Reserves will provide the necessary command, staff, country, and technical knowledge necessary for continuity in stability and recovery operations. Further, those Individual Ready Reserves (IRRs) living in a target nation can be extremely valuable if they are carefully screened to ensure that they have the language, technical skills, and civil affairs experience. During Just Cause some Reservists who volunteered provided excellent civilian technical skills and language support, but others did not have the necessary training or field experience. Nevertheless, several of the Ready Reservists contributed significantly and their political, social, and civilian job connections with key Panamanians enabled them to be excellent coordinators for the Task Force and Ministerial support teams.

Fourth, concerning intelligence, the Task Force was so understaffed that not only was it unable to process and forward all useful information to other operational elements, but was barely able to address its own requirements. Just Cause highlighted a number of areas where future intelligence support capabilities need to be improved.

Another critical problem at the onset of any military operation is the prompt treatment and evacuation of civilian casualties. While Just Cause was unique in that adequate medical facilities and personnel were available, there was a critical shortage in Panama's medical supplies and an inadequate distribution system. The Task Force health team and Southern Command worked together to obtain the most critical supplies, and the team helped the government to establish a more effective medical distribution system. Some of the initial coordination delays could have been averted if an experienced civil affairs medical officer had been assigned to execute contingency plans for civilian casualties, coordinate distributing medical supplies, and evaluate Panama's medical requirements. Some consideration should be given to establishing an emergency medical fund to handle the most critical medical shortfalls in future operations.

Finally, service war colleges and foreign service schools should provide seminars to enhance the general understanding of civil affairs doctrine. The revitalization of a government administration course at the Army's J.F. Kennedy Special Warfare School and greater emphasis on the study of evolving Third World governments would improve the understanding of the complexities in dealing with new governments. A short course on civil-military operations for other Reservists, especially those technical personnel living and working in Third World countries, would make them more valuable in future crisis situations.

SUMMARY

In conclusion, the Civil Affairs Task Force contributed significantly to achieving U.S. goals and objectives in Panama. It developed at least nineteen major engineering projects and over 220 nationwide civic action projects that focused on improving Panama's health, education, and economic conditions. While aggressive plans and projects have been developed, the U.S. ability to provide the necessary foreign aid to support them in the coming years will be among the more difficult U.S. foreign policy challenges of the 1990s.

10 Assessing Press Access to Information

Assessing press access to information during <u>Just Cause</u> is not possible without considering the institutional context and the history of U.S. military-press relations. In the institutional context, the military-press relationship has often been adversarial. For the press, the ideal situation is total access to information, as journalists continue their relentless pursuit of news. In this light, any denial of information is an impediment, a hurdle that must be overcome if the story is to be reported. Alternatively, the military often seeks to restrict information. Most often this concerns information that it wishes to deny the enemy; information that can endanger U.S. lives if it is made public. Less often, information is withheld if it will have an adverse affect on the war effort. This occurred, for example, during the British invasion of the Falkland Islands, when the Royal Navy lost ships at the beginning of the war. The combat situation was soon reversed and the British prevailed, but to have reported the losses in the early days of the war might have prompted the opposition in Parliament to call for curtailing subsequent operations. In that case, the war might not have been won. In <u>Just Cause</u>, the deliberate restriction of information concerned the facts that the operation was to occur and the time it was to occur. No official attempt was made to deliberately restrict news concerning the hostilities.

This adversarial relationship and the history of military-press relations also must be considered in an assessment of press access to information during <u>Just Cause</u>. The relationship was very hostile during the Vietnam War, producing many journalists who were jaundiced by the military's manipulation of information, and many servicemen who believed that the press was a danger, an antagonistic group that had been a factor in America's loss of the war. The situation had not improved in Operation <u>Urgent Fury</u>, the U.S. intervention in Grenada, when press access was deliberately restricted and many journalists were prevented from reaching the island during the hostilities.

Following Grenada, attempts were made to establish a better relationship that would provide journalists with information, but would still guarantee the security of sensitive information. Based on the experience of <u>Just Cause</u>, while the military did not actively oppose the press' access to information, there were so many problems and bottlenecks that press access was sorely restricted. The result was that this entire process went unsatisfactorily and was the least successful aspect of Just Cause. Further, much work remains if an acceptable balance is to be established. Finally, in spite of what might be termed "over-attention to security," there were security leaks. While these did not compromise the operation, they nonetheless reflected that existing procedures were inadequate.

As was mentioned in this book's preface, those who participated have every right to be proud of the conduct of Just Cause. An extremely complex operation, it was hallmarked by competence and professionalism. In the context of the U.S. military's record of mixed success in previous joint operations, in all but a few aspects, Just Cause was a resounding success. Unfortunately, one of those aspects concerned the press. The major concerns were for maintaining the secrecy of the operation and providing the press access to information. In both cases, there were problems. The following first presents the progression of events, then considers the cause of the problems and the measures that have been recommended to prevent them in the future. It concludes by assessing whether these recommendations are adequate to provide better news coverage in the future.

THE PROGRESSION OF EVENTS

The Problems with Press Access

In the aftermath of Just Cause, the government realized that the problems related to the sixteen-member press pool were of such magnitude that Peter Williams, the Assistant Secretary of Defense for Public Affairs, called for an investigation. The inquiry, conducted by Fred Hoffman, was extensive, and Hoffman's conclusions were profound.[1] These were released in a "Memorandum for Correspondents" on March 20, 1990.[2] Because Hoffman's study is not only the sole investigation into the access that was provided, but also continually assesses responsibility for each problem, this chapter relies heavily on his findings and assesses his judgments.

Table 10.1 (found at the end of this chapter) presents a chronology of the Pentagon's program to support the press during Just Cause. The plan was begun on November 13, 1989, when the Joint Staff asked U.S. Southern Command (SOCOM) to submit a public affairs plan. Failing to submit a full plan on November 22nd, SOCOM merely submitted a bare bones outline, probably believing that it would have primary responsibility for the press pool drawn from correspondents stationed in Panama. In this case, it was merely providing an outline of what would be accomplished. However, the Pentagon did not understand this relationship and assumed that SOCOM had deferred responsibility to the Joint Staff. When the Pentagon Public Affairs Office began to staff the SOCOM plan, an action that might have been successful, it was told by the Inter-American Affairs Office that the issue was so sensitive that the plan should not be disseminated. The Public Affairs Office then stored the plan and planning was effectively halted until mid-December. Thus, a concern for secrecy delayed any planning considerations for almost a month, no helicopters or aircraft to carry equipment were requested, and no provisions were made to provide adequate communications for reporters who would deploy to Panama.[3]

The existing procedure called for establishing a Pentagon press pool to report on operations in a remote area where there was no other U.S. press presence. In other situations, it was either assumed that U.S. reporters in the area would report independently or would be assembled in a local press pool. Although Panama definitely fell into the second category, this apparently was not understood in Washington, because in the days before the operation, the question of whether to form a Pentagon press pool or to instruct SOCOM to assemble a pool of reporters in Panama was deliberated continually. On December 17th, when President Bush ordered that Just Cause be executed, he also asked about the press issue and was told by Secretary of Defense Dick Cheney that a press pool would come from the Pentagon. Bush expressed his concern for security. On December 18th, Cheney told Peter Williams that a Pentagon press pool would cover Just Cause, but told him that he could not tell anyone. On the same day, Colonel Ron Sconyers, the SOCOM Public Affairs Officer, was told that a military operation might occur, but that he could not tell anyone. Sconyers assumed that he would assemble a pool of correspondents in Panama, as he had done during earlier U.S. operations in Panama.[4]

During the morning of December 19th, less than 17 hours before H hour, Williams finally briefed his staff and serious planning began. However, the debate concerning using Panama- or Washington-based correspondents continued into the afternoon, and it was not until 5 p.m. that Williams informed Sconyers that a pool would be coming from Washington. Sconyers now had a problem. He had planned on using surface transportation to convey the Panama-based pool and had not asked for helicopters. However, these were needed to transport the larger Washington-based pool, and other logistical arrangements--housing, food, work area, communications, office support, and so on--were infinitely more complex. Sconyers asked for helicopter support, but by this time, all helicopters were committed for operational missions. Possibly hoping to be able to salvage success from the approaching disaster, he did not inform Washington of any of these problems, thereby cutting himself off from any help that Secretary Cheney, General Colin Powell, the Chairman of the Joint Chiefs of Staff, or the White House might have provided.[5] However, without high level attention that could cut through the red tape and override other demands on the available resources, there was no way that the pool could be supported adequately. Thus, the pool was inevitably destined to suffer very severe difficulties.

All this amounts to a tremendous bureaucratic error that had resulted from a concern for secrecy. This concern continued to affect the pool even more adversely. At this point, the pool was certain to face a frustrating nightmare when it reached Panama because no provisions had been made for its support. However, the government would now make decisions that would guarantee its late arrival, hours after the inception of Just Cause.

In the inquiries following Just Cause, Secretary Cheney took full responsibility for using the Washington pool and for its late arrival. He said that his first priority was safeguarding the security of the operation and that he "was aware of the conflict" between that imperative and the goal of getting the pool to Panama in time. However, he believed that he had a "sense of special loyalty to people who cover the Pentagon" and "it was important that there be that kind of coverage." In the final analysis, he said, "we were very concerned about the situation--that the PDF might be waiting for us," and decided to notify the pool after the Tuesday evening national news broadcasts to minimize the possibility of leaks. The 7:30 p.m. callout guaranteed that the pool would reach Panama after Just Cause began, and Cheney said, "I did it with full knowledge" of what this decision would mean to the pool. Additionally, he acknowledged that Generals Powell and Kelly were left out of this decision-making.[6]

Those familiar with military exercises and operations will attest to the fact that, when an endeavor is poorly planned, a negative momentum can set in because those involved become myopic, seeing and solving immediate problems without considering what affect their solutions may have on other action officers further down the line. As a result, the entire project often snowballs to disaster. Just such a momentum was present in the case of the press pool. The pool members were supposed to report to Andrews Air Force Base at 9:30 p.m. for an 11 p.m. departure. Such a schedule meant that the reporters would arrive in Panama at approximately 5 a.m., four hours after Just Cause began and thus would miss much of the initial conflict. This delay could have been shortened if the processing at Andrews were accelerated and if high-level attention were focused on assuring that adequate and timely transportation was available when the press plane arrived in Panama. However, no such measures were taken. Rather, the actions at Andrews only delayed the departure. During the call-out of reporters, the pool was expanded when each service was invited to send a reporter and a photographer. Additionally, Williams allowed NBC news to bring a satellite dish and two independent technicians. The plane finally departed at 11:26 p.m. and arrived at Howard Air Force Base in Panama at 5 a.m. A helicopter did not arrive to transport the reporters until 6:30 a.m. and did not depart for Fort Clayton until 7 a.m.[7]

It was now over six hours since Just Cause had started, and no reporters had yet reached the scene of reportable news.

In short, the pool was now bogged down, but Williams did not notify General Powell for another 30 hours, although he did urge Colonel Sconyers to get the pool to the action. The question was what to do with them. No helicopters were available and there were no provisions for transporting the pool safely by car, truck, or bus to the action. The helicopter situation would not be solved for another 36 hours. A briefing by John Bushnell, U.S. Embassy Charge d'Affaires provided little information on the operation. At 10 a.m. it was decided to keep the pool together for the day and not split it into two groups until Thursday. The reporters were taken to Fort Armador, but arrived there when the action was largely over. While there, reporters saw fires at the Commandancia and asked to go there, but were told that it was too dangerous. They were also told that it was too dangerous to take a helicopter tour of the city. Southern Command Public Affairs Officers (PAOs) tried to find what they called "story ideas," but too many of these turned out to be disappointments. Thus, they had little success in getting the pool to any remaining newsworthy action in the mop-up of the defeated Panamanian forces. Over the longer term, the Southern Command PAOs failed to provide regular operational briefings for the pool to keep it informed of developments. There was only one such briefing, more than 24 hours into the pool's four-day deployment. The result of all this was that the pool produced stories and pictures of essentially secondary value.[8] To add insult to injury, when Sam Donaldson arrived the day after the main attacks, pressure from Washington afforded him preferential treatment. "When Sam Donaldson arrived, it was like the President had walked into the media center," said one military escort. Sconyers was "given over basically to supporting Sam Donaldson."[9]

All of this meant that press access to the story was sorely restricted. The failure to provide administrative support then came into play and delayed greatly much of the news that the journalists did prepare. The Pentagon's faxing machine malfunctioned, causing obstacle after obstacle for newspaper, wire service and magazine reporters and photographers. In Panama, there were only enough phones for the original pool and no additional phones were requested. Thus, when more reporters arrived on December 21st, the situation became impossible. No arrangements were made to fly film material to the United States, and the first material, sent on Thursday, did not arrive until Saturday. The situation was no better in the Pentagon, where the small staff had no experience in pool matters. No augmentation was requested and two-person teams worked 12 hour shifts, with a major on one of the teams also serving duty in the Pentagon watch center. Additionally, there were no standard procedures for handling pool products other than print reports and there were no provisions for sharing still photography with other services. While Hoffman noted that the two teams worked professionally and valiantly, it was impossible for less than four full-time people to provide adequate service.[10]

138

Assessing the Problems of Press Access

As Hoffman noted there were two primary causes for the problems in Panama--a lack of competence or professionalism and, in his terms, "an excessive concern for secrecy."

In respect to professionalism, there is certainly cause to blame almost all involved. While SOCOM could claim that existing procedures did not call for a Pentagon-based press pool to deploy to Panama, this does not excuse the lack of preparation concerning communications and administrative support. The fact that the SOCOM PAO staff was not informed of the operation on Tuesday, December 19th, presented a crisis. However, there appears to have been little reaction to this crisis. Office and administrative systems were not checked out and backup systems were not provided. Faced with an impossible situation, it appears that the reaction was to "tough it out." But having made this decision, little preliminary work was done, so that problems were only exacerbated as time passed.

Similarly, in the Pentagon, little appears to have been done. In one of the world's largest office buildings in which thousands of people are employed and task groups are formed frequently to provide the necessary support for crisis situations, it seems unbelievable that no augmentation could be found for four competent but terribly overworked people.

Hoffman also criticized the concern for secrecy, which he considered a major problem. However, the United States was about to embark on a very complex exercise, one in which surprise was crucial not only in saving the lives of hundreds of troops, but also to the success of the entire operation. In retrospect, Just Cause, like Urgent Fury in Grenada, was tremendously successful politically, achieving all the political goals envisioned and providing a context in which subsequent U.S. policy would be much more successful. But it could have gone the other way. Noriega's forces could have been prepared and U.S. losses could have been much higher. Noriega could have escaped to wage a guerrilla war. The Panama Canal could have been interdicted, creating great economic problems for many nations that would justifiably blame the United States for their difficulties. Finally, the United States might have found itself in a much weaker position to influence Panama's role in the drug trade, with consequent negative results.

Hoffman also noted that a distrust of the press was evident in the actions of the White House on down to personnel in the field and that this was a significant factor. For example, helicopter pilots did not want to fly journalists over Panama for fear of ground fire, journalists were "sometimes diverted from a promising objective by the presence of Special Operations soldiers who are under orders to shun the press," some unit commanders refused to check with the press until gaining approval from their superiors, photographers were not allowed to film damaged helicopters because they might photograph classified gear, and initially photographers were not allowed to film the caskets of the American dead. Hoffman stated that "as a result, there were suggestions that the pool was being manipulated to serve the Bush Administration's political and diplomatic interests," and commented that "over the five-year history of Pentagon-sponsored pools, including a year-long series in the Persian Gulf, hundreds of newsmen and newswomen demonstrated they could be trusted to respect essential ground rules, including operational security." He concluded that "unless the Defense Department's leaders are prepared to extend that trust in hot war situations, the pool probably will be of little value."[11]

The Problem of Security

In the final analysis, the actions of everyone from the White House, who had left the issue to Secretary Cheney to resolve, to Cheney who deliberately called the pool out too late to arrive in Panama on time, to the reticent people in the field, there was a concern for security and a distrust of the press.

One does not have to look back too far in history to find a cause for such distrust. From the military's perspective, the press' role in Vietnam, that was occasionally characterized by fabricating news and was increasingly anti-military as the war progressed, was unconscionable and probably caused the deaths of many Americans. Such distrust was evident in Urgent Fury, the U.S. operation on Grenada, when both the White House and U.S. operating forces actively inhibited reporting from the scene. But times had changed and a new generation of reporters were in the field in 1989. The press mellowed its stance to one that could be considered as having been very favorable toward President Reagan. Thus, there was reason to question whether such distrust was still deserved.

The issue of secrecy is an independent and related matter. Those concerned with military operations, whether they be in the White House, in the Pentagon, or in the field, are constantly reminded of security. Indeed, such an emphasis is placed on secrecy that breaches can destroy one's career. Entire systems, involving established procedures and thousands of people, are in place to attempt to ensure that secrecy is maintained. And yet there are leaks, constant leaks of information in which secrets are divulged. When they occur, the press feels justified in reporting them under the belief that the public has a right to know. Freedom of the press is one of our nation's great freedoms, but it can also endanger American lives. Additionally, the press is not indoctrinated into the security system and is not sensitive to the importance of classified information. In fact, a good reporter might view a tenet of his or her job as breaching this security whenever possible in order to make a scoop, or when in his or her mind, it is the "public's right to know."

Thus, there is a delicate balance of opposing forces and principles at work here and the ideal solution is to provide the maximum amount of information without endangering U.S. lives or policy. The Pentagon press pool was established to provide such a balance. The question then is whether based on the events in Just Cause the system worked. In terms of press access to information we have seen that the answer is a resounding "no." However, did the system work in terms of safeguarding information. Here again, the answer is "no," because of the many violations of operations security that occurred, four were caused by the press. On December 19th, despite U.S. governmental attempts to maintain secrecy, reports of unusual military activity at U.S. bases in Panama appeared on national television. The second breach of security occurred when the Time magazine staff discussed who would go as a member of the press pool at a Christmas party. The final two violations occurred with the full realization of government personnel. Peter Williams allowed NBC news representatives in the pool to bring a satellite dish with them to Panama. This required bringing two technicians from an outside company to service the dish. Neither of them had been briefed on security ground rules, which was a breach of security. Finally, one pool correspondent was allowed to call home from Andrews Air Force Base before the press plane departed for Panama and before Just Cause had begun.[12]

The fact that these violations occurred and that other violations might have occurred and went unreported--one assumes that the major services went into planning their coverage and sending additional reporters to Panama as soon as they were notified--that the attempts at secrecy were less than totally successful. While Hoffman notes that none of these breaches alerted the Panamanians, this does not detract from the fact that they occurred and that they reflect an imperfect system. In this light, Secretary Cheney was actually faced with a very difficult decision, and finally decided to favor security with the full realization that he would suffer criticism from the press.

RECOMMENDED SOLUTIONS

Thus, the current system is imperfect and if left unchanged might create similar problems in the future. When we consider amending the system, we should first examine Hoffman's recommendations and note which of these the government has chosen to implement. We can then assess whether the solutions offered and accepted will create a better system.

On March 20, 1990, the Assistant Secretary of Defense for Public Affairs (ASD(PA)) released Hoffman's report, which contained 17 recommendations. At that time, he stated that five recommendations would be implemented immediately.[13] These were:

   o   the ASD(PA) must work aggressively with the
         Secretary of Defense and the Chairman, Joint Chiefs
         of Staff, to overcome secrecy and other obstacles

to the prompt deployment of a pool to the scene of action.

o   the ASD(PA) must be kept informed after a pool is deployed and must act immediately to break through any obstacles that are encountered by the pool.

o   the ASD(PA) should consider deploying two pools. The first would be small and would have reporters and photographers. The second would have supporting equipment, such as satellite dishes.

o   the pool should never be kept together, but should be split up and then reassembled to share information.

o   there should be regular briefings for pool reporters to provide current information.[14]

Additionally, Williams accepted six other recommendations "in principle," but stated that they required refinement:[15]

o   the Secretary of Defense should issue a directive to be circulated throughout the Armed Forces stating his official sponsorship of the pool and requiring everyone to assist it in its reporting.

o   the ASD(PA) should have prepared and should review public affairs plans to assure that the pool is fully supported. These plans should be briefed to the Chairman, Joint Chiefs of Staff, and to the Secretary of Defense.

o   before an exercise, the Chairman, Joint Chiefs of Staff, should send a message to all commanders and all personnel involved directing them to cooperate with the media pool and provide all necessary resources, including helicopters, vehicles, and communications equipment.

o   the pool should be exercised at least quarterly. The Pentagon organization must be restructured so that ASD(PA) can assure that there is enough support (personnel and equipment) in the Pentagon to assure the timely processing of reports from the pool.

o   Public Affairs Officers from Unified Commands should meet periodically with reporters assigned to pools.[16]

Finally, Williams noted that the following recommendations would "require further consideration and coordination with the Joint Chiefs of Staff, the Unified Commands, and pool members":[17]

o   all Joint Staff operational plans must have an annex to insure that pool members will move in with the earliest forces and cover the earliest stages of operations.

o   the ASD(PA) should consider assigning a Pentagon editor to interface with staff officers handling pool reports.

o   the pool escorting system should be overhauled to

> o   ensure that escorts are from the proper service and
>   properly dressed for the combat environment.
> o   the ASD(PA) should require all pool organizations
>   to share their products.
> o   needed equipment, such as darkrooms and satellite
>   uplink gear, might be stored permanently at Andrews
>   Air Force Base so that it is ready for deployment.
> o   all pool-assigned reporters and photographers should
>   attend quarterly Pentagon sessions where problems,
>   rules, and responsibilities can be discussed.[18]

ARE THESE ADEQUATE?

Press Access

Given that Hoffman's recommendations are the current attempt to correct the problems encountered in _Just Cause_, the question is whether his recommendations are adequate to solve the problems of access and security. Based on the March 20th memorandum, those recommendations already put into effect will guarantee that the Chairman, Joint Chiefs of Staff, and the Secretary of Defense will bear a portion of the responsibility for the success of the pool, that the ASD(PA) will bear continuous responsibility for the smooth operation of the pool, that a smaller first party of the pool will deploy rapidly, that pool members will be split up, and that there will be regular briefings to provide information. These recommendations should go a long way toward resolving the delays and problems that were encountered concerning the rapid movement of the pool to Panama and its subsequent deployment.

We can assume that the second six recommendations, those "accepted in principle" but "requiring refinement," will be implemented in the near future, if they have not already been implemented. These will require all combat personnel to cooperate fully with pool reporters, thereby preventing the withholding of information, and will ensure that the reports that the pool files will be disseminated expeditiously.

Finally, the six recommendations requiring "further consideration and coordination" will require lengthy deliberation before they are implemented and some may not be implemented. However, if they are, then they would further ensure that pool members have the greatest access to the news and that their reports are disseminated as widely as possible.

Security

None of Hoffman's recommendations addresses the issue of secrecy. Rather, the tenor of his report seems hostile concerning security to the extent that it inhibits the flow of information. As such, it can be considered to be aimed at improving the Pentagon's role in the relationship. This is correct to the extent that it was the stated purpose of Hoffman's investigation. However, it does not address the problem of security and ignoring this issue will not make it go away. Rather than denigrating security, either explicitly or implicitly, it would be more beneficial to recognize that security is a legitimate factor in the entire equation. If Hoffman's recommendations are accepted, then the resulting situation will not have improved the security situation in any manner and we can expect that future presidents, secretaries of defense, and chairmen of the Joint Chiefs of Staff will be presented with the same dilemma. Additionally, in the final analysis, the majority of the American public can be expected to side with their decision to restrict or inhibit press access in order to protect American lives and ensure the success of American endeavors. The press demonstrated, through security violations in Just Cause, that such concern is warranted, and, while it may be loud in its criticism of the issue, the next time it arises (this time being able to implicate the Chairman of the Joint Chiefs of Staff and the on-scene commander as well), it will not get the access it seeks and will not solve the problem.[19]

Thus, we are left with providing a recommended solution. The answer appears to be one of affording the military the ability to deploy journalists without creating suspicion. One opion might be to ask the major news services to assign reporters to the Unified and Specified Commands on a full-time basis. These people would have much less visibility than the Washington pool and could be briefed and isolated immediately before an operation. They would then be able to report the outbreak of hostilities without arousing suspicion. Equipment could also be in place to assure the greatest coverage. Realizing that these might be the news services' more junior reporters, they might want to replace them with more prominent journalists. Such replacements could be collected after an operation began, briefed at the Pentagon or elsewhere so that they had the latest information, and transported expeditiously to the combat arena.

An alternative might be have a pool of reporters in isolation and sequestered from their news services. They could be relieved periodically, so as to minimize the inconvenience of such a detail. In times of non-crisis, their employers could assign them to non-time critical staff stories concerning defense affairs that would be filed after they left their isolation. However, when an operation was about to occur, these people could be briefed exhaustively as the operation unfolded and could even prepare reports concerning the buildup to hostilities. Since their services would not know where they were, they could be moved privately to the crisis arena before hand in sufficient time to insure that they had all the support and access that they needed to report responsibly. These recommendations are likely not to be accepted, since they involve restricting reporters' freedom and would involve an expense to the news services. However, continuing the current arrangement seems to assure that there will be similar problems in the future. In this light, it would appear that seeking a more acceptable solution would benefit all concerned.

144

NOTES

1.   United States, Department of Defense, <u>Review of Panama Pool Deployment, December 1989</u>, prepared by Fred S. Hoffman (Washington, DC: Office of the Assistant Secretary of Defense Public Affairs, 1990).

2.   United States, Department of Defense, "Memorandum for Correspondents" (Washington, DC: Office of the Assistant Secretary of Defense Public Affairs, March 20, 1990), p. 1.

3.   <u>Review of Panama Pool Deployment</u>, pp. 4-6.

4.   Ibid., pp. 2, 6-8.

5.   Ibid., pp. 4, 7-9.

6.   Ibid., pp. 1, 7-8.

7.   Ibid., pp. 10-11.

8.   Ibid., pp. 1-3, 11-12.

9.   Ibid., p. 14. While Hoffman's report was very critical of the treatment afforded to Donaldson, he seems to have been unfair. From his perspective---existing regulations and procedures---Donaldson should have received no such treatment. However, the reality was that Donaldson was special. Not only was he known for his pressing interviews of U.S. presidents, but he also represented a potentially wide audience, much wider than many of the pool members. A similar concession had been made to NBC news when it was allowed to bring along a satellite dish. The major news media are very competitive and ABC certainly outflanked NBC and CBS when it sent Donaldson, and definitely expected this to bring results. This was journalistic hardball and it seems that, under the circumstances, it would have been difficult for the military to treat Donaldson as just another journalist.

10. Ibid., pp. 14-16.

11. Ibid., pp. 1,5.

12. Ibid., pp. 6, 10.

13. "Memorandum for Correspondents."

14. <u>Review of Panama Pool Deployment</u>, pp. 17-18.

15. "Memorandum for Correspondents."

16. <u>Review of Panama Pool Deployment</u>, pp. 17-19.

17. "Memorandum for Correspondents."

18.   <u>Review of Panama Pool Deployment</u>, pp. 17-19.

19.   One would have expected this issue to have become a problem during the next operation, which was Operation <u>Desert Shield</u> in Saudi Arabia in 1990.   However, the potential problem was defused quickly when the Pentagon addressed the issue of press access, noting that the Saudi Arabians had different views concerning freedom of the press than did Americans and that their approach was much less open.   Thus the issue became whether the Saudis would allow reporters access.

TABLE 10.1

Problems Associated with Press Access
to Information During Just Cause

Date	Event	Significance
Nov 13	Joint Staff asked Southern Command (SOCOM) to submit a Public Affairs Plan.	A plan was needed for organized and complete newscoverage.
Nov 22	SOCOM Public Affairs Office (PAO) sent a Top Secret fax to Pentagon Public Affairs Plans unit. It was not a fully developed plan. Rather, it just provided bare bones guidance.	The plan was inadequate and needed development in order to assure a successful operation.
	LCDR Gregory Hartung took the fax to Colonel Peter Alexandrakos, who began to staff it in the Pentagon.	
	The Pentagon's Inter-American Affairs Office told Hartung that Deputy Assistant Secretary of Defense Richard C. Brown had ordered the fax "close-hold" until it became necessary to have such guidance and then staffed at at that time. Hartung was told to "stick it in the safe and forget about it." Williams was never told of Brown's objections.	Brown's concern for security prevented the necessary planning. The document could have alerted officers that a full plan was necessary. At a minimum, this meant that there were no helicopters or aircraft scheduled and adequate communications planned.
Dec 17	President Bush asked about reporters. Secretary Cheney relied that a pool would go from Washington. Bush indicated his concern for security.	Cheney was left with the responsibility.

Dec 18	General Stiner arrived in Panama. He would later say that he could have taken a small pool with him, which could have been briefed sequestered, and positioned to witness the opening attack.	Reporters would have been present when the operation began.
Dec 18	Cheney told Assistant Secretary of Defense for Public Affairs Peter Williams of <u>Just Cause</u> and that a pool would be used to cover it. "You can't tell this to anybody," said Cheney. Williams only informed two people on his staff because of the secrecy rule. Some "brain storming" was done, but there was no de- tailed planning.	24 hours planning time had been lost because of the concern for security.
	Southern Command PAO Colonel Ron Sconyers was told that a mili- tary operation might occur, but that he could not tell anyone. He in- tended to use a Panama- based pool and did not need helicopters because he intended to position the pool below Quarry Heights and possibly at Fort Amador.	The concern for secrecy prevented Sconyers from making adequate preparations.
Dec 18-Dec 19	Cheney and Williams decided on a press pool from Washington, but no one told Sconyers until 5 p.m.	Believing that he would use a Panama-based pool, Sconyers made no prepa- rations to support the incoming Pentagon pool.
Dec 19, a.m.	Williams briefed his staff but did not begin talking with Sconyers until later. The debate over whether to use the Panama-based pool or send one from Washington continued into the	The project now was so far behind that nothing less than the involve- ment of Secretary Cheney or the White House could have saved it from disaster.

afternoon.

The cutoff time for
deciding to successfully
use a Washington-based
pool had passed.

p.m.	Vice President Quayle asked if a pool could be organized in Panama. No one had a good answer. Bush and Quayle remained skeptical about secrecy, but left the press issue to Cheney.	
p.m.	Despite attempts to maintain secrecy, reports of unusual military activity at U.S. bases in Panama appeared on U.S. television.	
5 p.m.	Williams informed Sconyers that a pool would come from Washington. Sconyers then asked for helicopter support, but all the helos were obligated to transport troops.	Only high-level intervention by Generals Powell, Kelly, or Stiner, or the White House could have salvaged the operation.
7:30 p.m.	The Washington-based pool was called out.	
p.m.	_Time_ magazine staff members breached security when they discussed who would go to Panama at a Christmas party. This did not compromise the operation.	The government's fears concerning security appeared warranted.
	During the callout, the pool was expanded so that each service was invited to send a reporter and a photographer.	This caused a further delay of a pool that already would not reach Panama until hours after the operation began.
	Williams allowed NBC to bring a satellite dish and two technicians from an outside company. The technicians were not briefed on security	Further delay and an additional security violation.

ground rules, which was
a breach of security.

9:30 p.m. Pool members were to   Another security
report to Andrews Air   violation.
Force Base for an 11
p.m. departure. One
correspondent called
home from Andrews,
which was a breach of
security.

11:26 p.m. The pool departed Andrews.

Dec 20   The pool landed at Howard
5 a.m.   Air Force Base, Panama,
over five hours after
Just Cause began.

6:30 a.m. A helicopter arrived to
transport the pool.

7 a.m.   The helicopter departed   Additional delays
and proceeded to Fort   were certain because
Clayton. The pool was   of a lack of high-
now bogged down, but   level attention.
Williams did not notify
General Powell for
another 30 hours. He
did urge Sconyers to get
the pool to the action.

a.m.   Shortly after landing,
the pool was briefed by
John Bushnell, U.S.
Embassy Charge d'Affaires.
One reporter described
it as a history lesson.

10 a.m.   It was decided to keep   Not splitting the pool
the pool together for a   meant limiting the
day. It was not split   scope of its coverage.
into two groups until   Not transporting the
Thursday. It was taken   pool to the combat
to Fort Armador, where   action meant that they
the action was largely   would report on only
over. While there,   items of secondary
reporters commented on   interest.
fires at the Commandancia
and asked to go there,
but were told it was too
dangerous. They were also
told it was too dangerous
to take a helicopter

tour of the city.

Late on Dec 20 The pool had a news conference with the U.S. ambassador. One reporter reporter deemed it "worthless." SOCOM PAO stated that it was done because it was "either doing that or hanging around the press center."

Dec 21 through Dec 24 The media center filing facilities, particularly the telephone lines, were inadequate and overwhelmed.

This meant that any news the pool did file was delayed.

The media were not allowed to take pictures of the wounded or of caskets containing U.S. casualties.

The media initially could not photograph Panamanian prisoners.

The media could not photograph damaged helicopters at Howard Air Force Base for fear that they would photograph classified equipment.

Sam Donaldson of ABC news arrived the day after the main attacks. There was pressure from Washington to give Donaldson favored treatment.

Faxing problems continually impeded newspaper, wire service, and magazine reporters and photographers from reporting.

Caused further delays.

No arrangements were made to fly film material to the United States. The first material, sent Thursday, did not arrive until Saturday.

PART IV

The Aftermath

Mark P. Sullivan

11 The Future U.S. Role in Panama

INTRODUCTION AND OVERVIEW

Will there be a stable and democratic political system? Will drug trafficking and the laundering of drug money be curbed? Will the economy rebound so that Panamanians can regain the standard of living they enjoyed before their political crisis began in 1987? These are questions important not only for Panamanians, but also for U.S. policymakers, both in the executive branch and Congress, who supported the military mission to return democracy to Panama and to halt Panamanian involvement in drug trafficking and money laundering. U.S. efforts to support the new Panamanian government and prevent future Noriegas will be important not only because of significant U.S. interests in Panama, particularly the Panama Canal, but also because if democracy fails, then the rationale behind Operation Just Cause would be called into question, even by supporters of the intervention. The "liberation of Panama" would have a dubious connotation for both Panamanians and Americans.

The U.S. military intervention in Panama ensured a significant U.S. role in Panama for the foreseeable future. In the short to medium term, U.S. efforts will be concentrated on supporting the new government of Guillermo Endara in its five-year term of office through 1994. Soon after the U.S. intervention, First Vice President Ricardo Arias Calderon announced that the new government was committed to five goals: 1) to immediately establish democracy as expressed in the May 1989 elections; 2) to continue the process of transferring the canal to the Panamanian people according to the Torrijos-Carter Treaties; 3) to reorganize public forces so that they can play a professional and constitutional role in supporting democracy under legitimate civil authority; 4) to undertake economic reconstruction; and 5) to eliminate drug trafficking and money laundering.[1] U.S. support and cooperation will be essential in achieving these five objectives.

In each of these five areas, the United States will be faced with tremendous challenges. There will be significant chances for success, but along the way there will be abundant opportunities for failure. A particularly sensitive issue for U.S. policymakers will be how to provide effective assistance and support to Panama without infringing on its sovereignty.

As Panama's Archbishop Marcos McGrath has commented, "History will tell whether this invasion, or military action, in addition to liberating us from oppression, has shown full respect for the inalienable rights of the Panamanian people and their territory."[2] Considerable sensitivity will be required as the new Panamanian government struggles to overcome the legacy of the Noriega dictatorship and to build a truly democratic political system.

A longer term issue relates to the future U.S. military role in providing for the defense of the Panama Canal and perhaps for maintaining a U.S. military presence in Latin America. The chances for a continued U.S. military presence in Panama beyond 1999 would be augmented if the United States played a significant role in helping the Endara government achieve its fundamental objectives. More important, however, is the quality of U.S. support and cooperation. If the United States increasingly comes to be perceived as dominating or unduly influencing the Endara government, then a future U.S. military presence will be difficult to maintain. Any U.S. military role in Panama beyond the end of this decade will have to be negotiated with a Panamanian government that has proven itself to be independent and not under the control of the giant colossus to the north. A cooperative U.S.-Panamanian relationship, based on mutual respect, could augment the chances for a continued U.S. military presence. To a large extent, the quality of the U.S. role in Panama in the short to medium term will determine the ultimate success of Operation Just Cause, and it could well determine whether there will be a longer-term U.S. military role in Panama.

SUPPORT FOR THE NEW GOVERNMENT

As already noted, the new Panamanian government is going to face many challenges in overcoming the legacy of Noriega's rule. In particular, there are five areas in which U.S. support or cooperation will be essential, and which correspond to the basic goals of the Endara government: establishing and strengthening democracy; undertaking economic recovery; eliminating drug trafficking and money laundering; continuing the process of transferring the canal to Panama; and establishing a new public security force under civilian control. These five topics, discussed in detail below, point out the tasks ahead for the Panamanians, possible problems which might be encountered, and areas of U.S. support or cooperation.

Establishing and Strengthening Democracy

The creation of meaningful political institutions in Panama is going to be a difficult task, one which will not occur overnight. As former Ambassador Sol Linowitz has aptly stated: "Panama has no history of democratic rule." From its establishment as an independent nation in 1903 until 1968, power was concentrated in the hands of a few leading families known as the oligarchy or the rabiblancos (white tails). This changed in 1968 when a coup by Panama's National Guard ousted the nation's civilian president, and commenced the rise to power of Omar Torrijos, commander of the National Guard.

Torrijos' rule changed Panama's political system in two important ways. It moved beyond the narrow interests of the white urban elite, and opened the political and economic systems to the lower and rural classes. At the same time, the rule of Torrijos institutionalized the political role of the military. Beginning in 1978, Torrijos initiated political liberalization, but his death in a plane crash in 1981 effectively ended the chances for democratic reform. At that time, a power struggle ensued among factions of the National Guard as well as civilian political groups, and by August 1983, Manuel Noriega assumed control of the National Guard.

Noriega not only continued the Torrijos tradition of behind-the-scenes control of the political system, but he went further to ensure military control of most aspects of Panamanian life. He expanded the military's control of the country by creating the Panama Defense Forces (PDF) which incorporated numerous institutions under a single command. He turned the military into a corrupt enterprise involved in numerous illegal activities, ranging from selling passports to contraband trade to prostitution. Although not comparable to the repression of some Latin American dictatorships, the Noriega regime was, by Panamanian standards, the most repressive in the nation's history. It did not hesitate to use violence against its opponents as evidenced by the 1985 murder of Dr. Hugo Spadafora, a forceful Noriega critic.[3] When Panama's political crisis erupted in 1987, it soon became clear that a majority of Panamanians from all sectors, races, and social classes opposed the Noriega regime. This was confirmed by the May 1989 elections when an opposition coalition overwhelmingly defeated the pro-Noriega coalition.

Given the legacy of Panama's oligarchical rule and of both the benign and repressive dictatorships of the Torrijos and Noriega regimes, the new government of Guillermo Endara is faced with the difficult task of establishing meaningful democratic institutions. A significant challenge for the new government will be to demonstrate that it does not represent a return to pre-1968 Panama and the rule of the oligarchy, and that there is no possibility that the corrupt and repressive practices of the Noriega regime could resurface in other forms. In order to heal the divisiveness among Panamanians fostered by the Noriega regime, the new government needs to reach out to all classes and races. As the president of Panama's new Legislative Assembly noted in commenting on Panama's new democracy: "It is not just another democracy that the Panamanian people need, but an overall democracy that includes all of society and is based on an open, pluralistic, and free community; on the will of the majority; and, above all, respect for differences of opinion."[4]

In the first months after the military intervention, the Endara government took significant steps toward building

democratic institutions in Panama. In order to begin the
process of restoring the judicial system (which under the
Noriega regime had been totally dominated by the military and
the executive branch) President Endara appointed a new Supreme
Court. According to Endara, "the Supreme Court is obliged to
safeguard the integrity of the constitution and ensure a free,
expeditious, and uninterrupted administration of justice."
He pledged to respect the Supreme Court's independence, and
vowed not to meddle in their actions.[5]

In the past, a major problem hindering the judicial
system's independence was that appointments were dominated by
the executive branch which in turn was controlled by the
military. The constitution required the legislature to
confirm the Supreme Court's judges, but under the Noriega
regime, that government body merely rubber-stamped the
nominees of the executive branch. The net effect was that
military domination of the executive and legislative branches
sabotaged chances for judicial independence. In appointing
the Supreme Court justices, President Endara stated that he
only took into account the capabilities, experience, and
honesty of each magistrate.[6] The new members, however, were
appointed before Panama's Legislative Assembly had been
reconstituted and therefore were not confirmed by the
legislative branch. Legislative confirmation of these
magistrates would not only enhance the political power of the
legislative branch, but could be an important measure to
insure the political independence of the judicial branch, now
and in the future.

On March 1, 1990, Panama's Legislative Assembly was
reconstituted based on the results of the May 1989 elections
with a five-year term of office until 1994. In speaking at
the Assembly installation, President Endara noted that the
legislature "is a branch of government whose formation is so
basic for the exercise of a genuine democracy." He vowed to
fully respect legislative prerogatives and other legislative
functions assigned by the constitution and called for mutual
respect from the legislature for the rights and duties of the
executive branch.[7]

Of the 67 Legislative Assembly seats, 51 will be
controlled by the government coalition of the Democratic
Alliance of Civic Opposition (ADOC) that consists of three
parties: the Christian Democratic Party (PDC), the party of
First Vice President Ricardo Arias Calderon; the Nationalist
Liberal Republican Movement (MOLIRENA), the party of Second
Vice President Guillermo Ford; and the Authentic Liberal Party
(PLA). The largest bloc, 27 seats, will be controlled by the
PDC whereas MOLIRENA will have 15 seats and the PLA will have
nine seats. Six of the Assembly seats will go to the
Democratic Revolutionary Party (PRD), the party that served
as the political machine of General Noriega and which headed
the pro-Noriega National Liberation Coalition (COLINA) in the
May 1989 elections. Of the ten remaining Assembly seats, one,
popularly known as the Lone Ranger seat, will, according to
Article 141(6) of the Panamanian constitution, go to the party

which received the most votes of those parties which did not win an Assembly seat.[8] It will probably go to the Labor Party (PA), a party of the pro-Noriega COLINA electoral coalition.[9] For the remaining nine legislative seats, Panama's electoral tribunal did not have enough returns to estimate the results. New elections will be held for those seats, although no timetable had been set as of May 1990.

Some observers have noted discord within the ruling coalition, but President Endara has stressed that competition and conflict are natural in life and that conflict within the coalition will not affect the government.[10] One element of discord within the government involves the rank and file followers of the late Dr. Arnulfo Arias (Panama's firmly nationalistic and populist politician who dominated Panamanian politics for over 40 years until his death in 1988.) Arias' followers, known as Arnulfistas, supported the ADOC coalition in the 1989 elections largely because Guillermo Endara himself was an Arnulfista, but they were unable to participate directly in legislative elections because their party, the Authentic Panamenista Party (PPA), had been hijacked by a minority faction with the approval of the Noriega regime. As result, Arias' rank and file followers feel left out of the democratic process even though they believe they were largely responsible for ADOC's victory.

In speaking before the Legislative Assembly, President Endara, a long term spokesman for Arias, proclaimed himself to be an Arnulfista, "born from the nationalist womb of the party of Dr. Arnulfo Arias Madrid."[11] As such, Endara will be secretary general of the new Arnulfist Party (PA), a new legal party slated to represent those Arnulfistas who were denied the right to run candidates in the 1989 elections. Future tension within the government could result from strains between the Arnulfistas, traditionally the largest of Panama's political groups, and the Christian Democrats, who control the largest bloc in the Legislative Assembly.

An important sign of the health of Panama's newfound democracy will be the development of robust opposition to the ruling coalition, whether it will be the PRD or other political parties in the post-Noriega environment. Although it was evident that the ADOC coalition won the May 1989 elections overwhelmingly by a three-to-one margin, it is important to remember that some 25% of the nation's voters supported the pro-Noriega coalition of parties for various reasons. The PRD, the largest party of the pro-Noriega coalition was first established in 1978 as a party unifying political groups and forces loyal to General Omar Torrijos. It proclaimed itself the upholder of Torrijismo, the populist political ideology of Torrijos, and although it became, under Noriega's rule, a repressive political machine closely linked with the PDF, it still tried to wrap itself in the cloak of Torrijismo in order to gain the support of the lower and rural classes. While it is unclear if the PRD will be able to successfully carry the Torrijos mantle in a post-Noriega Panama, what is clear is that Torrijismo remains an important legacy in Panamanian politics and for many represents the overthrow of the Panamanian oligarchy and the empowerment of the lower classes.

In the aftermath of the military intervention, some Latin American nations called on the new government to hold national elections, but President Endara rejected that notion, claiming that his government was "overwhelmingly elected" for a five-year term in the May 1989 elections. In early February, U.S. officials reportedly were urging the Endara government to hold some type of referendum or ballot question, instead of a presidential election, as a means of seeking the public's view on the new government.[12] Soon after, Panamanian Foreign Minister Julio Linares, in response to a reporter's question on the U.S. proposal, pointed out that Panama has a right to act independently because it is sovereign and independent. Linares also noted, however, that if the Panamanian government considers it necessary "to hold a plebiscite, then we will hold it, but it will be a sovereign act of Panama, and not because we are being pressured by anyone."[13]

By early March, however, President Endara announced that in the next few months the government would hold a referendum to legitimize his electoral mandate. The President noted that he would submit various constitutional reforms, first subject to approval by the Legislative Assembly, and then to a direct referendum by the people.[14] According to Endara, the referendum on the constitutional amendments would demonstrate the popular support that his government enjoys.

U.S. Support for Democracy. Immediately after the intervention, U.S. support for the new government was provided in part by civil affairs units of the U.S. military. These units--comprised mainly of Army Reservists who hold full-time civilian jobs--specialized in almost two dozen fields of public service, including support for local government and the judicial system. Known as "nation builders," the civil affairs units provided support to rebuild the nation's shattered government services and institutions. According to U.S. officials, the members of the civil affairs units served as advisers and planners for the new government, but were not involved directly in the operation of Panamanian government institutions.[15]

As a further measure of support for Panama's new democracy, on January 2, 1990, President George Bush announced that he would appoint veteran diplomat Deane R. Hinton as the new U.S. Ambassador to Panama, replacing Arthur Davis who had served in the post since 1986. At the time of his appointment, Hinton was serving as Ambassador to Costa Rica, and in the past he had served as U.S. Assistant Secretary of State for Economic and Business Affairs. According to some observers, he was appointed because of his extensive economic background, a capability which would prove helpful in leading the major economic recovery program needed if Panama's fledgling democracy is to flourish. Observers have also noted that Hinton had served in two highly sensitive posts (El Salvador and Pakistan) that involved encouraging deeply entrenched militaries toward support of civilian democratic rule.[16]

U.S. support for Panama's new democratic institutions will require a combination of technical assistance and diplomatic skill. U.S technical assistance could be instrumental in carrying out needed institutional reforms. Already, a portion of this assistance has been slated for the Supreme Court and the Ministry of Government and Justice. Administration proposals for future economic assistance include funds to support judicial reform, fiscal management and accountability, and the restoration of public service.

It will be important to make known to the Panamanians that the United States does not support a return to the pre-1968 elitist rule of the oligarchy. As Panamanian expert Steve Ropp noted in late 1989, "Civilians will have to do much more than simply return to power. They will have to learn to govern in such a way as to be supportive of the future democratic process."[17] U.S. diplomacy should reinforce this notion. Likewise, U.S. diplomats should warn Panamanians against any possible resurgence of corrupt and anti-democratic forces, both civilians and former PDF members associated with the Noriega regime. R.M. Koster, an American writer living in Panama, has noted, "General Noriega did not tyrannize by himself."[18]

Given all this, however, it is extremely important that the United States let Panama develop its own institutions without undue U.S. influence. It is important that governmental decisions are made by Panamanians and that the U.S. Embassy does not become in itself a political power base in Panamanian politics. Central American historian Richard Millet aptly commented in a 1988 article that "the United States has neither the ability nor the right to create a political system in Panama that responds automatically to U.S interests."[19] In the past, nationalism and a liberal dose of anti-American sentiment have often been used by Panamanian politicians to garner popular appeal. No matter how much Panamanians supported the U.S. military intervention, perceived U.S. infringement on Panama's sovereignty could erode popular support for the Endara government. Endara could come to be perceived as yet another Panamanian puppet president, not of the Panamanian military as during the Noriega regime, but of the United States. U.S. respect for Panamanian sovereignty would go a long way in helping the development of a healthy democratic political system in Panama, which in turn would be the best means for protecting U.S. interests.

Revitalizing the Economy

A formidable task for the new government will be revitalizing the ailing Panamanian economy. Even before the military intervention, it had been severely damaged by two years of strong U.S. economic sanctions and economic disruption caused by the political crisis. Unemployment was

in the 20%-30% range and the Gross Domestic Product (GDP) had
declined some 25% since 1987. Panama's once thriving
international banking sector had been severely affected, with
deposits dropping to $15 billion from a previous peak of $40
billion in the mid-1980s.[20] By December 1989, the Panamanian
government's arrears to international financial institutions
(World Bank, International Monetary Fund, and Inter-American
Development Bank) were over $500 million with a total foreign
debt of almost $6 billion.

The military intervention added further to the economic
decline. Some sections of Panama City were heavily damaged,
leaving thousands homeless, and subsequent looting left
businesses with damages of more than $1 billion. Some
economists have estimated that Panama will need as much as
$1.5 billion-$2.0 billion over the next year just to get the
economy moving, and Panamanians are expecting a significant
amount of this to come from the United States. The Panamanian
government itself requested $1.5 billion in U.S. economic
assistance.

Some observers believe that the United States has a
special responsibility to help rebuild Panama's economy
because of the importance of the canal to the United States.
In the year 2000, Panama alone will have the responsibility
of operating the canal. Others believe that the United States
should help Panama since U.S. economic sanctions contributed
heavily to Panama's economic decline. They argue that
Congress overwhelmingly supported the imposition of economic
sanctions in 1988, and that Congress should now take action
to clean up the economic dislocation brought about by them.
Others argue that it was the United States that helped build
up the Panamanian military in the past, even keeping Noriega
on the CIA payroll for many years, and that because of this,
should now help build a democratic Panama. Still others
stress that unless there is substantial assistance, there will
be direct disillusionment of Panamanians with the United
States and a reassessment of the wisdom of the intervention
which could increase chances for anti-American sentiment in
Panama.

Some skeptics, however, believe that large amounts of
assistance will only result in further Panamanian dependence
on the United States, both real and perceived. Others
question the wisdom of providing large amounts of assistance
to Panama, a moderate income country, when U.S. assistance
could be spent in helping poor African nations that face
problems far worse than Panama. Still others point out that
there is only so much U.S. foreign assistance available
worldwide, and that it seems improbable that the United States
would be able to infuse large amounts of aid to Panama over
a sustained period given such other high-need areas like
Africa and Eastern Europe.

Both the Bush Administration and Congress have expressed
a commitment to help rebuild the Panamanian economy. On the
day of the invasion, Bush stated that "the United States is
eager to work with the Panamanian people in partnership and

friendship to rebuild their economy."[21]   Well before the intervention, Congress went on record on several occasions indicating that if democratic conditions were restored to Panama, then not only would aid be restored, but increased levels would be considered.[22]   The important questions remaining to be answered are how much can be effectively used, how much can the United States afford to provide, and how quickly can it be delivered.

In early January 1990, a team of U.S. officials led by Deputy Secretary of State Lawrence Eagleburger visited Panama to discuss future economic assistance. As a result of that visit, on January 25, 1990, Bush announced an economic recovery program for Panama potentially worth over $1 billion. The economic recovery program includes a package worth up to $500 million in loans, guarantees, and programs to stimulate market access and private investment incentive. In addition, the President announced that the administration would request $500 million in supplemental economic assistance for Panama for fiscal year 1990, to be offset from other programs. This would include assistance for: balance of payments support and business credit; a public sector investment program; public sector restructuring; and assistance to clear Panama's arrears with the international financial institutions. Moreover, in the immediate future, the U.S. Agency for International Development would provide $42 million in assistance for housing, public works, small business rehabilitation, and technical assistance, including a small amount of assistance, $1.2 million, for training the civilian police. Another $9 million in military assistance funds would provide equipment for the police.

By February 7, 1990, Congress took action on the $51 million in immediate economic and police assistance and restored Panama's eligibility for aid and trade benefits by waiving a number of legislative restrictions on assistance to Panama. Action on the $500 million in new economic assistance was delayed until March with both the executive and legislative branches blaming each other for the delay. Some members of Congress noted that the administration did not formally present its request until mid-March when it was combined with a $300 million supplemental request for Nicaragua, whereas the administration argued that Congress could not decide what Department of Defense programs should be cut to fund the additional foreign assistance requests for both Panama and Nicaragua (a part of the so-called "peace dividend"). On March 13, 1990, President Bush called for urgent action, by April 5, 1990, on assistance for both Panama and Nicaragua.

By that date, however, only the House of Representatives had taken legislative action on the administration's request by approving $420 million in foreign aid appropriations for Panama, some $80 million short of the administration's request. To be fair, however, the shortfall from the administration's request was really only $50 million since the administration and Congress had agreed to restore $30 million

in assistance to sub-Saharan Africa that had been used to fund
the emergency economic assistance to Panama approved in
February. Action in the Senate met with opposition from those
Members who believed that $500 million was far too much money
for such a small nation as Panama and who believed that more
money should be directed toward Eastern Europe. Moreover,
Senate Majority Leader George Mitchell announced in early
April that he would not support the full amount until the Bush
administration produced a "meaningful long-term foreign aid
plan" instead of approaching foreign aid "in one-shot
increments."[23] Thus, as the Senate began its Easter recess on
April 5, 1990, no action had been taken to appropriate the
assistance for Panama. As of mid-April, the future of foreign
assistance to Panama was uncertain.

Panamanian reaction to the announcement of U.S.
assistance plans was generally favorable, but some, including
President Endara, had wanted to see even more U.S. aid.
Although Congress and the administration acted quickly in
lifting economic sanctions and in approving $51 million in
urgent economic and police assistance, the aid did not start
flowing until mid-March 1990. Panamanians expressed
frustration at the slowness of the U.S. funding process,
particularly for the anticipated $500 million. In early March
1990, Endara went on a 13-day hunger strike in Panama City's
Metropolitan Cathedral as an act of compassion and solidarity
with the Panamanian poor. Although he insisted that the
hunger strike was not directed against the U.S. government,
he noted that its slowness in providing aid was creating a
dangerous situation because of widespread unemployment and
unrelieved poverty. Toward the end of March, after it became
clear that the anticipated $500 million would probably be
scaled down and would not be approved by early April, Second
Vice President Guillermo Ford warned that a U.S. pledge for
financial assistance was needed within 60 days to prevent
Panama's poor from rioting.[24]

In describing the $500 million in proposed assistance to
the Endara government, both U.S. and Panamanian officials
characterized it as a means of jump-starting the Panamanian
economy. They noted that before the political crisis took its
toll, the economy was well-developed with a sophisticated and
educated work force and the institutional structures needed
to help support a rapid recovery. They reasoned that once the
economy got back on its feet, high levels of U.S. assistance
would not be needed. This reasoning is not without merit, yet
considering Panama's dismal economic situation, U.S. officials
might be expecting too much. Some observers believe that it
will take years for the economy to rebound from the economic
devastation wrought by the political crisis and economic
sanctions as well as the military intervention itself and
subsequent looting. Despite the removal of the sanctions,
observers are skeptical about Panama's bouncing back to its
pre-political crisis standard of living. According to Dr.
Riordan Roett, a Latin American expert at Johns Hopkins
University, "We've done some quite lasting damage to the

Panamanian economy, which will take well into the 1990s to reverse."[25]

And if expectations of a jump-start for the Panamanian economy are off-base, then what does this mean for future U.S. assistance? The Bush administration's fiscal year 1991 budget does not include any economic assistance for Panama, so theoretically, unless another supplemental assistance package were requested for fiscal year 1991, Panama would not be eligible for additional aid until fiscal year 1992. Is the administration realistically thinking ahead? And what about the reaction of Congress toward sustained levels of economic assistance for Panama over the next several years? Given the growing foreign assistance needs of other parts of the world and increasing U.S. domestic budgetary pressures, would there be enough Congressional support for supplying aid to Panama over a number of years? Richard Millet argued in late 1989 that "maintaining needed levels of aid will require political courage and bipartisanship to a degree largely unknown in recent history."[26] In times of domestic budget pressures and increasing foreign assistance needs, it may have been easier to have reached a consensus in Congress to oust Noriega by military force than it will be to find consensus to support the recovery of the Panamanian economy over a sustained period. And if recovery is slow and that consensus is not achieved, resentment among Panamanians could grow along with anti-American sentiment.

Eliminating Drug Trafficking and Money Laundering

An important issue for U.S. policy-makers, including many Members of Congress, will be the measures that Panama takes to eliminate drug trafficking and to prevent laundering drug money. Under the Noriega regime, Panama was an important transshipment site for illicit drugs such as cocaine and marijuana and for the chemicals used to process cocaine. More importantly, however, it was also a center for laundering drug money, largely because of the nation's banking secrecy laws that reportedly allowed launderers to pass billions of dollars through the Panamanian banking system over the last decade.[27] Although the actual level of money laundering in Panama probably had decreased by 1989 as a result of deteriorating economic conditions and the unstable political environment, it still remained a serious problem.[28]

Nevertheless, some Congressmen have warned that future aid to Panama could be jeopardized if the new government does not move quickly enough to either enforce existing laws or make changes to Panama's banking system to prevent laundering. On February 7, 1990, in passing an urgent foreign assistance package for Panama (P.L. 101-243), Congress required a Presidential report, by April 15th, on specific actions taken by the Endara government to halt money laundering. Future foreign aid legislation for Panama could include a condition requiring demonstrated efforts by the government to prevent Panama from being a money laundering center. As

Representative George Miller noted in a House floor debate in early February, "We should all be very cautious--and on notice,--about voting to spend our own taxpayer money to any government that cannot, or will not, take aggressive action against the drug cartels that are pouring billions of dollars in narcotic poison into the United States."[29] Moreover, the House Committee on Foreign Affairs noted in a February 1990 report that it would closely monitor progress on bank secrecy laws and other areas of cooperation before approving further aid.[30]

In mid-January 1990, Second Vice President Guillermo Ford indicated that Panama would adopt any mechanism that would help control money laundering. According to Ford, "Panama will no longer be a money laundering center."[31] On January 10th, in an action commensurate with the new government's rhetoric, Panama and the United States signed an "umbrella" drug trafficking agreement committing the two nations to improve cooperation in the war on drugs, including actions to end trafficking and laundering and to control the transshipment of chemicals used to process cocaine. As a further demonstration of cooperation, the Endara government froze approximately 300 bank accounts which U.S. officials believed were being used for laundering drug money. Because of these actions, on January 26th, Bush certified to Congress that Panama was fully cooperating in the war on drugs, a measure that lifted certain legislative restrictions on aid and trade with Panama. In further actions, the Panamanian government in mid-February approved further regulations to curb money laundering, regulations similar to U.S. banking practices, which require a report on every banking transaction in excess of $10,000, including deposits and withdrawals.

Nevertheless, some observers have questioned the commitment of Panamanian authorities to take effective measures to prevent laundering. A controversial New York Times article in early February claimed that Panamanian government officials were resisting U.S. pressure to alter their banking laws, and that many senior Panamanian officials (including President Endara and Vice President Ford), "while never accused of money laundering, have had strong ties to corrupt banks."[32] Endara described the newspaper account as unfair and noted that his government was fighting drug trafficking.[33]

Some observers believe that Panama's system of banking secrecy should be changed to eliminate possibilities for laundering, while others argue that Panama's banking industry, once an important pillar of the economy, is dependent on banking secrecy, and could not be revived unless secrecy were ensured. According to Edgardo Lasso Valdes, president of Panama's private National Banking Association, "the end of banking secrecy would be the end of the financial center in Panama."[34] Others believe that the enforcement of existing laws would be adequate to prevent laundering. Some officials have suggested a banking model similar to that of Switzerland, which, while maintaining banking secrecy, accedes to U.S.

requests to identify and freeze assets of suspected money
launderers.

The issue could become a source of tension in U.S.-
Panamanian relations, particularly since some members of
Congress and some U.S. officials fear that Panama again could
become an important laundering center for the drug cartels of
neighboring Colombia. In late February 1990, U.S. officials
backed away from efforts to bring about a change in Panama's
bank secrecy laws. Instead, they agreed, at least for the
time being, to accept a pledge from Panama to cooperate with
U.S. investigators on drug probes.[35] Panamanian officials have
expressed concern over inordinate U.S. pressure on the
laundering issue, pressure which could be considered to be an
affront to Panama's sovereignty. In early March 1990, Vice
President Ford warned that Panama would not accept any foreign
economic aid if the country was pressured into easing its
banking secrecy laws. Ford noted that "nobody pressures" the
current government and that the "government was not kneeling
before anybody."[36]

Continuing the Process of Transferring the Canal to Panama

A critical task for the Endara government in
demonstrating its legitimacy and independence from the United
States is continuing the process of transferring the canal to
Panama, which is scheduled to culminate at the end of 1999
when Panama assumes control for its operation and defense.
At that time, the Panama Canal Treaty will terminate and the
Panama Canal Commission, the U.S. agency charged with
operating the canal, will be abolished.

An important step in the process is the appointment of
a Panamanian as Administrator of the Panama Canal Commission.
Under the terms of the Panama Canal Treaty, Article III(3)(c),
the United States was required to appoint a Panamanian,
proposed by Panama, as canal administrator beginning January
1, 1990. In addition, U.S. implementing legislation for the
Commission (P.L. 96-70) requires that the administrator be
appointed "by and with the advice and consent of the U.S.
Senate." In early December 1989, President Bush had announced
that in order to comply with the Panama Canal Treaty
requirement, he would appoint Fernando Manfredo, Deputy
Administrator of the Commission since its establishment in
1979, as acting administrator until Panama's political crisis
was settled. In following through with that announcement, on
January 1, 1990, Bush appointed Manfredo as acting
administrator until the Endara government could recommend a
qualified candidate.

In early March 1990, Endara announced the nomination of
its own candidate, Gilberto Guardia Fabrega, as the new
Panamanian Administrator. The nomination was forwarded to
Washington on March 13th, thereby beginning the process of
confirming and appointing the new administrator. The
appointment of a new administrator chosen by the Endara
government will be a significant step in demonstrating the

U.S. and Panamanian commitments to follow through with the Panama Canal Treaties. During Panama's political crisis, Noriega had attempted to portray the opposition as ready and willing to terminate the treaties, allowing the United States to retain control of the canal. The Endara government has maintained, however, that it will faithfully fulfill the Panama Canal Treaties. On the U.S. side, President Bush has stated that he is "fully committed to implement the Panama Canal Treaties and turn over the Canal to Panama in the year 2000."[37]

In addition to the administrator issue, there will be numerous areas of U.S.-Panamanian cooperation needed to ensure the successful transferral of the canal in the year 2000. One important issue is that of continuing to train Panamanians to take over the canal's operation. When the Panama Canal Commission was first established in 1979, around 69% of the permanent work force was made up of Panamanians, whereas U.S. citizens comprised around 26% of the force. Ten years later, the canal's permanent work force was almost 86% Panamanian and just 13% American.[38] A continued emphasis on hiring and training Panamanians will be important in achieving a 100% Panamanian work force by the year 2000. In particular, emphasis will be needed to train them as canal pilots and in the professional and managerial fields. As of September 1989, Panamanian canal pilots accounted for only 27% of the total number of pilots and Panamanians in the professional and managerial fields accounted for 43% of the total number of commission employees in those fields.[39]

Other important areas of U.S.-Panamanian cooperation relate to the future viability of the canal. These include measures to prevent landslides that could shut it down. In 1914, the Canal had been forced to close for more than nine months and in October 1986, a major landslide in the Gaillard Cut limited ship traffic to one-way passage for two months. Another possible cooperation measure includes a widening of the canal to allow two-way passage of all vessels through the Gaillard Cut, regardless of beam size, thereby removing a potential limitation to the canal's transit capacity. Finally, U.S.-Panamanian cooperation relating to the canal's defense beyond the year 2000 could become a significant issue in bilateral relations, if not during the tenure of the Endara government, then possibly during the next Panamanian administration, scheduled to be elected in 1994.

Establishing a New Public Security Force

Perhaps the most difficult task for the new government is demonstrating that it can effectively provide public security throughout the country. Soon after the U.S. intervention, President Endara stated that Panama's new public security force would be a modern police force with minimal military functions. First Vice President Arias Calderon, who also serves as Minister of Government and Justice, was charged with organizing the new force. On February 10, 1990, Panama's

Cabinet Council approved Decree No. 38, which abolished the old PDF and established a new Public Force until Panama's Legislative Assembly can debate and adopt a new organic law regulating the duties and organization of the new force. In effect, by abolishing the PDF, the decree stripped the new force of jurisdiction over key government agencies, including the immigration office which had been a lucrative center of corruption under the Noriega regime.

Under the decree, the Public Force is "organized to bear the technical and legal responsibility for public security and national defense" and is "directly subordinate to the executive branch." The President of the Republic is designated the supreme chief of the Public Force and each member of the force is required to take an oath vowing to obey the Constitution and Panamanian laws in "defense of democracy." The force consists of a National Police, a National Air Service (replacing the PDF air force), and a National Maritime Service (replacing the PDF navy). Each has separate commands and is under the authority of the executive branch through the Ministry of Government and Justice. In addition, special units may be organized within the National Police for several reasons: to guard the country's borders and protect the integrity of the national territory; to protect the Panama Canal (pursuant to the Canal Treaties); and to safeguard and support democratic institutions. All military schools from the Noriega regime were abolished, and a new Police Academy is to be established.

The former National Department of Investigations (DENI), which operated as a kind of secret police for many years, was replaced by the Judicial Technical Police (PTJ), and will be under the authority of the Ministry of Government and Justice. It will not be part of the Public Force. The former Presidential Guard, which used to be part of the National Guard in the PDF, has been expanded and renamed the Institutional Protection Service. It will be under the authority of the Ministry of the Presidency.

As of March, the new Public Force consisted of around 13,000-14,000 men, compared to the 16,000-man PDF under Noriega. The largest component of the new force is the National Police which has an estimated membership of around 12,000. Some officials have indicated that the Public Force will eventually be scaled down to around 10,000, but that will be determined by Panama's Legislative Assembly when it approves a new law concerning the Public Force.

Some observers have expressed concern that in building a new force, the government runs the risk of creating a new PDF that could threaten Panama's nascent democracy. Critics believe that many former PDF members are beyond reform, and note that these are the same people who were involved in electoral fraud and institutionalized corruption. As an example, they point to the first head of the new Public Force, Col. Roberto Armijo, who lasted only twelve days on the job until Endara fired him for links to corruption. Even Armijo's successor, Col. Eduardo Herrera Hassan, has been severely criticized by some observers. According to Panamanian professor Miguel Bernal, Herrera "was chief of the worst repression ever seen in the history of Panama" because of his role in brutally crushing an opposition demonstration in July 1987.[40]

Other critics of the new force believe that it should be strictly limited to having a police function, and should not have any military capability that could potentially threaten the nation's political system. They favor the Costa Rican model of military demobilization. Breaking the legacy of military intrusion into civilian rule, however, will be a tricky task for the new government. As Costa Rican President Oscar Aria noted in January 1990. "It is not enough to change the name of the armed forces. It is necessary to change the minds of those people who only yesterday wore a military uniform."[41]

Some Panamanian observers have long maintained that getting rid of Noriega would not automatically solve Panama's endemic political crisis. They viewed the crisis not as a political system dominated by a single corrupt leader, but as a political system stunted by the intrusion of the military as an institution. Central American historian Richard Millet argued just days after the intervention that "incorporating officers and enlisted men from the old PDF into any new force means that some of the corruption and political thinking that characterized the old body will survive long after Noriega's demise."[42]

In response to criticisms of the new Public Force, First Vice President Arias Calderon claimed in late March 1990 that great progress had been made in transforming the Panamanian military from an "army of domination" under Noriega to a national police modeled after that of Costa Rica.[43] The Vice President stated that all elements of the PDF had been disbanded or reorganized under separate civilian authorities in order to create a system of checks and balances, and that it would therefore be virtually impossible for a new military leader to come to power again in Panama.[44] As evidence of this, in late March 1990, Vice President Arias Calderon announced that Col. Eduardo Herrera, chief of the Public Force, would instead become director general of the National Police and would not have any authority over the other components of the Public Force for which director generals would also be appointed. According to Arias Calderon, "the only person who will have the title of chief of the Public Force is the president of the Republic."[45]

U.S. Support for the New Public Force. The United States has provided training and equipment for Panama's new Public Force and has provided U.S. military support to assist the force in carrying out its police functions. In early February 1990, Congress approved funds for training and equipping Panama's civilian police. It approved up to $1.2 million for both judicial and police training under the Administration of Justice program, and approved the use of previously obligated military assistance pipeline funds (estimated at $9.3 million) to procure law enforcement equipment. Not more than $500,000, however, is to be spent on lethal equipment. Moreover, an unspecified portion of the administration's $500 million request for Panama would be spent on building up and training the Public Force, including anti-narcotics laundering training. As of early April 1990, more than a dozen professional U.S. trainers, mostly former FBI agents, arrived in Panama under the Administration of Justice's International Criminal Investigations and Training Assistance Program (ICITAP). Through 1990, it is expected that between 1,000 and 1,200 Public Force members will receive training in police procedures.[46]

In the aftermath of the intervention, the world's attention focused on the withdrawal of the U.S. forces involved in Operation Just Cause. Resolutions in both the Organization of American States and the United Nations condemned the intervention and called for U.S. combat forces to withdraw. Some observers believed that resentment against U.S. intervention forces could grow if they stayed too long, and that they could cause significant problems for the Endara government, particularly in demonstrating its legitimacy and independence. Others believed that the continued presence of U.S. combat forces could jeopardize the future of U.S. relations with Latin America, as well as Latin America's relations with the Endara government. For example, Venezuela linked its recognition of the government with the withdrawal of U.S. combat forces.

By the end of January, the issue was well on the way to becoming moot as thousands of U.S. combat forces had returned from Panama. On January 31, in his State of the Union address, President Bush announced that the remaining troops involved in the intervention would be home "well before the end of February." Sure enough, by February 13, 1990, the U.S. troop level in Panama dipped below the pre-invasion level of around 13,600 troops. That action helped improve Panama's relations with several Latin American nations and also took some domestic pressure off the Bush administration from those calling for the removal of the forces. The timely removal of troops also permitted the administration to avoid any possible conflict with Congress over the War Powers Resolution.[47]

In a sense, however, the focus on the number of U.S. forces in Panama drew public attention away from a more important issue, the role of the troops that remained in Panama. Traditionally, the U.S. Southern Command (USSOUTHCOM) has had two main activities. It has had responsibility for all U.S. military activities in Central and South America. It has also fulfilled, pursuant to the Panama Canal Treaty, the U.S. responsibility for defending the canal until the year 2000. In the aftermath of Just Cause, however, the role of the U.S. military in Panama expanded significantly. U.S. forces not only had their traditional role of defending the canal, but they also assumed the function of helping to provide police services for the nation. U.S. military officials indicated that the troops would continue patrolling and would only return to their bases once the new Public Force was fully operational.

In January and February 1990, in the aftermath of the intervention, a crime wave in Panama City raised doubts about whether the Public Force would be able in the near future to take over the police duties being performed by U.S. troops. The crime wave appeared to be the work of common criminals, rather than remnants of pro-Noriega support, and included such incidents as bank robberies, restaurant holdups, bomb scares, and the murder of a senior U.S. official of the Panama Canal Commission.[48] In response, in early March 1990, U.S. forces participated with Panamanian police in a massive anti-crime operation known as "Operation to Recover Tranquility Amid Democracy" in which hundreds of Panamanians were detained. Four more massive sweeps were conducted through March 1990 in which hundreds of U.S. troops participated and hundreds of Panamanians arrested. Some observers questioned whether the raids violated Panama's constitutional norms. The head of Panama's new Judicial Technical Police reportedly admitted that the raids violated the "letter but not the spirit of the law."[49] In addition, U.S. military support for police security has included the deployment of small teams of green berets (U.S. Army 7th Special Forces Group) to the countryside that reportedly are involved in investigating crimes and acting as backups for the Panamanian police.[50]

For U.S. policymakers, important questions remaining are how long and to what extent will the U.S. military continue to provide police support for the Public Force. The longer U.S troops retain a police role in Panama, the greater the chances are that anti-American sentiment could arise. While it is clear that Panamanians overwhelmingly supported Operation Just Cause, it is less clear that they would support a continued U.S. military presence in their sovereign territory. As times goes by with U.S. troops performing police functions, chances of a nationalistic backlash will increase, at least among some sectors, with a resurgence of anti-American sentiment.

On March 2, 1990, one U.S. soldier was killed and 15 other U.S. servicemen were injured along with 12 Panamanians in a grenade attack on a disco in Panama City. Although an alleged pro-Noriega guerrilla group, known as the "December 20th Movement" (M-20), claimed responsibility for the attack and announced that it would take additional actions against U.S. targets and President Endara, Panamanian officials stated there was no evidence of an organized guerrilla movement in the country. The incident, however, highlights the predicament of a continued high-profile U.S. military presence in Panamanian territory. While on the one hand, continued U.S. operational support for the Public Force serves as a critical stabilizing factor for the new government by giving it time to successfully train and build-up a new force, at the same time a continued U.S. police role could provoke guerrilla or terrorist actions against Americans as well as against the new government. Some observers believe that the government's legitimacy would be enhanced if U.S. troops returned to their bases and concentrated their efforts on defending the canal.

ROLE OF THE U.S. MILITARY IN PANAMA BEYOND 1999

A longer-term issue relates to the future role of the U.S. military in Panama beyond the year 1999. Current U.S. rights under the Panama Canal Treaty allow for U.S. forces to maintain bases and to remain in Panama until the end of this century to carry out the U.S. responsibility of defending the canal (according to Article IV of the Panama Canal Treaty and the Agreement in Implementation of Article IV). On December 31, 1999, when the Panama Canal Treaty terminates, Panama will then have primary responsibility for the defense of the canal. The so-called Neutrality Treaty, officially known as the Treaty Concerning the Permanent Neutrality and Operation of the Panama Canal, guarantees that the canal shall remain open to ships of all nations on terms of equality, and has no expiration date. The Neutrality Treaty, however, does not give the United States a legal right to retain military forces in Panama. According to Article V of the treaty: "After the termination of the Panama Canal Treaty, only the Republic of Panama shall operate the Canal and maintain military forces, defense sites and military installations within its national territory."
Nevertheless, a condition to the Neutrality Treaty added by the U.S. Senate, makes clear that the two nations can negotiate future U.S. base rights in Panama. According to the second condition to the Neutrality Treaty:

> Nothing in the treaty shall preclude the Republic of Panama and the United States of America from making, in accordance with their respective constitutional processes, any agreement or arrangement between the two countries to facilitate performance at any time after December 31, 1999, of their responsibilities to maintain the regime of neutrality established in the treaty, including agreements or arrangements for the stationing of any United States military forces or the maintenance of defense sites after that date in the Republic of Panama that the Republic of Panama and the United States of America may deem necessary or appropriate.

Some observers, including some members of Congress, believe the United States should start negotiations with the Panamanians for a U.S. presence in Panama beyond 1999, particularly in light of Panamanian reluctance to reconstitute an army to defend the canal because of the potential threat to the nation's newly established democracy. They believe that Panamanians would welcome a U.S. presence into the next decade, and cite a post-invasion poll of January 1990 that claims that 70% of the Panamanian population favors a U.S. military presence in Panama beyond the year 2000.[51]

Some Panamanians point out that it would take a force at least as large, if not larger, than the old PDF under Noriega, for Panama to run the military bases in the year 2000, and that this is highly unlikely given the prohibitive cost of maintaining such a force and the government's and public's opposition to recreating such a large military. They argue that a reasonable alternative would be for Panama to lease the military bases to the United States on terms similar to other U.S. basing arrangements around the world. They note that Panama would reap substantial economic benefits from the leasing arrangements from the rent paid on those bases as well as from the economic benefits to the local Panamanian economy. Currently the U.S. military employs approximately 5,500 Panamanians (with wages of around $80 million annually) and makes purchases (both official and personal) of around $120 million on the local Panamanian economy.[52] Without future U.S. military bases in Panama, they point out that Panama would loose $200 million in national income annually that could not be easily made up from alternative sources.

Other observers, however, believe that current discussion of a permanent U.S. military presence could cause a nationalistic backlash in Panama and significant political problems for the Endara government, particularly in its efforts to prove that it is an independent government and not unduly influenced by the United States. They note the Panama Canal Treaties, more than any other issue, can raise patriotic fervor in Panama, and that any perceived action by the United States to alter the intentions of those treaties could spark anti-American sentiment not only within Panama, but throughout Latin America. Moreover, some observers believe that a U.S. presence beyond the life of the Panama Canal Treaty could be detrimental to Panamanian sovereignty. They point out that a continued large U.S. presence in Panama, given the historical record of U.S. military intervention in Panama (dating from Panamanian independence in 1903), could distort any sense of Panamanian national identity, and contribute to an excessive Panamanian dependence on the United States, both economically and politically.

Some U.S. political observers point out that it would be politically difficult for a U.S. administration to negotiate foreign base arrangements when so many domestic U.S. bases have been closed or are faced with the prospect of closure. Domestic economic interests would almost certainly prompt some members of Congress to oppose the additional use of tax revenues to fund additional foreign bases.

For its part, the new Endara government has indicated that it is dedicated to completely fulfilling the Panama Canal Treaties, which according to Article V of the Neutrality Treaty, means that U.S. forces must be out of Panama by the year 2000. On the question of negotiating with the United States for bases beyond the end of 1999, the Endara government has not indicated its position, but has not ruled out the possibility. In mid-February 1990, Vice President Arias Calderon stated that negotiations for U.S bases "was not an issue at this time."[53]   U.S. officials have not formally broached the issue with the Endara government and have even indicated that doing so might be counterproductive at this juncture given the challenges ahead for the Panamanians. Nevertheless, some U.S. officials have reportedly indicated privately that there will be future negotiations on U.S. bases and facilities, perhaps as official guarantors of Panama's neutrality or as a primary component of an international force.[54]

In addition to debate over a future U.S. military presence in Panama is the issue of the U.S. right to take military action in Panama after 1999 when the Panama Canal Treaty expires, no matter where the U.S. troops are located. Under the terms of the Neutrality Treaty, both the United States and Panama have the responsibility to assure that the Panama Canal will remain open and secure to ships of all nations.   In other words, both nations are responsible for maintaining the canal's "regime of neutrality" (Article IV). According to Amendment No. 1 to the Neutrality Treaty, which clarifies Article IV, "the correct interpretation of this principle is that each of the two countries shall, in accordance with their respective constitutional processes, defend the Canal against any threat to the regime of neutrality, and consequently shall have the right to act against any aggression or threat directed against the Canal or against the peaceful transit of vessels through the Canal." Understanding No. 2 of the Neutrality Treaty further clarifies Article IV by stating that either Panama or the United States "may, in accordance with its constitutional processes, take unilateral action to defend the Panama Canal against any threat, as determined by the Party taking the action."

Nevertheless, while the United States clearly has the right to take military action in Panama beyond 1999, the scope of this action is limited by other provisions in the Neutrality Treaty. U.S. military actions can only be taken if the canal itself is threatened or if ships passing through the canal are threatened, and if the actions do not constitute an intervention into Panama's internal affairs. According to Amendment No. 1 to the Neutrality Treaty, the U.S. right to defend the canal "does not mean, nor shall it be interpreted as, a right of intervention of the United States in the internal affairs of Panama." The amendment further states that "any United States action will be directed at insuring that the canal will remain open, secure, and accessible, and it shall never be directed against the territorial integrity or political independence of Panama."

Some observers, including some Panamanians, believe that the Neutrality Treaty gives the United States the right to intervene in Panama for reasons other than armed attack against the canal. This includes Panama's Foreign Minister, Julio Linares, who believes that Condition No. 1 to the Neutrality Treaty (the so-called DeConcini condition) gives the United States the authority to take whatever measures it deems advisable to keep the canal open, even for reasons other than armed attack. According to Condition No. 1, "if the Canal is closed, or its operations are interfered with, the United States of America and the Republic of Panama shall each independently have the right to take such steps as each deems necessary, in accordance with its constitutional processes, including the use of military force in the Republic of Panama, to reopen the Canal or restore the operations of the Canal." Linares warns that if, after the year 1999, the canal becomes uncompetitive economically, then the United States could theoretically, under the authority of the DeConcini condition, take control of the canal and operate it in place of Panama.[55]

While this interpretation might seem extreme to many U.S. observers, it demonstrates the inherent distrust shared by many Panamanians of U.S. intentions regarding the canal. It also points to how much work lies ahead in order to improve the bilateral relations between the two nations regarding the canal. Continued U.S.-Panamanian cooperation in fulfilling the Panama Canal treaties, particularly the appointment of a Panamanian Administrator, would go a long way to allaying fears among some Panamanians that the United States has ulterior motives of attempting to retain control of the canal.

NOTES

1. "Arias Notes Basic Objectives," in Foreign Broadcast Information Service, Daily Report: Latin America (December 22, 1989): 23.

2. "Catholic Paper Assesses Reaction to Invasion," in Foreign Broadcast Information Service, Daily Report: Latin America (January 22, 1990): 40-41.

3. Ricardo Arias Calderon, "Panama: Disaster or Democracy" Foreign Affairs (Winter 1987/88): 335.

4. Foreign Broadcast Information Service, Daily Report: Latin America (March 5, 1990): 25.

5. "Endara Speaks at Assembly Installation," in Foreign Broadcast Information Service, Daily Report: Latin America (March 2, 1990): 35.

6. Ibid.

7. Ibid., p. 33.

8. "Electoral Tribunal Picks Legislature," Foreign Broadcast Information Service, Latin American Weekly Report (March 8, 1990): 5.

9. Ibid.

10. "Endara Plays Down Differences Within ADOC," Foreign

Broadcast Information Service, Daily Report: Latin America (February 20, 1990): 44.

11. "Endara Speaks at Assembly Installation, p. 33.

12. Paul Bedard, "U.S. Urges Panama's Endara to Call New Elections," Washington Times, February 5, 1990, p. A3.

13. "Foreign Minister on U.S. Pressure, Treaty," Foreign Broadcast Information Service, Daily Report: Latin America (February 18, 1990): 30-31.

14. Article 308 of the Panamanian constitution outlines the process of constitutional reform. As described, there are two procedures for amending the constitution. The first method would be for two consecutively-elected Legislative Assemblies to approve identical reforms by absolute majority. The second method would also be for two consecutively-elected Legislative Assemblies to approve the reforms by absolute majority, but in this procedure, the text of the reform can be modified by the second Legislative Assembly. Furthermore, this second method also requires the constitutional reform to be subjected to popular referendum. See: Constitucion politica de la Republica de Panama (Panama: Editorial Alvarez, 1984), pp. 125-126.

15. Molly Moore, "U.S. Seeks To Rebuild Structure," Washington Post, December 29, 1989, pp. A1, A16.

16. Joe Pichirallo and John M. Goshko, "New Ambassador to Panama Named," Washington Post, January 3, 1990, pp. A1, A24.

17. "Letter to the Editor," La Prensa Digest (Washington), vol. 7/1989(November 30, 1989): 9-10.

18. R.M. Koster, "In Panama, We're Rebuilding Frankenstein," New York Times, December 29, 1989, p. A35.

19. Richard Millet, "Looking Beyond Noriega," Foreign Policy (Summer 1988): 59.

20. David Asman, "Panama's Hong Kong Vision," Wall Street Journal, February 15, 1990, p. A14.

21. United States, White House, Office of the Press Secretary, Statement by the President, 7:20 A.M., December 20, 1989, p. 2.

22. In foreign aid appropriations legislation in 1987, 1988, and 1989, Congress stated that increased aid levels to Panama should be considered in the event that democratic conditions were restored. Moreover, on October 21, 1988, the Senate approved a bipartisan resolution (S.Con.Res. 140) sponsored by Senator Kennedy which, in the event of the restoration of

democracy in Panama, called on the United States to consider
assistance to revive the Panamanian economy.

23. Helen Dewar, "Mitchell Hits Emergency Aid Request,"
Washington Post, April 3, 1990, p. A9.

24. James M. Dorsey, "Panamanian Veep Lobbies Here For $500
Million, One-Shot Deal," Washington Times, March 22, 1990, p.
A12.

25. Paul Blustein and Steven Mufson, "Economic Recovery Could
Take Years," Washington Post, December 21, 1989, p. A35.

26. Richard Millet, "Once the Cheering Stops," Miami Herald,
December 24, 1989, pp. 1C, 4C.

27. Frank Greve, "U.S. Quits War With Panama Bankers," Miami
Herald, February 22, 1990, pp. 1A, 16A.

28. United States, Department of State, Bureau of
International Narcotics Matters, International Narcotics
Control Strategy Report (Washington, D.C.: U.S. Department
of State, March 1990), p. 31.

29. Congressional Record, February 7, 1990, p. H 317.

30. United States, Congress, House of Representatives,
Committee on Foreign Affairs, Urgent Assistance for Democracy
in Panama Act of 1990, Report to accompany H.R. 3952, 101st
Cong., 2nd sess., February 7, 1990, House Report 101-401, Part
1.

31. Andres Oppenheimer, "Panama May Restrict Cash
Laundering," Miami Herald, January 18, 1990, p. 13A.

32. Stephen Labaton, "Panama is Resisting U.S. Pressure to
Alter Inadequate Bank Laws," New York Times, February 6, 1990,
p. A1, D24.

33. "Endara Views American Newspaper Article, Aid," Foreign
Broadcast Information Service, Daily Report: Latin America
(February 20, 1990): 42.

34. "Legislation to End Money Laundering Approved," Foreign
Broadcast Information Service, Daily Report: Latin America
(February 15, 1990): 29.

35. Greve, pp. 1A, 16A.

36. "Ford Says Nobody Pressures Nation With Aid," Foreign
Broadcast Information Service, Daily Report: Latin America
(March 8, 1990): 29.

37. Statement by the President, 7:20 A.M., December 20, 1989,

p. 2.

38. Panama Canal Commission, <u>10 Year Report: FY1980 to FY1989, A Decade of Progress in Canal Operations and Treaty Implementation</u> (Washington, D.C., 1990), p. 27.

39. Ibid., p. 28.

40. Alexander Cockburn, "Beneath a Park in Darien: The Conquest of Panama," <u>The Nation</u>, January 29, 1990, pp. 114-115.

41. Oscar Arias Sanchez, "Panama, Without an Army," <u>New York Times</u>, January 9, 1990, p. A23.

42. Millet, "Once the Cheering Stops," pp. 1C, 4C.

43. William Branigin, "Panama Faces Troubled Economy, Rising Crime," <u>Washington Post</u>, March 24, 1990. pp. A23, A27.

44. Ibid.

45. "Arias Announces Changes in FP Organization," Foreign Broadcast Information Service, <u>Daily Report: Latin America</u> (March 29, 1990): 34.

46. Brook Larmer, "Police Grapple With Crime Wave," <u>Christian Science Monitor</u>, April 3, 1990, p. 3.

47. For more information on the War Powers Resolution as it relates to Operation <u>Just Cause</u>, see: U.S. Library of Congress, Congressional Research Service, <u>War Powers Resolution: Presidential Compliance</u>, [by] Ellen Collier [Washington]. CRS Issue Brief 81050. (Updated regularly.)

48. Michael R. Gordon and David Pitt, "Panama Crime Waves Shakes Faith in Police," <u>New York Times</u>, February 2, 1990, p. A14.

49. Larmer, p. 3.

50. Gordon and Pitt, p. A14.

51. "Poll Reports Public's View of U.S. Invasion," Foreign Broadcast Information Service, <u>Daily Report: Latin America</u> (January 22, 1990): 39.

52. "Possible Leasing of Bases," Foreign Broadcast Information Service, <u>Daily Report: Latin America</u>, February 5, 1990, pp. 54-55.

53. "Arias Says No Renegotiation of Canal Treaties," Foreign Broadcast Information Service, <u>Daily Report: Latin America</u> (February 16, 1990): 38.

54. Joanne Omang, "Neutrality For Panama Suggested," <u>Washington Post</u>, December 30, 1989, p. A17.

55. "Linares Criticizes Amendment to Canal Treaty," Foreign Broadcast Information Service, <u>Daily Report: Latin America</u> (April 2, 1990): 46.

12 The International Implications

While as a U.S. military operation it has been overshadowed by <u>Desert Shield</u>, the U.S. operation in Saudi Arabia in 1990, <u>Just Cause</u>, the U.S. invasion of Panama in December 1989, was a very successful and sustained use of U.S. military power. Because of the moral, psychological, military, and political defeat in Vietnam and the disaster in Lebanon, doubts have persisted concerning the U.S. ability and will to employ sustained military power in pursuit of national objectives. While Panama hardly proved to be a national trial (indeed it may be the century's splendid little war), it is an antidote to Vietnam. At a minimum it will have a rehabilitative effect on the U.S. Armed Forces, particularly the Army, and will instill confidence in Army planners and commanders as they experience the difficult adjustments attendant to the post-cold war era. For this reason, <u>Just Cause</u> will have some positive international impact on U.S. foreign relations.

The international implications of failing to oust the provocative and corrupt ruler of Panama, General Manuel Noriega, clearly would have had an adverse impact on U.S. foreign policy and prestige. For months prior to the invasion Noriega had taunted, provoked, insulted, and in the end, brutalized U.S. citizens. He was apparently involved in profiting from illegal drug trafficking in a time of great public concern over narcotics. His regime was obligated in January 1990 to appoint the first Panamanian administrator of the Panama Canal, and the security of the canal was in potential jeopardy. He also manipulated a free election in order to retain power. In the face of his tactics to humiliate the United States, the Bush administration demonstrated great restraint for an extended period. Finally, the manifest failure of the Organization of American States (OAS) to move Panama toward democracy after Noriega's fraudulent manipulation of the election impelled some action from the United States. Diplomatic pressure clearly was not sufficient to influence the regime and remove Noriega, while U.S. national interests and prestige required a response. The military operation was swift and successful. After experiencing some difficulty in locating Noriega, U.S. forces accomplished their mission of forcing a change in the regime, and once order was restored and the arms caches were uncovered, the invading troops were gradually withdrawn.

THE NEAR-TERM REACTION

The immediate international reaction to the invasion was moderate, and, on balance, its impact would probably have a positive effect. A preliminary assessment of this impact must consider the Latin American sensitivity concerning U.S. intervention into Central and South American affairs and the dramatic political events in Europe in the waning months of 1989.

On the negative side, the invasion revived opposition to U.S. military intervention in the hemisphere. This was reflected in the December 30, 1989 U.N. General Assembly resolution deploring the U.S. intervention that passed by a margin of 75 to 20, with 40 abstentions. The mixed results of this vote reflected the international response. In Latin America and the Caribbean basin, only the Dominican Republic and El Salvador voted with the United States against the resolution, while Costa Rica, St. Lucia, St. Vincent, and the Grenadines abstained. With the exception of Spain, America's major European, Asian and Middle Eastern allies—Great Britain, France, the Federal Republic of Germany, Italy, Turkey, Israel, Japan, and Australia—voted against the resolution. The Islamic nations either voted in favor or abstained, with the abstentions including Saudi Arabia and Oman. The Soviet Union and China voted in favor of the resolution and the Chinese were harsh in their condemnation of the United States. Soviet spokesman Gennady Gerasimov said that "no state has the right to take the law into its own hands" because "that's basically lynch law."[1] However, Moscow also stated that it saw no reason why the action should damage East-West relations.[2]

While nearly uniformly negative, the Latin American reaction did not have major international repercussions. The thirty-two members of the OAS "regretted" but did not condemn the U.S. operation. A sampling of the statements that were made provides an insight into the tenor and intensity of this response. The Mexican government opposed the action and stated, "The fight against international crimes cannot be a motive for intervention in a sovereign nation."[3] This criticism was echoed by many Latin American leaders, who seemed to concur that it was necessary to rid the region of a thug, but disapproved of the manner in which this was accomplished. Shortly after the invasion, a spokesman for President Salinas characterized his nation's relations with the United States as good, but noted that the two nations had "agreed to disagree" on Panama.[4] Brazilian President Jose Sarney said that he also was opposed to "any solution by force" and called the U.S. action "a real regression with respect to international relations on the continent."[5] In mid-January, Mexico and Venezuela said that it was too soon after the invasion for Vice President Dan Quayle to visit them, warning that his trip could prompt anti-U.S.

demonstrations.[6] Peru was strongest in its denunciation, with President Alan Garcia temporarily declining to meet with President Bush at the Drug Summit in Colombia. Other nations also issued statements that opposed the intervention. In Argentina, President Carlos Menem called for the withdrawal of U.S. troops so that the "Panamanian people could develop an adequate political solution that would allow the restoration of a representative democracy."[7] Bolivian spokesmen claimed that the intervention violated the sovereignty and jeopardized the independence of all the peoples of all Latin American countries. They called for the immediate establishment of a provisional government and the holding of free, democratic elections, reiterating the Bolivian position concerning its support for the self-determination of all nations and non-intervention in the affairs of others. On December 21, 1989, Costa Rica issued a cautious statement decrying the use of force. Carlos Jose Guiterrez, its Ambassador to the United Nations, said that his country's "reaction had been one of regret for the new blow to the inter-American system, but relieved because the nightmare lived by the Panamanian people had ended."[8] Ecuador charged that the United States had acted in "flagrant violation of international principles," but said that it was Noriega's "undemocratic stubbornness that caused the situation to deteriorate to this point."[9] Peruvian President Alan Garcia described the invasion as "brutal, excessive, and arrogant," and as reopening "a chapter that we all believed had been closed in Latin America."[10] The Peruvian Ambassador to Panama stepped down in protest and Peru withdrew from the list of attendees to the February Drug Summit in Colombia. (It later reversed this decision.)[11] Finally, in Venezuela, President Carlos Andres Perez said that Latin America had failed to rid the region of Noriega, which led to the U.S. action. "We lacked the necessary determination to create a collective situation to force the Panamanian de facto government to change its stance and permit the free exercise of the people's sovereignty," he said. Perez added that he condemned the invasion, but that the Endara government would be recognized by Venezuela after the U.S. forces were withdrawn.[12]

The international press also criticized the invasion. In La Paz, Bolivia, the Roman Catholic newspaper, Presencia, had the following reaction:

> After an avalanche of astonishing events..., one makes an effort to put the facts into perspective. But the way that things turned out continues to amaze us... It astonishes us when [Panamanian President] Guillermo Endara speaks of forgiving Latin American countries for not supporting the invasion in which he took part and after which he was installed as Panama's head of state by the American command. U.S. Vice President Dan Quayle produced a special chapter of amazement when he was

designated by President George Bush to tour Latin
America to convince us of the goodness of the
invasion and other wrongs.[13]

Reflecting these sentiments, the governments of Latin America
were slow to recognize officially the new Panamanian
government.
  In Canada, the independent <u>Toronto Star</u> remarked:

> Every once in a while, the condescension of the
> United States toward Latin America reaches dizzying
> new heights. The visit of Vice President Dan Quayle
> to the region is a perfect case in point. ...
> Virtually all Latin American states were glad to be
> rid of General Manuel Noriega. But the gregarious
> excesses committed by the United States to
> accomplish this goal have simply reinforced Yankee
> imperialism run amok. Latin America,
> understandably, would prefer a change in attitude,
> not a pat on the head from Dan Quayle.[14]

In spite of the existing mood, only two months after the
invasion Quayle visited Latin America without incident. By
this time, Washington was confident that much of the Latin
American denunciation of the intervention was rhetoric, and
that behind the scenes, the democratic nations of Latin
America approved of the U.S. goal, which was to restore
democracy.
  Thus, <u>Just Cause</u> seemed destined to be ranked with other
recent U.S. positions and actions in Latin America. For
example, when Washington supported Great Britain against the
military dictatorship in Argentina, Buenos Aires observed that
"the United States destroyed its position not only in
Argentina but in all of Latin America, for several
millenniums." In truth, U.S. relations with Argentina are
better now than they have been in decades. Similarly, the
U.S. interventions in the Dominican Republic in 1965 and
Grenada in 1983 caused no lasting damage to U.S. regional
interests.[15]
  In Europe, the comments were more focused on the legal
aspects of Just Cause. Frankfurt's <u>Frankfurter Allgemeine
Zeitung</u> stated:

> The impression is growing that U.S. justice
> authorities do not have ironclad evidence of
> Noriega's involvement in the drug trade... The
> administration could have spared itself
> embarrassment had Noriega been turned over to
> Panamanian justice, which has enough to put him on
> trial from election fraud to murder.[16]

FACTORS SUPPORTING THE OPERATION

A number of events preceding and following the invasion

served to mitigate the negative impact on U.S. relations with Latin America. First, the operation succeeded in toppling a corrupt dictator who was an embarrassment to Latin America. With the exception of Cuba's Castro and Nicaragua's Ortega, virtually all of Latin America's leaders wished Noriega would peacefully step down from the presidency. The surgical military operation and the successful installation of President Endara was another victory for democracy when democracy was emerging triumphant throughout the world. Secondly, the drug summit in February 1990, attended by President Bush and the presidents of Colombia, Peru, and Bolivia showed that leaders who had been critical of Just Cause were still willing to meet with Bush to discuss the issues. Finally, Violeta Chamarro's victory in the Nicaraguan election drew regional attention away from Just Cause. As the U.S.-backed choice in the election, her victory enhanced U.S. prestige in the region and isolated the only remaining communist, Fidel Castro.

Future events may not continue to favor the United States. Terrorism or insurgency in Panama would call into question the success of the operation, while Noriega's trial will focus attention again on the former strongman. Another intervention, if it took place, would be denounced more harshly coming as it would after Panama, and if it were perceived as unwarranted, could have enduring negative effects on U.S. regional relations.

The world continues to monitor U.S. actions in Panama. In this respect, the process of rebuilding an economy that has suffered severely from past U.S. sanctions, as well as the massive destruction that occurred on December 20, 1989 will have a major influence on future judgments of Just Cause. A failure to adequately fund the rebuilding of Panama will lead to the rise of serious anti-U.S. sentiment and groups inimical to U.S. interests. U.S. budget constraints could limit the scope of such economic assistance to Panama. Likewise, the Latin American governments will be watching the restoration closely to determine whether Washington is interfering and micromanaging Panamanian affairs. If this appears to be the case, then Panamanians might seek a change in government which the hemisphere's U.S. critics could exploit. As the United States restores Panama's economy, it has a chance to minimize anti-U.S. rhetoric throughout Latin America by providing discrete guidance and maintaining a low profile. Here every effort should be made to defer to Panamanian leadership and institutions as long as they retain their democratic character.

THE INFLUENCE OF THE WORLDWIDE MOVE TOWARD DEMOCRACY

The year 1989 was remarkable in that there was a general movement worldwide toward democracy. And in no place was this trend more dramatic than in the Warsaw Pact. In the weeks preceding the invasion, world attention was riveted on these events. On November 10th, Bulgarian Communist Party chief

Zhikov resigned after 35 years in power. On December 4th, tens of thousands of East Germans marched in the streets of Leipzig demanding German reunification. On December 5th, Erich Honeker was arrested. On December 10th, a new cabinet with a non-communist majority was sworn in Czechoslovakia. On December 11th, Croatia's Communist Party called for free multi-party elections in Yugoslavia. On December 12th, U.S. Secretary of State James Baker visited East Germany, and on December 14th, the Western governments announced that a $1 billion emergency fund had been created for Poland and a $1 billion loan had been granted to Hungary. On December 14th, Zhivkov was expelled from the Bulgarian Communist Party, and on December 17th, several thousand Romanian demonstrators clashed with security forces, and there were reports of several hundred casualties. On December 18th, Czechoslovakian opposition leader Vacal Havel received the endorsement to become a candidate for President, and on December 22nd, two days after the Panama invasion, the last hardline Warsaw Pact dictator, Nicolai Caucescau, was ousted from power.

In this context, the capability and willingness of the United States, a status quo power with a vital interest in international stability, to successfully use its power to preserve its interests and promote its democratic values will have a benign effect. The reason that this effect is important was best summarized in an editorial in the _Economist_. Although it did not specifically address Panama, it reflected on the required role of the United States in international affairs:

> ...America is still number one. Its dominance may
> be declining a little, because Japan is catching up
> and several countries are now political powers in
> their regions. But only the United States has the
> complete mixture of economic, military, and
> diplomatic powers to qualify as a superpower.
> ...American interests very much include stability
> and prosperity throughout the world. The prize...a
> world in which America does not have to fight wars
> in order to defend its values and further its
> interest.[17]

CONCLUSIONS

Superpower obligations are not easy to shed. The political consequences of reduced power and influence and an increasingly multipolar international environment will increase the risks to U.S. friends and interests worldwide. U.S. power applied to further national interests and in support of democratic alternatives lends aid and comfort to friends and allies worldwide.

Even with the dramatic changes in domestic and international power, U.S. interests will remain oriented toward Europe, Japan and the Pacific, the Middle East-Persian Gulf-Indian Ocean region, and Latin America. The good hemispheric relations coupled with the centuries that tie North and South America together create a combination that will not change as a result of the heat generated by Operation Just Cause. As George Fauriol at the Georgetown Center for Strategic and International Studies has stated, "...For all its current problems, Latin America will remain a source of U.S. economic interest as it has for more than a century. The region's political and security proclivities and manifold development problems will ensure the existence of a unique relationship."[18]

Seven decades ago, Woodrow Wilson's fourteen points lent brief encouragement to war ravaged and oppressed peoples and nationalities around the world. The world went through a great upheaval after World War I and the United States retreated into isolationism. We have made progress since World War I and World War II. Great change is now taking place thus far without a great war. The final patterns of power in world affairs are uncertain, but the United States is a force for stability during this time of dramatic change. Success at home and abroad will help fortify the United States while it continues to play a major role in the conduct of foreign affairs. The confidence that derives from Panama is surely preferable to disillusionment and disappointment. Free people know they have won another small round because of U.S. intervention in Panama. They also know that a confident and outward looking United States is a leading force for a safer, more democratic world.

NOTES

1. Washington Post, January 5, 1990.

2. Time Magazine, January 1, 1990.

3. UPI, December 20, 1990.

4. Time Magazine, January 29, 1990.

5. UPI, December 20, 1989.

6. New York Times, January 18, 1990.

7. The Times of the Americas, January 10, 1990.

8. Ibid.

9. Ibid.

10. Ibid.

11. Ibid.

188

12. Ibid.

13. <u>World Press Review</u>, March 1990, p. 8.

14. Ibid.

15. Elliot Abrams, <u>Los Angeles Times</u>, January 10, 1990.

16. Ibid.

17. <u>The Economist</u>, February 24, 1990.

18. "America and the World," <u>Foreign Affairs</u> (1989/1990).

13 Summary and Conclusions

The magnitude of Operation Desert Shield, the U.S. deployment to Saudi Arabia that was begun in August 1990, was such that it overshadowed Just Cause. However, as Colonel McCall noted in his discussion of the use of air power in Just Cause, one should neither make too much nor too little out of an operation. In this respect, although many of the aspects of Just Cause were unique and will probably not recur in future operations, there are several relevant military and political lessons to be gleaned from it.

MILITARY LESSONS

It has been noted that, as a military operation, Just Cause was an anomaly in that the United States had troops stationed in Panama at the beginning of the operation and that many of the forces were well rehearsed for their combat roles. One might add an additional factor that made the operation unique: while it was a joint exercise, in respect to ground combat operations it was basically an Army show with some participation from the Marines, Navy SEALs, Army special forces, and the Air Force. Future exercises probably will not be weighted so heavily in favor of one service.

In spite of this, there are some important military lessons in Just Cause and most of these are traditional ones. In this respect, one cannot consider the operation without addressing an earlier operation, Urgent Fury, the 1983 U.S. intervention in Grenada. While Urgent Fury was a resounding political success, it was rife with problems on the military side that reflected the Army's relatively low state of preparedness. The preliminary feedback from Just Cause indicates that many of these problems have been addressed and resolved. In this respect, alone, Just Cause is important as an indicator of how far the Army had come since Urgent Fury and might indicate how it would perform in Desert Shield.

Leadership

Just Cause was hallmarked by good leadership from the commanders at the top downward to the officers and noncommissioned officers in the field. One must start by mentioning President Bush, who, having ordered the execution

of the operation, had such confidence in his military leaders
that he stood aside and let them do their jobs. This lack of
political interference prevented a distraction that could have
interfered with the operation. From here, one must note the
maturity of the Joint Chiefs of Staff and other senior leaders
in relevant joint service positions. The service rivalries
were put aside, and the choice of the forces that were used
was made on whether a force was necessary and appropriate,
rather than on the color of its uniforms. The result was a
combined force that functioned well in combat.

Proceeding further, one must be impressed with the
leadership of those directly involved--General Colin Powell,
Chairman of the Joint Chiefs of Staff, Lieutenant General Carl
Stiner, General Maxwell Thurman, Lieutenant General T.W.
Kelly, and others. Together they developed a very successful
plan and provided a lean command and control system that was
responsive to those in the field. Finally, one must address
the leaders in the field. To accomplish a politically-laden
operation such as Just Cause with such restrictive rules of
engagement required the very best in leadership, and this was
provided by the tactical leaders. Lorenzo Crowell's vignette
about U.S. forces entering a room full of Panamanians and not
firing reflected the leadership and control that was
characteristic of the entire operation. The fact that so few
Panamanians were killed--far below that predicted by the
planners and very low for the type and dimensions of the
operation that occurred--reflects the discipline and
professionalism of the soldiers in the field.

Training

Very little went wrong in Just Cause and, when one
considers the complexity of the operation, the reason--good
training--soon becomes evident. During Urgent Fury, a
national television crew interviewed two soldiers in the
field. It was obvious that the soldiers were less than highly
motivated and the vignette ended with the two shuffling off
into the field while dragging their weapons in the dirt.
Those in Just Cause performed in vivid contrast to this
earlier, embarrassing demonstration. The reporting from
Panama showed consistently the professionalism and motivation
of those involved. It was obvious that they had been trained
well, were confident of knowing their assignments, and
performed excellently. One can conclude that the Army learned
well from the problems encountered in Grenada and had improved
considerably the professionalism of its forces.

When considering training, one also must mention the
impressive performance by the Air Force. An organization such
as the Military Airlift Command does not simply come forth out
of the blue and provide the highly professional service seen
in Just Cause. Rather, such superb service was the result of
constant training and high standards of professionalism that
were aspects of a daily routine. Thus, when a unique
situation such as Just Cause occurred, the forces were

prepared to respond. The training and professionalism of the Military Airlift Command and the Air Force were evident, because without them these organizations simply could not have fulfilled their missions so competently.

Elsewhere, one has to mention the high quality of the service provided by the medical and logistical personnel involved. For the most part, the wounded were treated promptly and professionally, resulting in fewer fatalities.

Discipline

Just Cause was a politically laden operation that placed significant requirements on the combat soldier. The political goal was to defeat decisively the Panamanian Defense Forces in a way that these same forces could be quickly reorganized into a democratic, hopefully pro-American force that would help rather than hinder the new Endara government. Thus it was very important to minimize the loss of life on the Panamanian side, and this meant using minimal force with overwhelming forces, while taking risks. The instinct for survival runs very high on the battlefield, and accomplishing the aims of Just Cause ran counter to that feeling. The result was a very low loss of life, directly reflecting the great discipline and high professional standards of the combat forces involved.

POLITICAL LESSONS

Domestic Political Lessons

There were two domestic political lessons that resulted from Just Cause. The first pertained to the actions of the President. When President Reagan was not awakened during U.S. Naval and Air Force strikes on Libya in April 1986, he changed the relationship between the White House and the Pentagon. Reagan believed that the on-scene military commander was best equipped to make an accurate decision and the further away from the battlefield that decisions were made, the greater the chances for error. His performance in other crisis situations during his administration reflected this belief. President Bush seems to advocate the Reagan approach, in that, once having made the decision to conduct Just Cause, he left it to his military officers to carry it out. The lesson is not a new one--President Abraham Lincoln was noted for interfering in the Civil War campaigns, and Tsar Nicholas II of Russia insisted on going to the front in World War I, leaving the nation's political matters in the hands of his troubled wife, Alexandra. However, it appears that the White House has again discovered the lesson, and the ongoing Operation Desert Shield and the nation's future military operations can only profit from this approach.

The second lesson pertains to the press. The unsatisfactory treatment of the press during Just Cause reflects that press access to information remains a serious problem. The issue of national security versus press access is a serious one, and the measures that the Pentagon has recommended will not provide a solution that both protects the nation's secrets and provides the public with the news. In Just Cause, the President left the issue to Secretary Dick Chaney, who took the blame when things went badly. However, the problem remains unresolved and the Pentagon cannot offer a permanent solution. Rather, it is of such sensitivity that it requires an answer from the White house, after due deliberations with both the press and the military.

International Political Lessons

In one sense, Just Cause stands as yet another incident in the U.S.-Panamanian relationship in which the United States again intervened in Panamanian affairs. Confronted with Noriega, a dictator who taunted Washington and could not be tolerated, the United States intervened, forcing a change in government. In addition to the destruction incurred during the actual invasion, years of economic sanctions and measures that were designed to put pressure on Noriega had also done tremendous economic damage. The immediate result of Just Cause was a traditional one in that the United States had forced a transfer of power to a person more to Washington's liking.

The long-term result, however, is harder to predict. Just Cause could be the beginning of a new more responsible, more active U.S. role in Central America. Here Panama could be used as an example where responsible assistance increased considerably the standard of living and offered a serious alternative to drugs and money-laundering. Negative U.S. economic measures in 1987, 1988, and 1989 and the destruction that occurred during Just Cause certainly established partial U.S. responsibility concerning Panamanian conditions.

However, there is much to argue against such a revision in the U.S. role. First, there is the fact that many in the United States view Just Cause as a measure that solved the problem. An intolerable dictator who taunted Washington had been removed and no further action was necessary. Second, there is the traditional U.S.-Panamanian relationship that was described fully by Donald Mabry and William Drohan. This pictures U.S. concern in Panama as centering on the canal. The canal is again secure and there is little reason for further involvement. Third, there is the problem of funding, as the United States faces a growing and critical debt and the huge expense of Desert Shield. Thus the money available for foreign aid is restricted and must be divided among many very pressing requirements. In essence, there appears to be much to argue for a continuance of the past policy.

Thus Just Cause could offer a promise of a better U.S.-Panamanian relationship in the future, but whether this promise will be fulfilled remains to be seen.

.

Chronology

1502   **(historical entry)**
Panama was first sighted by Rodrigo de Bastidas who was sailing with Columbus.

1513   **(historical)**
Balboa crossed the Isthmus of Panama with a force of 300 heavily armed Spaniards and several hundred Indians, some of whom knew the way to the Pacific.

1671   **(historical)**
Panama was sacked and burned by the pirate Morgan. The present city was begun three years later with more concern for defense, and it was situated on a tongue of rock surrounded by water on three sides.

1821   **(historical)**
Panama became a province of Columbia.

December 12, 1846   **(historical)**
Benjamin Alden Bidlack, U.S. charge d'affaires in New Grenada (Colombia), signed a treaty that guaranteed the United States the exclusive right of transit across the Isthmus of Panama.

January 7, 1849   **(historical)**
The first group of Americans, about 200 people heading for California, started across the Isthmus of Panama. All survived the journey.

1850   **(historical)**
Construction was begun on the Panama Railroad as a link to the California gold fields. It cost $8 million, and was completed five years later.

February 1, 1880   **(canal)**
The Compagnie Universelle du Canal Interoceanique under the leadership of Vicompte Ferdinand de Lesseps began work on a canal across the Isthmus of Panama.

March 31, 1885   **(historical)**
The town of Colon, situated on the Atlantic Ocean side of the Isthmus of Panama, was consumed in flames.

February 4, 1889   (canal)
The Compagnie Universelle du Canal Interoceanique was placed
in the hands of a liquidator.

May 15, 1889   (canal)
The liquidator ordered that all work cease on the canal.

1890   (canal)
The Influence of Sea Power by Alfred Mahan was published. In
it Mahan stressed the importance of a canal to U.S. security.

October 4, 1894   (canal)
The Compagnie Universelle du Canal Interoceanique was
incorporated into the French properties in Panama.

March 19, 1898   (canal)
The battleship USS Oregon arrived in time to participate in
the battle of Santiago Bay. However, its voyage from the U.S.
west coast would have been much shorter had there been a
Panama Canal.

November 18, 1901   (canal)
A second Hay-Paunceforte Treaty was signed between Great
Britain and the United States. It granted the United States
the right to build and operate a canal across the Isthmus of
Panama. The treaty did not forbid fortifications along the
canal, and the United States was free to do whatever it
considered necessary to protect the waterway.

December 16, 1901   (canal)
The U.S. Senate ratified the Hay-Paunceforte Treaty.

January 28, 1902   (canal)
The U.S. Congress authorized President Theodore Roosevelt to
acquire the French property in Panama at a cost not to exceed
$40 million.

June 19, 1902   (canal)
The U.S. Senate, in a vote of 42 to 34, voted in favor of
building a canal through Panama rather than through Nicaragua.

June 26, 1902   (canal)
By a vote of 259 to 8, the U.S. House of Representatives
passed the Spooner Act, which called for building a canal
across the Isthmus of Panama.

June 28, 1902   (canal)
President Roosevelt signed the Spooner Act.

January 21, 1903   (canal)
The Hay-Herran Treaty was signed between the United States and
Colombia. It authorized the sale of the French properties in
Panama to the United States and granted the United States
control of a canal zone six miles wide from Colon to Panama

City, but did not include either of those cities. The United States was to pay Colombia $10 million in gold and an annual rent of $250,000.

March 17, 1903   (canal)
By a vote of 73 to 5, the Hay-Herran Treaty was ratified by the U.S. Senate without amendments.

August 12, 1903   (canal)
By a unanimous vote, the Hay-Herran Treaty was rejected by the Colombian Senate.

November 3, 1903   (canal)
Manuel Amador declared the creation of the Republic of Panama and its independence from Colombia. The United States intervened to help Panama gain its independence by sending the USS _Dixie_ followed by nine other warships in the succeeding weeks.

November 1903   (canal)
The Hay-Bunau-Varilla Treaty (1903) was extremely generous in giving away Panamanian authority. The new Panamanian government reluctantly accepted it, fearing either Colombian or U.S. military intervention if it did not. Panama had no right to tax in the zone or fix the toll rates on the canal. The rent on the zone was fixed by treaty, thus making it extraordinarily difficult to change, and inflation reduced the value of the rent the U.S. paid.

1904   (U.S. policy)
The fledgling Panamanian Army was disbanded in 1904 on the grounds that the U.S. Army was all the protection needed by the nation. This prevented the creation of any Panamanian counterforce.

May 4, 1904   (canal)
Lieutenant Mark Brook took possession of the French properties in Panama for the United States.

July 26, 1905   (canal)
John Stevens arrived at Colon to assume responsibility for work on the Panama Canal.

February 12, 1907   (canal)
President Roosevelt received a letter from Stevens. While it was not a formal resignation, Stevens said that he was not "anxious to continue in service." Roosevelt accepted Stevens' resignation.

February 26, 1907   (canal)
Lieutenant Colonel George W. Goethals, U.S. Army, was appointed as head of construction of the Panama Canal. Goethals had graduated second in his class from West Point in 1880. He officially relieved Stevens on March 31, 1907.

May 1911   (canal)
Construction was begun on the Gatun Locks. The Pedro Migal
Locks were completed later this year.

May 1913   (canal)
The Gatun and Miraflores locks were completed.

August 15, 1914   (canal)
The Panama Canal was opened.

1918   (U.S. policy)
The United States intervened militarily in Panama City and
Colon to settle an election dispute. U.S. troops occupied
Chiriqui province from 1918 to 1921.

1921   (canal)
o   The United States paid an indemnity of $20 million to
       Colombia for its loss of Panama.
o   In order to prevent a boundary dispute between Panama and
       Costa Rica, the United States threatened Panama by
       sending a battleship and four hundred Marines.

1925   (U.S. policy)
U.S. troops, at the request of the Panamanian government,
intervened in an election dispute.

January 1936   (U.S. policy)
The United States guaranteed Panamanians equal opportunity
with Americans in the zone, a promise never completely
fulfilled.

1936   (canal)
In the Hull-Alfaro Treaty, Washington renounced the right to
intervene militarily to guarantee Panamanian independence and
the right to maintain police in Colon and Panama City. The
annuity was raised to $430,000 to offset the devaluation of
the dollar in 1933. Panama obtained the right to control
immigration. Most important, Article III stipulated that the
Canal Zone was the sovereign territory of the Republic of
Panama under the jurisdiction of the United States. The U.S.
Senate, however, refused to ratify the treaty until 1939 and
then only after Panama agreed to allow the United States to
continue military intervention when the latter thought it
necessary.

1941   (Panamanian politics)
President Arnulfo Arias was overthrown by the National Guard.
A pro-U.S. government took his place.

1947   (canal)
A renewal treaty ignored demands for better treatment of
Panama, and nationalistic riots erupted in Panama City. The
Panamanian government quelled them with its National Guard,
but not before the rioters turned their fury against the

United States.

<u>1955</u>   (canal)
A new treaty provided Panama with important concessions: it
could now tax zone employees who were Panamanians; the United
States gave up monopoly rights over railroad and highway
construction and control of sanitation in Colon and Panama
City; zone commissaries were restricted to selling only to
U.S. citizens and to canal employees who worked and lived in
the zone; Panamanians were granted a large share in supplying
goods to zone markets; Panama obtained some zone land; and the
rental annuity was raised to $1,930,000. In an informal,
separate "Memo of Understandings Reached," President Dwight
Eisenhower agreed to create equality of opportunity in the
zone and end wage discrimination against the Panamanians
working for the canal company.

<u>May 1958</u>   (anti-U.S. sentiment)
University students entered the zone under Operation
Sovereignty to plant some fifty Panamanian flags as an
assertion of Panamanian sovereignty. Rebuffed in a brief
confrontation, they withdrew. When they returned on November
3, 1959, American personnel resisted, and more than 120
students were killed or wounded, nine of them by U.S.
soldiers.

<u>1960</u>   (U.S. policy)
President Eisenhower opened skilled positions in the zone to
Panamanians and ordered the Panamanian flag flown in parts of
the zone.

<u>January 1964</u>   (anti-U.S. sentiment)
Panamanian national pride provoked a serious confrontation
between Panama and the United States. Panamanian students had
long insisted that the United States recognize Panamanian
sovereignty over the zone. In January 1964, U.S. high school
students refused to fly the Panamanian flag over their high
school and flew the U.S. flag by itself in violation of U.S.
law. Panamanian students swarmed into the zone to assert
Panamanian rights. During the riot which ensued, twenty-four
persons (three of whom were U.S. soldiers) were killed and
hundreds were injured.

<u>1964-1967</u>   (canal)
President Lyndon Johnson and President Marco Robles agreed to
negotiate three new canal treaties. Johnson, however,
announced that the United States was also exploring the
possibility of building a canal across Nicaragua or Mexico.
Panamanian leaders got the message that they should accede to
U.S. wishes lest Panama be stuck with a white elephant. The
1967 treaties were never ratified.

<u>October 1968</u>   (Panamanian politics)
Colonel Omar Torrijos, the commander of the National Guard,

exploited this widespread dissatisfaction with the political
system to overthrow the Robles government in a bloodless coup
d'etat and created a populist, nationalistic military
dictatorship.

1970   (money-laundering)
With U.S. technical advice, Panama instituted new banking laws
to make the country an offshore banking haven in an effort to
generate new revenues.

February 1974   (canal)
A joint "Statement of Principles" was signed by Panamanian
Foreign Minister Juan Antonio Tack and Secretary of State
Henry Kissinger in February 1974. The United States agreed
to a new treaty with a fixed termination date, to return the
zone to Panama in stages, to give the United States specified
rights to operate and defend the canal in conjunction with
Panama during the life of treaty, and to guarantee that Panama
would get a fair and equitable share of revenues.

March 1975   (canal)
The United States and Panama were deadlocked in negotiations.
Panama refused to give the United States a forty- or fifty-
year lease on military bases, to allow the United States to
occupy as much territory as it wanted, or to allow the U.S.
control of the canal to last as long as the Americans wanted.
Panama demanded complete control over the canal by the year
2000, and full control over police-fire protection and health
and sanitation. It also demanded that the United States
retain only the 4% of the zone's land that was used by the
canal itself, and that the United States retain land
sufficient for only three military installations.

Mid-1970s   (canal)
Technological change had gradually made the canal less
important. It and the zone no longer had as much economic and
strategic importance because the development of a two-ocean
U.S. Navy, nuclear submarines, carriers, long-range bombers,
and missiles had reduced, if not eliminated, the canal's
strategic importance and the necessity of maintaining military
bases there. Further, the development of excellent ground
transportation within the United States and the construction
of gigantic ships reduced the canal's commercial importance.
By the 1960s, approximately 80% of the canal's traffic was
Latin American, and by 1975, only 16% of total U.S. import and
export tonnage passed through the canal, and in monetary
terms, only 8%. The canal influenced less than 1% of the U.S.
GNP.

September 7, 1977   (canal)
President Jimmy Carter and Panama's General Torrijos signed
the Panama Canal Treaties in Washington, D.C.

April 18, 1978   (canal)
The U.S. Senate ratified the Panama Canal Treaties and added
a proviso that permitted U.S. intervention if the canal's
operation were interrupted.

October 1, 1979   (canal)
The first phase of the Panama Canal Treaties was implemented
as U.S. control over the Panama Canal Zone ended.

July 30, 1981   (Panamanian politics)
General Omar Torrijos was killed in a plane crash in western
Panama.

August 12, 1983   (Panamanian politics)
General Noriega became the commander of the Panamanian
National Guard and de facto ruler of Panama.

September 22, 1983   (drugs)
Drug dealer Steven Michael Kalish flew to Panama with $2.5
million to arrange for money-laundering services for his
marajuana smuggling operation. He gave Noriega a gift of
$300,000, made Panama a base of his operations, and grew so
close to Noriega that he described him as a "full-scale
conspirator in my drug operations."

January 1984   (anti-U.S. sentiment)
A Panamanian nationalist immolated himself in front of the
U.S. Embassy in January 1984 to protest U.S. violations of the
treaties and its Central American policies. Panama's National
Legislative Council declared him a national martyr, but did
little else.

1984   (Panamanian politics)
Arnulfo Arias was the presumed winner in the Panamanian
presidential election. However, Nicolas Ardita Barletta, a
former vice president of the World Bank, was installed. U.S.
Secretary of State George Schultz attended the inauguration.

1984   (U.S. involvement)
Panama insisted that the School of the Americas leave Panama,
and it was moved in 1984.

January 1985   (drugs)
Two percent of the U.S. respondents to a Gallup poll listed
drug abuse as the most important problem facing the United
States.

May 1985   (drugs)
Six percent of the U.S. respondents to a Gallup poll listed
drug abuse as the most important problem facing the United
States, a rise of four percent since January 1985.

September 14, 1985   (corruption)
The headless body of Hugo Spadafora was found stuffed in a

U.S. mail sack near the Panamanian-Costa Rican border. A medical doctor, he was also something of a revolutionary. He had served with Eden Pastora's (Comandante Zero's) guerilla unit in the Nicaraguan revolution, was a friend of Omar Torrijos (who made him Panama's deputy minister of health), and was an idealist. He made a fatal mistake when he decided to publicly accuse Noriega of drug trafficking and claimed that he had proof of his allegations. Spadafora had been kidnapped, tortured horribly, and beheaded. Noriega was accused of ordering the Spadafora kidnapping and murder.

September 27, 1985   (political corruption)
Noriega deposed Barletta, who wished to look into the Spadafora murder, and appointed First Vice President Eric Arturo Delvalle to replace him. In its first public opposition to Noriega, the U.S. condemned the pressure against Barletta.

March 10, 1986   (drugs)
Norman A. Bailey, a former Special Assistant to President Reagan for National Security Affairs, testified on Panamanian drug trafficking before the Subcommittee on Western Hemisphere Affairs of the Senate Committee on Foreign Relations during a hearing entitled "The Situation in Panama." He said, "There is a great deal of information, ranging from very hard to rather soft, concerning the use of Panama as a transhipment place for both illegal drugs as well as arms to various guerilla movements, both in Central America as well as Colombia and Peru. Much of this...is classified information."

June 6, 1987   (Panamanian politics)
PDF Deputy Commander Colonel Roberto Diaz Herrera exposed Noriega's involvement in illicit activities, accusing him of fraud in the 1984 presidential elections, drug trafficking, money laundering, and complicity in political assassinations. Widespread public demonstrations ensued, resulting in a state of emergency and violent repressions.

June 26, 1987   (U.S. response)
The U.S. Senate approved a resolution calling for democracy in Panama and threatened to cut off U.S. aid and military assistance. Military aid was cut off in July 1987.

July 1986   (drugs)
Eight percent of the U.S. respondents to a Gallup poll listed drug abuse as the most important problem facing the United States, a rise of two percent since May 1985.

March 1, 1987   (U.S. response)
President Reagan certified to Congress that Panama was "fully cooperating" in U.S. anti-drug efforts. Such certification was needed to qualify for U.S. assistance. On April 3, 1987, the Senate responded with a joint resolution (S.J.Res. 91) disapproving the President's certification of Panama.

June 11, 1987   (drugs, political corruption)
o   Colonel Roberto Diaz Herrera, a cousin of Torrijos,
     accused Noriega of drug trafficking. Noriega had been
     plotting against Herrera, who was serving as his chief
     of staff. The plotting was in its final phase and had
     become public. Herrera had been slowly isolated from his
     Panamanian Defense Force (PDF) support, while Noriega
     created a ruse of graceful retirement for Herrera but
     apparently intended to dishonorably discharge him from
     the PDF. Herrera, learning of this, struck back in the
     media, giving a television interview. He then launched
     into a series of interviews and press conferences in
     which he charged Noriega with engineering the outcome of
     the 1984 presidential elections; directing the slaying
     of Spadafora; planning the 1981 death of Omar Torrijos;
     participating in international drug trafficking, and
     selling visas to Cubans illegally.
o   The revelations touched off riots, and Panamanians
     attacked the U.S. Embassy with rocks and paint to protest
     U.S. support of Noriega. The revelations prompted the
     formation of the Anti-Noriega National Civic Crusade.
     Noriega clamped down on domestic opposition while
     marshalling his forces to protest the U.S. actions. The
     Panamanian Legislative Assembly demanded the expulsion
     of the U.S. ambassador and accused the United States of
     interventionist aggression. Noriega obtained an
     Organization of American States' resolution accusing the
     United States of unwarranted intervention in Panamanian
     affairs.

June 26, 1987   (U.S. response)
The U.S. Senate passed Senate Resolution 239, calling for
Noriega and other Panamanian officials to step down pending
the outcome of an investigation into Herrera's charges of
election fraud, criminal activity, and official corruption.
Reacting to this, Noriega turned his thugs loose to attack the
U.S. Embassy and the U.S. Information Service, doing much
damage. In response, U.S. Ambassador Arthur Davis suspended
all aid to Panama.

August 1987   (drugs)
Eleven percent of the respondents to a Gallup poll listed drug
abuse as the most important problem facing the United States,
a rise of three percent since July 1986.

September 24, 1987   (U.S. response)
The U.S. Senate approved an amendment to the Department of
Defense Authorization Act expressing the sense of the Senate
that within 45 days the government of Panama should take the
following steps or all U.S. aid would end and Panama's sugar
quota would be terminated: (1) return the PDF to effective
civilian control; (2) initiate an independent investigation
into certain illegal acts by the PDF; (3) establish a civilian
transition government not dominated by the military; and (4)

restore all rights guaranteed in the Panamanian constitution.

December 1987   (U.S. response)
The Reagan administration sent Assistant Secretary of Defense
Richard Armitage to Panama to explore the conditions under
which Noriega would step down. The mission failed in spite
of a U.S. offer to drop its ongoing investigation into
Noriega's drug trafficking. Meanwhile, the U.S. Congress
eliminated Panama's sugar quota.

December 22, 1987   (U.S. response)
The Omnibus Continuing Appropriations Resolution was signed
into law as Public Law 100-102. The Senate had amended it to
ban almost all aid to Panama, including funds for joint
military exercises. The resolution also directed the United
States to vote against Panamanian loan requests before
multilateral development banks and prohibited importation of
Panamanian sugar. This bar to aid could only be lifted by a
Presidential certification that democracy had been restored
in Panama.

February 5, 1988   (drugs)
Marijuana- and cocaine-trafficking and money laundering
indictments against Noriega were unsealed in Tampa and Miami,
Florida. The formal charges included: protecting cocaine
shipments; laundering drug money, and providing safe haven to
Medellin Cartel drug traffickers in exchange for a bribe of
$4.6 million; allowing the cartel to shift its drug operations
to Panama after the crackdown in Colombia; protecting a drug
laboratory; providing a safe haven in Panama for international
narcotics traffickers; arranging the shipment of chemicals for
cocaine processing; attempting to smuggle over 1.4 million
pounds of marajuana into the United States; buying a jet plane
that was used to transport illegal drug revenues to Panama
from the United States; and accepting a $1 million bribe from
drug traffickers in exchange for their use of Panama for
money-laundering and drug transhipment.

February 25, 1988   (political corruption)
President Delvalle's attempt to fire Noriega as the PDF
Commander failed. Hours later the Panamanian National
Assembly dismissed Delvalle, and Noriega replaced him with
Manuel Solis Palma. Delvalle went into hiding and later
appeared in Miami, Florida. The U.S. State Department
subsequently certified that Delvalle was still recognized by
the United States as the legitimate President of Panama.

March 1, 1988   (drugs)
Because of the two Federal indictments of Noriega that were
unsealed on February 5, 1988 and the mass of information on
the public record concerning high-level Panamanian involvement
in drug trafficking, the President did not certify to Congress
that Panama was fully cooperating with U.S. counternarcotics
efforts. This noncertification was well received by the

Senate. The Panamanian opposition then used this noncertification in U.S. Federal Courts to prevent Noriega's government from gaining access to Panamanian assets held by U.S. commercial banks. About $40 million in assets were frozen, and the U.S. operations of Air Panama were also suspended.

March 10, 1988   (U.S. response)
U.S. State Department officials expressed hope that PDF members would rebel against Noriega.

March 11, 1988   (U.S. response)
The White House announced a package of economic sanctions against Panama, suspending trade preferences granted under the Generalized System of Preferences and the Caribbean Basin Initiative, and placing all U.S. payments due to Panama into an escrow account to which President Devalle had access.

March 16, 1988   (political corruption)
Panamanian Police Chief Colonel Leonidas Macias led a coup against Noriega that was easily quashed. Noriega had Macias arrested and removed 12 of 54 majors then serving in the PDF.

March 25, 1988   (U.S. response)
o   The U.S. Senate passed a sense of the Senate resolution (S.Con.Res. 108), that provided that the "United States should act immediately to impose additional diplomatic, political, and economic pressure on General Noriega and should obtain his extradition from Panama."
o   Meanwhile, in Panama, Noriega rejected a U.S. offer to drop the drug indictments against him in return for his departure from Panama.

March 31, 1988   (U.S. response)
The U.S. government announced that it would place all funds owed to Panama into an escrow account that would be controlled by President Delvalle.

April 5-9, 1988   (U.S. response)
In response to Noriega's successive acts of tyranny, the Reagan administration sent in 1,300 additional troops to enhance security on U.S. bases.

April 8, 1988   (U.S. response)
President Reagan issued Executive Order No. 12635, declaring a national emergency with respect to Panama and invoking his authority under the International Emergency Powers Act. Under this order, the Treasury Department issued regulations blocking all property and interests of the Panamanian government under U.S. jurisdiction and prohibiting payments or transfers of currency to Panama. These Panamanian Transaction Regulations were strengthened further on June 3, 1988.

Early April 1988   (Panamanian politics)
The anti-Noriegan Authentic Panamanian (PPA) and Popular
Action (PAP) parties opposed the U.S. policy of working to
remove Noriega and stressed a national, popular solution.

May 11, 1988   (political corruption)
Noriega approved a provisional plan with U.S. authorities
under which he would leave power on August 12th in return for
withdrawing the drug indictments and other inducements.
Noriega finally refused to go along with the agreement,
complaining that the news leaks had turned his junior officers
against him and made it impossible to sell the deal to his
supporters in Panama.

June 1988   (U.S. response)
The United States sent an additional 1,300 troops to Panama.

June 16, 1988   (violence, corruption)
A U.S. Army private and his eighteen-year old wife were
assaulted by a probable PDF member. The private was beaten
and locked in the trunk of his car while his wife was raped
and battered by the assailant.

July 1988   (U.S. response)
President Reagan signed an intelligence finding authorizing
the CIA to work with former PDF Colonel Eduardo Herrera Hassan
to foment a coup in the PDF against Noriega. The Senate
Intelligence Committee objected because it feared that Noriega
would be assassinated.

August 1988   (Panamanian politics)
Opposition leader Arnulfo Arias, then 82 years old, died
without appointing an heir to lead his party in the May 1989
elections.

September 29, 1988   (U.S. response)
President Reagan signed the Department of Defense
Authorization Act, Fiscal Year 1989, as Public Law 100-456.
It contained provisions restricting U.S. aid to the Panamanian
Defense Force and expressing the sense of Congress that the
United States should not reach any agreement with Noriega
involving dropping the drug indictments against him.

October 1, 1988   (U.S. response)
President Reagan signed the Foreign Operations, Export
Financing, and Related Programs Appropriations Act, 1989, as
Public Law 100-461, and continued the economic sanctions
previously in place against Panama.

December 1988   (U.S. response)
The Senate Committee on Foreign Relations' Subcommittee on
Terrorism, Narcotics, and International Operations issued a
report entitled "Drugs, Law Enforcement and Foreign Policy,"
that contained extensive material on Panama's involvement in

the drug trade. This report was based in large part on
testimony given at the Subcommittee's previous series of
hearings. It asserted that Noriega had turned Panama's
political system into one that was controlled by personal
loyalties to Noriega, cemented by graft and corruption, and
substantially funded with narcotics money.

February 1989   **(U.S. response)**
President George Bush signed an intelligence finding
authorizing $10 million in covert aid to forces opposing
Noriega.

February 1989   **(Panamanian response)**
In accordance with U.S. economic sanctions against Panama, the
Canal Commission employees' taxes had not been transferred to
the Panamanian government. In response, in February, Noriega
enacted legislation authorizing the Panamanian government to
seize canal employees' automobiles and property for nonpayment
of taxes, and Panamanians were prohibited from leaving the
country without proof of having paid their taxes.

March 1, 1989   **(U.S. response)**
President Bush followed President Reagan's lead and refused
to certify that Panama was "cooperating fully" with U.S. anti-
drug efforts.

April 6, 1989   **(U.S. response)**
President Bush renewed the economic sanctions that Reagan had
imposed the year before.

May 7, 1989   **(political corruption)**
The Panamanian presidential elections were held. A count by
the Catholic Church showed that the opposition had won by a
three-to-one margin. No government count of the vote was ever
released. Noriega's candidate, Carlos Duque, claimed victory
and the following day government troops fired on thousands of
opposition demonstrators and raided ballot counting centers.
International observers and President Bush denounced the
elections and Noriega responded by charging foreign
interference and annulling the vote on May 10th.

May 10, 1989   **(violence, political corruption)**
Panamanian opposition leaders and their supporters were
brutally attacked by Dignity Battalion paramilitary groups
that included members of the police. The Panamanian electoral
tribunal nullified the election citing foreign interference.
Noriega's newly-constituted Dignity Battalions had overstepped
the bounds of acceptable Panamanian political practice, and
had done so in front of the international media. The
Panamanian Roman Catholic Church denounced the regime for
fraud and violence, calling for Panamanians to withdraw their
support of the dictator. The United States recognized the
victory of opposition leader Guillermo Endara. Panamanians
openly began suggesting that either a military coup or U.S.

military intervention might be the only way to oust Noriega.

May 11, 1989   **(U.S. response)**
President Bush announced that 1,900 troops were being sent to
Panama to augment the 10,000 troops already stationed there.
He also announced a seven-point plan concerning Panama in
which Washington supported the initiative of other
Organization of American States (OAS) governments and other
international groups, withdrew its ambassador, reduced its
embassy staff, and ordered U.S. employees and their dependents
to safe housing.

May 17, 1989   **(international response)**
The Organization of American States (OAS) adopted a resolution
condemning Noriega and calling for the "peaceful transfer of
power" to a democratically elected government.

July 1989   **(Just Cause)**
A series of joint exercises rehearsing parts of the Just Cause
plan began. After the operation was complete, General Stiner
reported that "We practiced every target." The troops that
were not in Panama or brought in for exercises practiced on
mock-ups at Fort Bragg. Significantly the junior ranking
personnel never realized that they were practicing a real
plan.

July 20, 1989   **(international response)**
The OAS proposed that a provisional government assume power
on September 1, 1989, when the current presidential term
expired, and that elections be held as soon as possible.

August 1989   **(U.S. response)**
Deputy Secretary of State Lawrence Eagleburger told an OAS
gathering that the United States estimated General Noriega was
worth $200 to $300 million. His assets included four
luxurious homes in Panama, 50 oil paintings, a farm in France,
an apartment in Paris, three Lear jet aircraft, a Boeing 727
aircraft, and three yachts, named Macho I, II, and III.

August 8, 1989   **(U.S.-Panamanian confrontation)**
U.S. troops detained nine PDF soldiers and eleven other
Panamanians for trying to impede maneuvers on U.S.-controlled
territory.

August 9, 1989   **(U.S.-Panamanian confrontation)**
In an exercise, SOUTHCOM deployed tanks to block the entrance
to Fort Amador, while helicopters overflew the southern end
of the canal.

August 10, 1989   **(U.S.-Panamanian confrontation)**
In an exercise, U.S. forces stormed a PDF gate and disarmed
its guard. SOUTHCOM reported that the action was in response
to the PDF's detention of two U.S. soldiers which, in turn,
had been in retaliation for the brief detention of 29

Panamanians.

<u>August 17, 1989</u>   (**U.S.-Panamanian confrontation**)
SOUTHCOM conducted joint maneuvers at eleven canal installations. While the United States said that it was enforcing its rights under the 1977 treaties, Panama claimed it was violating them. SOUTHCOM reported that the exercise was designed to train U.S. forces "to respond swiftly and decisively in defense of the Panama Canal and protection of U.S. lives and property."

<u>September 1, 1989</u>   (**U.S. response**)
Francisco Rodriguez was sworn in as Panama's new president. President Bush said that the United States would not recognize the new government or have any diplomatic relations with it.

<u>October 1, 1989</u>   (**Just Cause**)
General Maxwell R. Thurman the Southern Command Commander took command. The plan used in <u>Just Cause</u> was in existence at this time. Thurman would update the plan in the coming weeks.

<u>October 3, 1989</u>   (coup attempt)
Major Moises Giroldi Vega, the individual responsible for quashing the March 1988 coup attempt and chief of security for PDF headquarters, led a coup against Noriega with the aim of forcing him to retire. Although Noriega was reported to be a captive in his own headquarters, the rebellion was suppressed the same day. Noriega executed the leaders and reorganized the PDF to insure its loyalty. He also sought to neutralize other dissidents, some of whom fled to the zone and U.S. protection.

<u>October 3-December 1990</u>   (**Just Cause**)
o   The performance of PDF units in the failed coup of October 3, 1989, provided the U.S. planners with basic intelligence. The planners' analysis of the coup attempt identified priority targets. The PDF units most loyal to Noriega were the 6th and 7th Companies at Rio Hato and Battalion 2000 at Fort Cimarron, and in October the 7th Company flew to Panama City to come to Noriega's aid while Battalion 2000 arrived by truck. In light of this information, the planners made seizing the airports at Rio Hato and Panama City, disabling Panamanian aircraft, and seizing the bridges high priority targets. (The Rio Hato airport and PDF barracks were not even H-hour targets until after the October coup.)
o   In preparation for <u>Just Cause</u>, U.S. Southern Command conducted a series of exercises that permitted scouting target areas, rehearsing maneuvers, and masking increased activities. To familiarize the troops involved with their targets and operations, joint exercises, code named <u>Purple Storms</u>, and single unit exercises, code named <u>Sand Fleas</u>, were held weekly for several months prior to <u>Just Cause</u>.

October 12, 1989   **(negotiations with Noriega)**
Noriega's attorney, Frank A. Rubino of Miami, Florida, met
with Michael G. Kozak, Deputy Assistant Secretary of State for
Inter-American Affairs. Kozak presented the following U.S.
offer: Noriega would step down from power. In return, the
United States would not seek Noriega's extradition, but the
U.S. indictments would remain in force. In November, Rubino
presented this offer to Noriega, who replied that there was
no basis for agreement.

October 31, 1989   **(Just Cause)**
U.S. forces held maneuvers along the canal and obstructed
highways in a show of force that included tanks and aircraft.

November 1989   **(Just Cause)**
President Bush, Secretary of Defense Cheney, and General Colin
Powell, Chairman of the Joint Chiefs of Staff, all approved
General Thurman's updated plan.

November 13, 1989   **(Just Cause)**
The Joint Staff asked Southern Command (SOCOM) to submit a
Public Affairs Plan to ensure adequate press access during
Just Cause.

November 20-21, 1989   **(U.S.-Panamanian confrontation)**
Southern Command used tanks to impede access to the Health
Ministry, arguing that PDF units had tanks blocking the U.S.
Gorgas Hospital. These forces remained in a standoff for two
days.

November 21, 1989   **(U.S. response)**
o   The U.S. Departments of Commerce, Justice, State, the
     Judiciary, and Related Agencies Appropriations Act, 1990,
     was signed into law, becoming Public Law 101-162. It
     contained a sense of Congress provision to the effect
     that the international drug summit's agenda should
     include consideration of how to remove Noriega from power
     and another provision calling upon the United States to
     intensify its efforts against Noriega.
o   President Bush signed into law the Foreign Operations,
     Export Financing, and Related Programs Appropriations
     Act, 1990, which became Public Law 100-167, and which
     continued the economic sanctions against Panama for
     another year.

November 22, 1989   **(Just Cause)**
Southern Command Public Affairs Office (PAO) sent a Top Secret
fax to the Pentagon Public Affairs Plans office. It was not
a fully developed plan, but merely provided bare bones
guidance. Colonel Peter Alexandrakos began to staff it, but
the Pentagon's Inter-American Affairs Office told him that
Deputy Assistant Secretary of Defense Richard C. Brown had
ordered the fax "close-hold" until it became necessary to have
such guidance and then to staff it at that time.

Late-November 1989   (**Just Cause**)
To have the needed helicopters available, late in November, six AH-64 Apaches equipped with 30mm chain guns in their turrets and a combination of Hellfire anti-tank missiles or 2.75 inch rockets were secretly deployed to Panama.

Early December 1989   (U.S. **response**)
The Bush administration banned Panamanian-registered ships from U.S. ports.

Early December 1989   (U.S.-**Panamanian confrontation**)
The PDF was ordered to arrest General Maxwell Thruman, the SOUTHCOM commander, and Major General Marc Cisneros, Commander of U.S. Army South, for failing to respond to summonses to appear in court on charges of disturbing the peace.   The charges alleged that military maneuvers conducted by their subordinate units were a constant harassment to Panamanian citizens.   Washington dismissed the accusation, explaining that all of its activities were within the limits of the Panama Canal Treaties, and SOUTHCOM said that it would consider any attempt to arrest the officers as an act of terrorism.

Early December 1989   (U.S. **policy**)
President Bush announced that in order to comply with the Panama Canal Treaty requirement, he would appoint Fernando Manfredo, Deputy Administrator of the Commission since its establishment in 1979, as Acting Administrator until Panama's political crisis was settled.   In following through with that announcement, on January 1, 1990, Bush appointed Manfredo as Acting Administrator until the Endara government could recommend a qualified candidate.   (Under the terms of the Panama Canal Treaty, Article III(3)(c), the United States was required to appoint a Panamanian, proposed by Panama, as Canal Administrator beginning January 1, 1990.   In addition, U.S. implementing legislation for the Commission [P.L. 96-70] requires that the Administrator be appointed "by and with the advice and consent of the U.S. Senate".)

December 14, 1989   (U.S.-**Panamanian confrontation**)
Noriega named himself "Maximum Leader" and declared his nation to be "at war" with the United States.

December 15, 1989   (anti-U.S. **activity/sentiment**)
In December 1989, Noriega, growing bolder by his seeming ability to act with impunity, allowed his forces to harass U.S. personnel and had the National Assembly assert that Panama and the United States were in a virtual state of war. Panama's National Assembly declared that Panama was "in a state of war" with the United States on December 15th, and named Noriega "chief of the government" and "the maximum leader of national liberation," formalizing his already sweeping powers in response to what it termed U.S. aggression.

December 15, 1989   (U.S.-Panamanian confrontation)
Ten PDF soldiers armed with .50 caliber machine guns stopped
a U.S. Military Police (MP) patrol car. One soldier "locked
and loaded a round" and aimed his weapon at an MP, but the
arrival of the MP's commander prompted the PDF to release the
Americans.

December 16, 1989   (anti-U.S. activity/sentiment)
o   First Lieutenant Robert Paz, U.S. Marine Corps, was shot
    and killed by Panamanian forces at a road block in Panama
    City, and a Navy officer and his wife who witnessed the
    murder were brutalized. In response to these incidents,
    U.S. military personnel in Panama were confined to U.S.
    bases, while U.S. troops were placed on maximum alert.
    The violence continued on Monday, when a U.S. Army
    officer, when threatened, shot and wounded a Panamanian
    police corporal.
o   In another incident, a PDF policeman accosted eight U.S.
    servicemen, aimed his assault rifle at them, and ordered
    them to leave the area. The Americans left, but returned
    with three MP units and arrested the policeman, holding
    him for ninety minutes before releasing him.
o   In a third incident, a U.S. soldier was stopped at a PDF
    checkpoint, arrested, taken to a PDF facility, and
    verbally abused by Panamanian soldiers. He was released
    when a friend in the PDF intervened on his behalf.

December 17, 1989   (Just Cause)
o   President Bush ordered the execution of Operation Just
    Cause. He or Secretary of Defense Cheney set H-hour at
    1 a.m. on Wednesday December 20, 1989.
o   President Bush asked about reporters. Secretary Cheney
    replied that the Department of Defense pool would go from
    Washington. Bush indicated his concern for security.

December 17-December 19, 1989   (Just Cause)
o   On notification of President Bush's decision, commanders
    immediately made pre-attack notifications putting troops
    and aircrews on alert, using an exercise as a cover
    story.
o   The Military Airlift Command (MAC) positioned transports
    at their departure airfields. MAC also notified its
    crews and put them into "crewrest" status twenty-four
    hours in advance.
o   A Sheridan tank platoon with four tanks from the 82nd
    Airborne Division, the augmented 4th Battalion of the 5th
    Infantry Division (Mechanized), and Navy SEAL (sea, air,
    land) Teams were deployed to augment Task Force Bayonet,
    which consisted of the 193rd Infantry Brigade (Light)
    permanently assigned to U.S. Army South in Panama.
o   K Company of the 3rd Battalion of the 6th Marine Regiment
    and D Company of the 2nd Light Armored Infantry Battalion
    equipped with amphibious vehicles, a detachment of the
    Brigade Service Support Group from Camp Lejeune, and the

Marine Corps' First Fleet Antiterrorism Security Team were deployed to Panama for the operation. These units were combined with the Marine Corps Security Force Company permanently stationed in Panama to form the 600-man Task Force Semper Fi.

o   C-5s brought 20 MH-6/AH-6 special operations forces scout/ attack helicopters in at night. These were kept in hangers until <u>Just Cause</u> began. The Air Force flew HH-53s and MH-60s in under their own power and also hid them in hangers during daylight.

o   The plan estimated that about 70 U.S. personnel would be killed and "several hundred" would be wounded. The largest anticipated cause of accidents would be due to paratroopers jumping from 500 feet onto runways. In peacetime training the U.S. Army normally suffers a six percent casualty rate on jumps that are made at 800 feet. Jumping at the lower altitude, while increasing the accident risk, reduced the exposure to hostile fire.

o   C-141s shuttled in and out of Howard Air Force Base with troops and supplies.

December 18, 1989   (Just Cause)
o   General Stiner arrived in Panama to make last minute adjustments with his commanders.

o   Between 24 and 48 hours before H-hour the National Security Agency intercepted a telephone call to Noriega. The unknown caller told him that a source in the U.S. State Department had said U.S. military intervention was imminent. Someone in the State Department reportedly placed a call to a member of the Canal Commission and warned that individual to keep his children home that night. The Canal Commission member supposedly warned his friends.

December 18, 1989   (anti-U.S. activity/sentiment)
A U.S. Army officer shot and wounded a Panamanian corporal near a U.S. military installation on the western edge of Panama City.

December 19, 1989   (Just Cause)
o   A notice was issued to U.S. civilians to restrict their movements.

o   Reuters reported that President Bush had met with key advisors Tuesday afternoon but reported that the subject was the war on drugs.

o   Military transport aircraft of the Military Airlift Command (MAC) began flights to Howard Air Force Base in Panama, in preparation for the initiation of the operation. NBC television broadcast footage of C-141s landing every 10 minutes in Panama while CBS reported the departure of transports from Fort Bragg. The same report included the Monday statement by the Defense Department that the 82nd Airborne's 18th Airborne Corps was participating in a readiness exercise.

o   7:30 p.m.   The Washington-based press pool was called out.

o   9:30 p.m.   Press pool members reported to Andrews Air Force Base for an 11 p.m. departure.

o   10:00 p.m.   Panamanians supposedly overheard two U.S. soldiers discussing H-hour.

o   11:26 p.m.   The press pool departed Andrews for Panama.

o   Warnings were aired on Panamanian radio that the United States would attack at 1 a.m. and that PDF units should report, draw arms, and prepare to fight. Noriega appears to have believed that something was happening without knowing just what or when. He increased his movements but did not put the PDF on alert although some units did increase their readiness on their own initiative.

Late on December 19, 1989

o   Special operations forces were sent into the field to observe assigned targets, including General Noriega.

o   Task Force Bayonet units moved into position before H-hour to be ready to attack the <u>Comandancia</u> (PDF Headquarters), the Presidential Palace, Fort Amador, the Patilla Airport, the small PDF fleet, and PDF facilities in Panama City. Task Force Bayonet was also responsible for protecting such U.S. facilities in Panama City as the Southern Command Headquarters, the housing area at Fort Amador, the embassy, and Fort Clayton. A small force, primarily military police, was positioned to assist Task Force Semper Fi to secure the Bridge of the Americas across the canal and to join U.S. Air Force personnel to protect Howard Air Force Base.

o   Task Force Black's teams conducted reconnaissance and moved out to positions near their targets to strike at H-hour or earlier.

o   Task Forces Bayonet, Atlantic, and Semper Fi units moved into their staging areas.

o   Task Force Red troops had been airborne for hours, while Task Force Pacific troops were loading onto their aircraft except where weather interfered.

o   Special operations teams of Task Force Black moved into position and started to strike. The first into action was the Delta Force team assaulting the <u>Carcel Modelo</u> (Model Jail) to free Kurt Frederick Muse. In April the Noriega regime had arrested Muse, an American who had grown up in Panama, for running a clandestine anti-Noriega radio station. Prison authorities had told Muse he would die if the United States went after Noriega. The Delta Force team arrived shortly after midnight in several armored personnel carriers and in a helicopter that landed on the roof. They struck so suddenly that the guards never touched their guns, but nearby PDF troops opened fire and killed a gunner in the first armored personnel carrier. The team reached Muse quickly and took him to the helicopter. The PDF poured heavy small arms fire into the helicopter, which went down breaking the pilot's leg and giving Muse a fracture. An armored personnel carrier then rescued Muse and carried him off at about 12:45 a.m., six minutes after Delta Force had begun its assault.

o   Task Force Bayonet deployed to three jumping-off points: Albrook Air Force Base, the Southern Command Headquarters compound at Quarry Heights on Ancon Hill, and Fort Clayton.

December 20, 1989   (**Just Cause**, **Endara government**)
12 a.m.   A new Panamanian government was sworn in at a U.S. military base in Panama City one hour before the U.S. attack. Guillermo Endara was sworn in as president and Ricardo Arias Calderon and Guillermo Ford as vice presidents by Osvalvo Velasquez, head of the Panamanian Commission for Human Rights. Endara, a labor lawyer, had studied law at New York University.

December 20, 1989   (**Just Cause**)
12:45 a.m. - H hour occurred.
o   Joint Task Force South hit 27 targets simultaneously at H-hour, which General Stiner had advanced fifteen minutes for fear of security leaks.
    --   **Task Force Semper Fi**, moved out to secure the Bridge of the Americas and provide Howard Air Force Base area security. It was also responsible for the Arraijan Tank Farm about five miles west of the city.
    --   **Task Force Pacific**, composed of forces in the United States, was airborne, scheduled to jump at H+1, after Rangers had secured Torrijos/Tocumen Airport.
    --   **Task Force Atlantic** proceeded to secure the electric distribution center at Cerro Tigre, the prison at Gamboa, Madden Dam, and the Colon area. While securing these facilities and areas, it neutralized the PDF 8th Infantry Company near Colon and a PDF naval infantry company near Coco Solo.
    --   A **Task Force Black** Army Special Forces team seized control of the Pacora River Bridge that was the choke point on the route from Fort Cimarron to Panama City and the Torrijos/Tocumen Airport.
    --   From their jumping-off points **Task Force Bayonet** simultaneously hit the Commandancia (PDF Headquarters), Fort Amador, the National Department of Investigations and the Department of National Transportation buildings, Patilla Airport, and other targets.
    --   **Task Force Red**, consisting of Rangers from Fort Lewis, Washington, Fort Benning, Georgia, and Hunter Army Airfield, Georgia, who had boarded their MAC transports before sunset on December 19, 1990 and had flown southward, jumped at H-hour into the airfield at Rio Hato, home of the 6th and 7th PDF Companies, and Tocumen/Torrijos Airport.

<u>12:45 a.m. onward</u>
o   **Task Force Bayonet**
    --   after defeating stiff resistance in which two
          helicopters, possibly MH/AH-6s, were shot down,
          captured the Commandancia and eliminated the
          organized resistance there during the afternoon of
          December 20th.
    --   another part of the 193rd Brigade assaulted Fort
          Amador, killing six PDF troops and wounding three,
          while suffering no U.S. casualties.
    --   Company C of 5th Battalion of the 87th Infantry
          assigned to the 193rd Brigade, secured the National
          Department of Investigations and National Department
          of Transportation buildings.
    --   Forty-eight Navy SEALs assigned to Task Force
          Bayonet attacked the Patilla Airport with the
          objective of controlling the airfield and
          incapacitating Noriega's airplane to ensure that he
          did not escape from Panama. The PDF defense was
          much stronger than expected, and the combination of
          a last minute change in plans and inaccurate
          intelligence was fatal. Advancing across the open
          airfield, the SEALs took heavy fire. Four SEALs
          died and three suffered severe wounds. The SEALs
          finally fired an AT-4 round into the cockpit of the
          aircraft, destroying it, the airport hanger, and at
          least two other aircraft. Eventually 82nd Airborne
          troops of Task Force Pacific relieved them.
    --   SEALs boarded and disabled patrol boats in the
          harbor to prevent Noriega's escape by that route.
    --   An element made up primarily of military police
          moved to the Bridge of the Americas and met Marines
          of Task Force Semper Fi coming from the west.
    --   Other task force elements seized the Presidential
          Palace and provided protection for Fort Clayton, the
          U.S. Southern Command Headquarters, and the U.S.
          Embassy during the opening phases of <u>Just Cause</u>.
    --   Task force elements seized control of the Panamanian
          television station.
o   **Task Force Atlantic**
    --   At Colon, task force Atlantic quickly defeated the
          8th PDF Company. The Task Force, including troops
          from the 82nd Airborne Division and the 7th Infantry
          Division, then moved to Coco Solo where they
          encountered a determined PDF Naval Infantry unit.
          During the Colon fighting, the PDF shot down a
          MH/AH-6 SOF helicopter, killing the pilot, but by
          the afternoon of the 20th, the resistance was
          reduced to sporadic firing.
    --   At H-hour, Hueys carried Task Force Atlantic troops
          from the second battalion into the El Renacer Prison
          near Gamboa, while a Cobra helicopter gunship
          attacked the PDF barracks. The paratroopers
          captured the barracks and then moved to protect a

housing area at Gamboa.

-- Troops from this same battalion moved to secure two other vital objectives. They seized the Madden Dam that provided the water to operate the canal locks. If saboteurs had been able to blow-up the dam, the canal could have been disabled for a year or more. The other objective seized was the electrical distribution center at Cerra Tigre.

o   **Task Force Pacific**

-- The Task Force Pacific drop started approximately one hour after H-hour at Torrijos/Tocumen Airport. Once on the ground, the task force relieved the Rangers at the airport and the nearby special operations elements of Task Forces Black and Bayonet.

-- The task force moved out from the airport and was prepared to deal with any PDF resistance including relieving the Rangers at the Pacora River Bridge or moving further east to combat PDF Battalion 2000 at Fort Cimarron.

-- Task Force Pacific also had responsibility for the PDF unit at Panama Viejo and the PDF 1st Infantry Company at Tinajitas. A small task force element jumped near Madden Dam and reinforced troops from Task Force Atlantic at that facility.

-- Task Force Pacific also provided the Joint Task Force South Commander with an operational reserve force in the vicinity of Panama City.

o   **Task Force Semper Fi**

-- Task Force Semper Fi secured U.S. Naval Station Panama (Rodman), Howard Air Force Base, the Arraijan Tank Farm, and the Bridge of the Americas. The Marines suffered one killed and two wounded.

o   **Task Force Red**

-- At Rio Hato, the action opened with two F-117As dropping 2,000 pound bombs near the PDF barracks to stun and disorient he defenders. Because of pilot error, the bomb reportedly landed more than 300 yards off the intended point. Despite the F-117A's action, the PDF was partially ready and firing started when the transports were about 1000 meters from the drop zone. The first U.S. combat casualty was a Ranger shot in the head by groundfire as his transport approached the drop zone. Someone had warned the PDF just minutes before the 850 Rangers arrived. Given this warning and the firing by the PDF, the decision to jump from 500 instead of 800 feet no doubt saved U.S. lives. Numerous sources describe the fighting at Rio Hato as among the hardest in Operation Just Cause. While U.S. losses were significant--four killed and 44 wounded, 41 of whom were injured in their parachute landing falls--they could easily have been much worse.

-- Task Force Red achieved an effective tactical

surprise in its jump at the Tocumen/Torrijos Airport. Noriega appears to have been either at a hotel or the officers' club at the airport and to have fled as approximately 700 Rangers (all of the 1st Ranger Battalion and one company of the 3rd Battalion) jumped from the sky. By dawn, U.S. forces had control of the airfield and had sent patrols out to the east, including patrols to reinforce Task Force Black special forces at the Pacora River bridge. The Rangers effectively blocked any possible surface movement by Battalion 2000 on the capital and any possible flight into the Tocumen/Torrijos Airport by PDF forces. Before the fighting ended at Tocumen/Torrijos Airport Task Force Pacific had started to jump into the airport.

o   **Task Force Pacific**

--   At 1:55 a.m. Task Force Pacific, built around the 82nd Airborne Division, jumped into the Tocumen/Torrijos Airport and near the Madden Dam to reinforce the troops already at those objectives. Half of the 20 C-141s carrying the approximately 2000 paratroopers from Fort Bragg were delayed three hours at Pope Air Force Base by an ice storm. They finally reached the drop-zone at 5:15 a.m.

o   The late arrival at Tocumen/Torrijos Airport of half of Task Force Pacific meant moving in daylight. Most of the 45 Army helicopters hit by hostile fire during Just Cause were hit during daylight operations the first day. These hits came largely from small arms, and most of the battle-damaged Army helicopters were back in service within twenty-four hours. Helicopters and surface transport moved the 82nd Airborne paratroopers out to their targets. They moved against a PDF company at Tiajitas and a cavalry squadron at Panama Viejo. They relieved the SEALs at Paitilla Airport and moved up the road to Fort Cimarron, relieving the Rangers at the Pacorra River bridge while en route. When Task Force Pacific reach Fort Cimarron, Battalion 2000 had disappeared.

5:00 a.m.
The press pool landed at Howard Air Force Base, Panama.

7:00 a.m.
President Bush held a news conference in which he announced that Operation Just Cause had begun.

7:45 a.m.
Secretary of Defense Richard Chaney and the Chairman, Joint Chiefs of Staff, General Colin Powell, held a news conference. The following was included in the information that they released:

o   Chaney stated that the plan had been in existence for some time.

o   the publicly announced U.S. political objective in <u>Just</u>
     <u>Cause</u> had four parts: (1) protect American lives; (2)
     protect American interests and rights under the Panama
     Canal Treaty; (3) restore Panamanian democracy; and (4)
     apprehend Noriega.

<u>4:40 p.m.</u>
o   General T.W. Kelly held a news briefing in which he
     reviewed the actions and objectives of each task force
     in Panama. He announced that organized resistance had
     ended but that the Dignity Battalions were still
     operating in Panama City. In response to reporters'
     questions, he asserted that troops would be working to
     restore order in Panama City and to apprehend Noriega.
     While Kelly was announcing that organized resistance was
     over, he was anxious to get the follow-on forces into
     Panama.
o   U.S. troops moved to secure Panamanian government offices
     and cut off Noriega's diplomatic escape routes. Among
     other objectives secured were the Foreign Ministry,
     Health Ministry, Finance Ministry, and Central Bank. To
     keep him from seeking political asylum, U.S. troops
     surrounded the Cuban, Nicaraguan, and Libyan embassies.
     One patrol investigating a reported arms cache searched
     the Nicaraguan Ambassador's house over his vehement
     objections.

<u>December 21, 1989</u>   **(international response)**
o   In retaliation for the stationing of U.S. troops around
     the Nicaraguan Embassy in Panama City, Nicaragua deployed
     troops around the U.S. Embassy in Managua.
o   Costa Rica issued a cautious statement decrying the use
     of force. Carlos Jose Guiterrez, its Ambassador to the
     United Nations, said that his country's "reaction had
     been one of regret for the new blow to the inter-American
     system, but relieved because the nightmare lived by the
     Panamanian people had ended."

<u>December 22, 1989</u>   **(Just Cause)**
o   Eliecer Gaytan, Noriega's security chief, took refuge in
     the Vatican Embassy in Panama City.
o   U.S. patrols moved systematically across Panama City, and
     U.S. Southern Command assigned police duties to about
     3,000 U.S. troops.

<u>December 23, 1989</u>   **(Just Cause)**
o   The 82nd Airborne swept Panama City from the northeast
     to the southwest while the 193rd Brigade and part of the
     6th Military Police Company swept in the opposite
     direction. Panama City suffered from the after effects
     of a battle that had eliminated the police force but had
     not yet replaced it. The PDF had melted into the
     civilian population, and looting and arson were
     widespread.

o   At 11:30 a.m., Noriega loyalists attacked the police
     headquarters near the Southern Command Headquarters at
     Quarry Heights, attacking with mortars, machine guns, and
     automatic rifles.   The attack lasted "at least ten
     minutes" and wounded "several."

December 24, 1989   (Just Cause)
o   When Noriega sought asylum in the Papal Nunciature, the
     large-scale operational military action of Just Cause was
     over. The streets of Panama City appeared to be calm for
     the first time. U.S. troops concentrated on looters and
     occasional snipers, and former PDF members participated
     in joint patrols with U.S. troops. About 1,000 of the
     former PDF members responded to a call to join a new
     Panamanian security force commanded by Colonel Roberto
     Armijo.
o   Just Cause produced casualties on both sides.   The
     twenty-three U.S. fatalities were much lower than the
     estimate of seventy, and the 324 wounded U.S. servicemen
     fell within the public estimate of "several hundred."
     The official U.S. estimate was 220 civilians and 314 PDF
     members, with some of those listed as civilians possibly
     PDF members in civilian clothes.

December 24, 1989   (search for Noriega)
o   Noriega took refuge in the Vatican embassy where Msgr.
     Jose Sebastian Laboa assigned him to the same spartan
     room that had been occupied by Noriega's enemies in the
     past.   The television set was broken and the air
     conditioning was cut off. The embassy also housed Gaytan
     and other Noriega supporters and four members of the
     Basque terrorist group ETA.
o   U.S. drug enforcement agents flew Lieutenant Colonel Luis
     del Cid to Miami to face charges.   del Cid had
     surrendered with 2,000 Panamanian troops in the Chiriqui
     and Bacos del Taro provinces near the Costa Rican border,
     which reduced the chances of subsequent guerrilla
     resistance considerably.

December 26, 1989   (Just Cause)
Following the initial action, airlift aircraft delivered
relief items, including medical supplies, food, and temporary
housing, to those Panamanians injured or made homeless during
the operation. By December 26th, the Department of Defense
had coordinated enough U.S. aid to feed 50,000 people for 30
days, and most of this was transported to Panama by MAC.

December 27, 1989   (U.S. response)
The U.S. Justice Department filed formal requests to freeze
Noriega's bank accounts in Great Britain, France, Luxembourg,
and Switzerland.

December 29, 1989   (Just Cause)
An eighty-man search team entered the residence of Nicaraguan

Ambassador, Antenor Ferry, where they found rifles, rocket launchers, and machine guns.

December 30, 1989   (international response)
The U.N. General Assembly passed a resolution deploring the U.S. intervention that passed by a margin of 75 to 20, with 40 abstentions.

January 1, 1990   (international response)
Twenty U.S. diplomatic personnel left Managua, Nicaragua for Miami, Florida. They were expelled by Nicaragua in retaliation for the December 29th U.S. raid on Nicaraguan Ambassador Antenor Ferry's house in Panama.

January 1, 1990   (Just Cause)
o   Approximately 140 U.S. combat troops departed Panama.
o   Between December 20, 1989 and January 1, 1990, the Military Airlift Command had flown 408 MAC flights (55 C-130 flights, 254 C-141 flights, and 99 C-5 flights) in Just Cause. A total of 19,500 personnel and 11,700 tons of materiel had been delivered. Concerning personnel transport, a total of 84 parachute drops had been made; 2 from C-5, 63 from C-141, and 19 from C-130 aircraft. Twenty-seven other MAC flights, 10 by C-5s, 14 by C-141s, and 3 by C-130s, delivered other troops.

January 2, 1990   (U.S. policy)
President Bush announced the appointment of veteran diplomat Deane R. Hinton as the new U.S. Ambassador to Panama, replacing Arthur Davis who had served in the post since 1986. Hinton was currently serving as Ambassador to Costa Rica and had previously served as U.S. Assistant Secretary of State for Economic and Business Affairs. He had an extensive economic background, a capability which would prove helpful in leading the major economic recovery program needed if Panama's fledgling democracy was to flourish. He had also served in two highly sensitive posts (El Salvador and Pakistan) that involved encouraging deeply entrenched militaries toward support of civilian democratic rule.

January 3, 1990   (corruption)
The newly appointed head of the Panama Public Forces (formerly the Panama Defense Forces) Colonel Roberto Armijo was arrested and forced to resign when authorities discovered that he had $1 million in a private bank account. He was replaced by Lieutenant Colonel Eduardo Herrera Hassan.

January 3, 1990   (U.S. economic assistance)
A team headed by Deputy Secretary of State Lawrence Eagleburger arrived in Panama to discuss U.S. economic assistance.

January 3, 1990   (search for Noriega)
Noriega, in full military uniform, walked out of the Vatican

Embassy and surrendered to U.S. Major General Marc Cisneros.
Noriega was transported to Howard Air Force Base where he was
arrested on drug charges.

January 4, 1990   (prosecution of Noriega)
Noriega was transported to Homestead Air Force Base, Florida,
and was transferred to U.S. jurisdiction in Miami where he was
lodged in a cell in the basement of the federal courthouse.
He was arraigned in U.S. District Court, where his defense
lawyer, Frank Rubino, challenged the jurisdiction of the
court.

January 10, 1990   (drugs)
Panama and the United States signed an "umbrella" drug
trafficking agreement committing the two nations to improve
cooperation in the war on drugs, including actions to end
trafficking and money-laundering and to control the
transshipment of chemicals used to process cocaine. As a
further demonstration of cooperation, the Endara government
froze approximately 300 bank accounts which U.S. officials
believed were being used for laundering drug money.

January 16, 1990   (international response)
Panama expelled Peru's charg d'affaires after Peru questioned
the legitimacy of the new Panamanian government.

January 17, 1990   (international response)
The U.S. vetoed a U.N. Security Council resolution condemning
the search the residence of the Nicaraguan Ambassador to
Panama by U.S. troops. Great Britain abstained, while the
other thirteen members of the Council supported the
resolution.

January 18, 1990   (money laundering)
Second Vice President Guillermo Ford was reported to have said
that Panama would adopt any mechanism that would help control
money laundering. According to Ford, "Panama will no longer
be a money laundering center."

January 25, 1990   (U.S. economic assistance)
As a result of the Eagleburger visit that had begun on January
2, 1990, President Bush announced an economic recovery program
for Panama that was potentially worth over $1 billion. The
program included a package worth up to $500 million in loans,
guarantees, and programs to stimulate market access and
private investment incentive. In addition, Bush said that his
administration would request $500 million in supplemental
economic assistance for Panama for fiscal year 1990, to be
offset from other programs and would include assistance for
balance of payments support and business credit, a public
sector investment program, public sector restructuring, and
assistance to clear Panama's arrears with international
financial institutions. Additionally, the U.S. Agency for
International Development would provide $42 million in

assistance for housing, public works, small business rehabilitation, and technical assistance, including a small amount of assistance, $1.2 million, for training the civilian police. Another $9 million in military assistance funds would provide equipment for the police.

January 26, 1990   (prosecution of Noriega)
Noriega appeared in full military uniform at a hearing before U.S. District Court Judge William M. Hoeveler. Through his attorney, Frank Rubino, a former secret service agent, he claimed prisoner of war status. He made the same claim in a letter to President Bush.

January 26, 1990   (drugs)
Because of the anti-drug actions of the Endara government, President Bush certified to Congress that Panama was fully cooperating in the war on drugs, a measure that lifted certain legislative restrictions on aid and trade with Panama.

January 29, 1990   (international response)
Vice President Daniel Quayle visited Jamaica where Prime Minister Manley said that the U.S. invasion of Panama violated international law.

January 31, 1990   (Just Cause)
In his State of the Union address, President Bush announced that the remaining troops involved in the intervention would be home "well before the end of February."

January and February 1990   (violence)
In the aftermath of Just Cause, a crime wave in Panama City raised doubts about whether the Public Force would be able in the near future to take over the police duties being performed by U.S. troops. The crime wave appeared to be the work of common criminals, rather than remnants of pro-Noriega support, and included bank robberies, restaurant holdups, bomb scares, and the murder of a senior U.S. official of the Panama Canal Commission.

Early February 1990   (Endara government)
U.S. officials reportedly urged Endara to hold some type of referendum or ballot question, instead of a presidential election, as a means of showing the public's support for the new government.

February 7, 1990   (U.S. economic assistance)
o   The U.S. Congress passed an urgent $51 million foreign
     assistance package for Panama (P.L. 101-243), and
     restored Panama's eligibility for aid and trade benefits
     by waiving a number of legislative restrictions on
     assistance to Panama. Congress required a Presidential
     report, by April 15th, on specific actions taken by the
     Endara government to halt money laundering. Future
     foreign aid legislation for Panama could include a

condition requiring demonstrated efforts by the government to prevent Panama from being a money laundering center. As Representative George Miller noted in a House floor debate in early February, "We should all be very cautious--and on notice,--about voting to spend our own taxpayer money on any government that cannot, or will not, take aggressive action against the drug cartels that are pouring billions of dollars in narcotic poison into the United States."

o   The House Committee on Foreign Affairs stated in a February 1990 report that it would closely monitor progress on bank secrecy laws and other areas of cooperation before approving further aid.

February 10, 1990   (Endara government)
Panama's Cabinet Council approved Decree No. 38, which abolished the old PDF and established a new Public Force until Panama's Legislative Assembly could debate and adopt a new organic law regulating the duties and organization of the new force. In effect, by abolishing the PDF, the decree stripped the new force of jurisdiction over key government agencies, including the immigration office that had been a lucrative center of corruption under the Noriega regime.

February 13, 1990   (Just Cause)
The United States completed withdrawing the military forces that had been flown in to participate in Operation Just Cause. A total of 13,504 personnel remained, in comparison to 13,597 who were there before the invasion. This action helped improve Panama's relations with several Latin American nations and also took some domestic pressure off the Bush administration from those calling for the removal of the forces. The timely removal of troops also permitted the administration to avoid any possible conflict with Congress over the War Powers Resolution.

Mid-February 1990   (money laundering)
In further actions, the Panamanian government approved additional regulations to curb money laundering. These were similar to U.S. banking practices and required reporting every transaction over $10,000, including deposits and withdrawals.

February 26, 1990   (Just Cause-press relations)
Lieutenant General Carl W. Stiner said that security around the U.S. invasion of Panama was compromised, resulting in prolonged fighting and higher casualties. The Pentagon placed the final casualty figures at 23 U.S. personnel killed and 124 wounded. PDF casualties were 314 killed and 124 wounded. The U.S. also estimated that 202 Panamanian civilians had been killed.

February 28, 1990   (U.S. policy)
In a six-to-three vote, the U.S. Supreme Court ruled that U.S. officials do not need a warrant to search the properties of

foreign citizens located abroad. This ruling allowed the United States to use the evidence gathered during <u>Just Cause</u> in its court case against Noriega.

<u>Late February 1990</u>   **(money laundering)**
o   U.S. officials backed away from efforts to bring about
     a change in Panama's bank secrecy laws. Instead, they
     agreed, at least for the near term, to accept a pledge
     from Panama to cooperate with U.S. investigators on drug
     probes.
o   Panamanian officials had expressed concern over
     inordinate U.S. pressure on the laundering issue, which
     they felt might be an affront to Panama's sovereignty.

<u>Early March 1990</u>   **(Endara government)**
Concerning the issue of the Endara government's legitimacy, President Endara announced that in the next few months the government would hold a referendum to legitimize his electoral mandate. He said that he would submit various constitutional reforms, first subject to approval by the Legislative Assembly, and then to a direct referendum by the people. He believed that the referendum on the constitutional amendments would demonstrate the popular support that his government enjoys.

<u>Early March 1990</u>   **(money laundering)**
Concerning the issue of money-laundering by Panamanian banks, Vice President Guillermo Ford warned that Panama would not accept any foreign economic aid if the country was pressured into easing its banking secrecy laws. Ford noted that "nobody pressures" the current government and that the "government was not kneeling before anybody."

<u>Early March 1990</u>   **(canal)**
In respect to the Canal Administrator, President Bush had appointed Fernando Manfredo as an interim Administrator until Panama appointed one. In early March 1990, Endara announced the nomination of Gilberto Guardia Fabrega as the new Panamanian Administrator. The nomination was forwarded to Washington on March 13th, thereby beginning the process of his confirmation and appointment. His appointment would be a significant step in demonstrating the U.S. and Panamanian commitments to follow through with the Panama Canal Treaties.

<u>Early March 1990</u>   **(violence)**
In response to the crime wave that had plagued Panama in January and February, in early March 1990, U.S. forces participated with Panamanian police in a massive anti-crime operation known as "Operation to Recover Tranquility Amid Democracy" in which hundreds of Panamanians were detained. Four more massive sweeps were conducted through March 1990 in which hundreds of U.S. troops participated and hundreds of Panamanians arrested. Some observers questioned whether the raids violated Panama's constitutional norms. The head of

Panama's new Judicial Technical Police reportedly admitted that the raids violated the "letter but not the spirit of the law." In addition, U.S. military support for police security had included the deployment of small teams of green berets (U.S. Army 7th Special Forces Group) to the countryside that reportedly were involved in investigating crimes and acting as backups for the Panamanian police.

March 1, 1990   (Endara government)
Panama's Legislative Assembly was reconstituted based on the results of the May 1989 elections with a five-year term of office until 1994. In a speech at the Assembly's installation, President Endara noted that the legislature "is a branch of government whose formation is so basic for the exercise of a genuine democracy." He vowed to fully respect legislative prerogatives and other legislative functions assigned by the constitution and called for mutual respect from the legislature for the rights and duties of the executive branch.

March 2, 1990   (anti-U.S. activity/sentiment)
One U.S. soldier was killed and 15 other U.S. servicemen were injured along with 12 Panamanians in a grenade attack on a disco in Panama City. Although an alleged pro-Noriega guerrilla group, known as the "December 20th Movement" (M-20), claimed responsibility for the attack and announced that it would take additional actions against U.S. targets and President Endara, Panamanian officials stated there was no evidence of an organized guerrilla movement in the country. The incident, however, highlighted the predicament of a continued high-profile U.S. military presence in Panamanian territory. While on the one hand, continued U.S. operational support for the Public Force served as a critical stabilizing factor for the new government by giving it time to success-fully train and build-up a new force, at the same time a continued U.S. police role could provoke guerrilla or terrorist actions against Americans as well as the new government.

March 1990   (U.S. economic assistance)
o   Action on the $500 million in new economic assistance that Bush had announced on January 25, 1990 was delayed until March with both the executive and legislative branches blaming each other for the delay. Some members of Congress noted that the administration did not formally present its request until mid-March when it was combined with a $300 million supplemental request for Nicaragua, whereas the Administration argued that Congress could not decide what Department of Defense programs should be cut to fund the additional foreign assistance requests for both Panama and Nicaragua (a part of the so-called "peace dividend").
o   In early March 1990, Endara went on a 13-day hunger strike in Panama City's Metropolitan Cathedral as an act

of compassion and solidarity with the Panamanian poor. Although he insisted that the hunger strike was not directed against the United States, he noted that its slowness in providing aid was creating a dangerous situation because of widespread unemployment and unrelieved poverty.

March 13, 1990   (U.S. economic assistance)
President Bush called for urgent action, by April 5, 1990, on assistance for both Panama and Nicaragua.

March 20, 1990   (U.S. economic assistance)
After it became clear that the anticipated $500 million would probably be scaled down and would not be approved by early April, Second Vice President Guillermo Ford warned that a U.S. pledge for financial assistance was needed within 60 days to prevent Panama's poor from rioting.

March 27, 1990   (U.S. economic assistance)
The U.S. House Appropriations Panel approved a supplemental spending bill for Fiscal Year 1990 that included $420 million in aid to Panama.

April 5, 1990   (U.S. economic assistance)
Senate Majority Leader George Mitchell announced in early April that he would not support the full amount ($500 million) that President Bush had requested until the Bush administration produced a "meaningful long-term foreign aid plan" instead of approaching foreign aid "in one-shot increments." Thus, as the Senate began its Easter recess on April 5, 1990, no action had been taken to appropriate the assistance for Panama. As of mid-April, the future of foreign assistance to Panama was uncertain.

December 31, 1999   (canal)
The Canal Treaties are scheduled to terminate. The process of transferring the canal to Panama is scheduled to culminate, as Panama assumes control of its operation and defense. At this time, the Panama Canal Commission, the U.S. agency charged with operating the canal, will be abolished.

About the Contributors

Editors

BRUCE W. WATSON served as a naval intelligence officer for twenty-two years. He currently is associated with the University of Virginia, and serves as an Adjunct Professor at George Mason University, the Defense Intelligence College, and the University of Maryland. He is a free lance writer and consultant on defense matters. He has served as Vice Chairman and as Chairman, Comparative Foreign Policy Section, International Studies Association, and is a Professor Emeritus at the Defense Intelligence College. The author of Red Navy at Sea, he has coedited three books on the Soviet Navy, has written several articles on the subject, and has written or coedited seven other books on defense and national security matters. Dr. Watson has just completed writing a comprehensive study of sea power since World War II, is writing a second book on Soviet naval operations, and is the editor-in-chief of the Garland encyclopedia series on military affairs.

PETER G. TSOURAS is an analyst at the U.S. Army Intelligence and Threat Analysis Center, Washington, D.C. He has written extensively on Soviet naval matters, contributing to two Westview studies on the subject. He is also the author of an incisive series of articles on Russian military history. He is currently writing a comprehensive study of ground-based military power since World War II, has just completed coediting an encyclopedia on U.S. Army terminology with Bruce Watson, and will soon begin a series of studies on German military strategy in World War II.

Contributors

E. MARIA BIGGERS is an intelligence analyst trainee at the U.S. Army Intelligence Threat and Analysis Center in Washington, D.C., and is a research assistant for Dr. Alan R. Goldman, the co-author of her chapter. She is the author of "NATO Force Reductions Past and Present," has written extensively on low intensity conflict, and participates in the production of the Army Global Forecast.

LORENZO CROWELL is an Assistant Professor of History at Mississippi State University specializing in twentieth century United States and U.S. military history. He is a fellow of the International Institute for Strategic Studies in London, the Inter-University Seminar for the Study of Armed Forces and Society, and the Center for International Security and Strategic Studies at Mississippi State University. He served

as an Air Force officer for twenty-three years retiring as a
lieutenant colonel. He is a command pilot with operational
experience in B-52s, HC-130s, HH-43s, and UH-1s. He served
on the faculty of both the Air Force Academy in Colorado
Springs and the Air War College in Montgomery, Alabama, where
he was Chief of Military History and Strategy and Director of
the Regional Security Issues Course. He has published in
Modern Asian Studies, Quarterly Journal of Ideology, and
Defense Analysis.

EDWARD F. DANDAR JR. is a Colonel in the active Army Reserves
and has served as a Military Intelligence officer for 25
years. He has spent the last fifteen years in strategic and
tactical psychological operations and civil affairs positions.
He served as the Deputy Commander of the first Joint Psyop
Task Force during the 1982 Joint Chiefs of Staff Ocean Venture
Exercise in the Caribbean and, most recently, as the Deputy
Commander/Chief of Staff of the Joint Civil Affairs Task Force
in Panama from December 26, 1989 until March 28, 1990. He is
currently serving as the Deputy Commander of the 5th
Psychological Operations Group. In his civilian life, he is
a senior Army representative and staff officer on the
Intelligence Producers Council (IPC) in Washington, D.C. and
is responsible for ensuring that national-level policy-
makers' needs are translated into responsive production
programs. Mr. Dandar's civilian assignments over the last ten
years have provided him with a unique perspective for
understanding Department of Defense, Joint Chiefs of Staff,
Unified and Specified Commands, and Service operational
requirements from both the producer's and the operator's
perspectives.

WILLIAM H. DROHAN currently works as an analyst at the Defense
Intelligence Agency. He received his Bachelor of Arts degree
in political science from Boston College and his Master of
Arts degree in history from Catholic University of America.
A major in the U.S. Army Reserve, Mr. Drohan was on active
duty from 1969 until 1978. Subsequently, he worked for the
Drug Enforcement Administration from 1979 until 1983, and the
Office of Enforcement, U.S. Customs Service from 1983 to 1989.
He is an authority on international drug trafficking and
money-laundering.

LAWRENCE S. GERMAIN retired from the Los Alamos National
Laboratory in 1985, having completed a thirty-year career in
the national laboratories. During his tenure, he contributed
to such diverse programs as nuclear weapons design and
testing, arms control issues, and alternative energy projects.
He is currently employed by R and D Associates and is working
primarily in support of the Defense Nuclear Agency on treaty
verification issues.

ALAN R. GOLDMAN received his Bachelor of Arts and Doctorate
degrees in political science from Brown University and his

Masters in political science from the University of Pennsylvania. He has taught international relations, national security affairs, and American government at Fitchburg State College. Dr. Goldman began his intelligence career as the NATO and EEC analyst at the Central Intelligence Agency, and has spent over ten years with Army Intelligence, first as the Chief of the NATO Branch, and more recently as Senior Analyst for all regions of the world. He has published numerous articles on U.S. national and military intelligence, and is a major in the Military Intelligence Branch of the U.S. Army Reserve.

MICHAEL R. HATHAWAY is a professional staff member of the United States Select Committee on Intelligence. He served as Minority Staff Counsel to the Senate Caucus on International Narcotics Control from 1987 to 1989, and was the Staff Director of the United States Commission on Security and Cooperation in Europe from 1985 to 1987. Previously, he was Legislative Assistant for National Security Affairs to U.S. Senator Alfonse D'Amato from 1981 to 1985, and served on active duty as a U.S. Army military intelligence officer from 1972 to 1975. He holds a Bachelor of Arts degree in political science from the University of California at Berkeley, a Master of Business degree from Jacksonville State University, and a Juris Doctorate degree with honors from Golden Gate University School of Law.

SUSAN G. HORWITZ is a Central America analyst for the Department of the Army and provided crisis support to the U.S. Army Staff during Operation Just Cause. Ms. Horwitz earned her Bachelor of Arts degree in International Studies from Emory University and a M.A.L.D. with a concentration in International Security Studies from the Fletcher School of Law and Diplomacy, Tufts University. She recently completed a two-year Department of Defense training program in advanced language and area studies, specializing in Latin America. The training enabled her to travel and work for Defense Attache Offices in Latin America.

DONALD J. MABRY is Senior Fellow in the Center for International Security and Strategic Studies and Professor of Latin American History at Mississippi State University. He received a Bachelor of Arts degree with honors from Kenyon College and a Doctorate of Philosophy in Latin American history from Maxwell Graduate School of Citizenship and Public Affairs, Syracuse University. A specialist on Latin American affairs, Professor Mabry has written numerous books and articles on the subject. His books include Latin American Narcotics Trade and U.S. National Security, The Mexican University and the State, and Neighbors--Mexico and the United States.

NORIS LYN MCCALL is currently assigned to the Office of the Secretary of Defense and is serving as a negotiator on the

U.S. delegation for the Conventional Forces in Europe Treaty talks in Vienna, Austria. A career Marine Corps Officer, Colonel McCall's assignments have included duty in Vietnam, where he flew 788 combat missions, and multiple tours with various Marine Corps aviation squadrons. He commanded Marine Heavy Helicopter Squadron 362, Jacksonville, North Carolina for two years. Colonel McCall is a graduate of the Air Force Command and Staff College, the Marine Corps Command and Staff College, the National Defense University Security Management Course, and the U.S. Naval War College. He holds a Master of Arts degree in Human Resource Management from Pepperdine University and a second Master of Arts degree in International Relations (Soviet Concentration) from Salve Regina College, Newport, Rhode Island.

MICHAEL E. SEITZ is a submarine analyst at the Naval Operational Intelligence Center, Washington, D.C. Lieutenant Seitz joined the Navy in 1983 through the Nuclear Propulsion Officer Candidate (NUPOC) program. After completing Officer Candidate School and nuclear power training, he served aboard USS Nevada (SSBN 733)(Blue) as a member of the commissioning crew. His duties included Communications Officer and several positions associated with operating and maintaining the submarine's nuclear-power plant. He holds a Master of Science in Strategic Intelligence from the Defense Intelligence College, Washington, D.C and a Bachelor of Science degree in Chemistry and Mathematical Sciences from Southern Methodist University, Dallas, Texas.

MARK P. SULLIVAN is a Latin American affairs analyst at the Congressional Research Service (CRS) of the Library of Congress, and has prior service in the Federal Research Division of the Library of Congress, where he contributed to several of its Latin American country studies. He attended Merrimack College, which included a year of language and academic studies at the University of Valencia, Spain, and received his Bachelor of Arts degree in political science in 1981. In 1983, he completed a Master of Science in Foreign Service degree at Georgetown University, where he specialized in Latin American Studies. Mr. Sullivan has written or has contributed to numerous Congressional studies and publications on Panama and Latin America, and wrote the chapter on the Bahamas for the Department of the Army's area handbook series study on the Commonwealth Caribbean.

JOHN W. TURNER is currently the senior Africa and Middle East analyst for USAIA. Dr. Turner received his master's degrees from The University of Michigan and Yale University, and his doctorate in Near East Languages and Literatures from Yale University. He has worked for the Federal government since 1982 as a specialist in Third World affairs and is the author of several papers in both government and private fora, the most recent being at a February 1990 Force Modernization Conference in Singapore. A recognized government expert on

Third World military affairs, Dr. Turner has travelled and studied extensively in his area of interest.

Selected Bibliography

Adkin, Mark. Urgent Fury: The Battle for Grenada. Lexington, MA: D.C. Heath and Co., 1989.

Almond, Peter. "Stealth Steals Some Applause for Panama Debut." Washington Times, January 8, 1990.

Aquilar, Eloy O. "U.S. Troops Comb City for Missing." Washington Times, December 22, 1989, p. A1.

"The Architect of 'Just Cause' LTC Carl Stiner Explains His Panama Plan." Army Times (March 12, 1990): 14+.

"Arias Announces Changes in FP Organization." Foreign Broadcast Information Service, Daily Report: Latin America (March 29, 1990): 34.

Arias Calderon, Ricardo. "Panama: Disaster or Democracy." Foreign Affairs (Winter 1987/1988): 328-347.

"Arias Notes Basic Objectives." Foreign Broadcast Information Service, Daily Report: Latin America (December 22, 1989): 23.

Arias Sanchez, Oscar. "Panama, Without an Army." New York Times, January 9, 1990, p. A23.

"Arias Says No Renegotiation of Canal Treaties." Foreign Broadcast Information Service, Daily Report: Latin America (February 16, 1990): 38.

Asman, David. "Panama's Hong Kong Vision." Wall Street Journal, February 15, 1990, p. A14.

Auster, Bruce B. "Military Lessons of the Invasion." U.S. News and World Report (January 8, 1990): 22-23.

Bailyn, Bernard, et. al. The Great Republic. 2d ed. Lexington, MA and Toronto, CA: D.C. Heath and Co., 1981.

Baker, Caleb. "Army Officials Credit Success in Panama to Planning, Few Bureaucratic Obstacles." Defense News, March 5, 1990.

Bedard, Paul. "U.S. Urges Panama's Endara to Call New Elections." Washington Times, February 5, 1990, p. A3.

Bernal, Miguel Antonio. Los tratados Carter-Torrijos: una traicion historica. 2nd ed. Panama: Edicones Nari, 1985.

Blustein, Paul, and Mufson, Steven. "Economic Recovery Could Take Years." Washington Post, December 21, 1989, p. A35.

Bond, David F. "Six F-117As Flown in Panama Invasion; Air Force Broadens Daytime Operations." Aviation Week and Space Technology (March 5, 1990): 30.

Borbon, Guillermo Sanchez. "Panama Fallen Among Thieves: Of General Noriega and a Country Convulsed." Harper's Magazine (December 1987): 62-65.

Branigin, William. "Panama Faces Troubled Economy, Rising Crime." Washington Post, March 24, 1990, pp. A23, A27.

_____. "U.S. Agent Rescued from Panama Cell Minutes Before Anti-Noriega Offensive." Washington Post, January 1, 1990, p. A12.

_____. "U.S. Embassy Staff Attacks Security." Washington Post, December 31, 1989, p. A20.

_____, Priest, Dana. "U.S., Panama Report Some Success in Restoring Order." Washington Post, December 24, 1989, p. A1.

Brown, Robert K. "U.S. Warriors Topple Panamanian Thugs: 'We Came, We Saw, We Kicked Ass'--82nd Airborne Graffiti, Balboa, Panama." Soldier of Fortune (April 1990): 57.

Burns, E. Bradford. "Panama: A Search for Independence." Current History (February, 1977): 67.

Bush, George. "Panama: The Decision to Use Force." Vital Speeches of the Day 56, no. 7(15 January 1990): 194-195.

"Bush Not Likely to Find Many Panama Wounded in San Antonio." Reuters, December 27, 1989, a.m. cycle.

"Catholic Paper Assesses Reaction to Invasion." Foreign Broadcast Information Service, Daily Report: Latin America (January 22, 1990): 40-41.

Church, George J. "Showing Muscle." Time (January 1, 1990): 20-23.

Cockburn, Alexander. "Beneath a Park in Darien: The Conquest of Panama." The Nation, January 29, 1990, pp. 114-115.

Constitucion Politica de la Republica de Panama. Panama: Editorial Alvarez, 1984.

Conte-Porras, J. Del Tratado Hay-Bunau-Varilla a los tratados Torrijos-Carter. Panama: Biblioteca Jose

Agustin Arango Ch., 1981.

Cooper, Nancy, et. al. "Drugs, Money and Death." Newsweek (February 15, 1988): 32.

Dewar, Helen. "Mitchell Hits Emergency Aid Request." Washington Post, April 3, 1990, p. A9.

Dinges, John. Our Man in Panama: How General Noriega Used the United States--and Made Millions in Drugs and Arms. New York: Random House, 1990.

Donnelly, Tom. "With So Many Weapons--Can Communists Be Far?" Army Times (January 8, 1990): 7.

Donovan, Elizabeth P. "Marines Seize Control of Panamanian Military Compounds." Navy Times (January 1, 1990): R3.

Dorsey, James M. "Panamanian Veep Lobbies Here For $500 Million, One-Shot Deal." Washington Times, March 22, 1990, p. A12.

"Electoral Tribunal Picks Legislature." Foreign Broadcast Information Service, Latin American Weekly Report (March 8, 1990): 5.

"Endara Plays Down Differences Within ADOC." Foreign Broadcast Information Service, Daily Report: Latin America (February 20, 1990): 44.

"Endara Speaks at Assembly Installation." Foreign Broadcast Information Service, Daily Report: Latin America (March 2, 1990): 35.

"Endara Views American Newspaper Article, Aid." Foreign Broadcast Information Service, Daily Report: Latin America, February 20, 1990. p. 42.

"Ford Says Nobody Pressures Nation With Aid." Foreign Broadcast Information Service, Daily Report: Latin America (March 8, 1990): 29.

"Foreign Minister on U.S. Pressure, Treaty." Foreign Broadcast Information Service, Daily Report: Latin America (February 18, 1990): 30-31.

Foss, General John W. "The Future of the Army." Army Times (March 5, 1990): 12.

Freed, Kenneth and Miller, Marjorie. "Panama Bands Stage Bloody Attack; Combat: Troops Believed Directed by Noriega Hit Downtown. Continued Resistance Mocks U.S. Claims that Situation Is Under Control." Los Angeles

Times, December 23, 1989, Home Edition, p. A1.

Fulghum, David. "Jamming with the Panamanians." _Air Force Times_, March 12, 1990.

Fullwood, Sam III. "Combat in Panama; Dignity Battalion Still Lurks in Shadows; Resistance: Many Call Paramilitary Groups Common Street Toughs; They Still Roam the Cities." _Los Angeles Times_, December 22, 1989, p. A7.

Gerstenzang, James and Miller, Marjorie. "Deadly Battles Continue in Panama; Fighting: 2000 Fresh Troops Bolster U.S. Forces. Capital in Near-Anarchy." _Los Angeles Times_, December 23, 1989, Southland Edition, p. A1.

Gertz, Bill. "Assault on Patilla Airport Costs Elite Navy Unit 4 Dead." _Washington Times_, December 22, 1989, p. A7.

_____. "Noriega Tipped Off by a Spy." _Washington Times_, January 2, 1990, p. A1.

_____, and Scarborough, Rowan. "Helms Asks State Probe of Panama Attack Leak." _Washington Times_, March 2, 1990, p. A3.

_____. "Noriega 'Tipped off' to U.S. Strike." _Washington Times_, December 29, 1989, p. A1.

Geyer, Georgie Anne. "Death in Panama." _Washington Times_, September 30, 1985, pp. 1D, 2D.

Gibbons, Gene. "U.S. Aircraft Reported Landing in Panama." Copyright Reuters, December 19, 1989, a.m. cycle.

Ginovsky, John and Fulghum, Davis. "A-7s, OA-37s Patrol over Panama." _Air Force Times_, January 1, 1990, p. R1.

Gordon, Michael R. "Inquiry into Stealth Performance in Panama Is Ordered by Cheney." _New York Times_, April 11, 1990, p. A19.

_____, and Pitt, David. "Panama Crime Waves Shakes Faith in Police." _New York Times_, February 2, 1990, p. A14.

Goldrich, Daniel. _Sons of the Establishment: Elite Youths in Panama and Costa Rica_. Chicago: Rand McNally, 1966.

Government of the Republic of Panama. _Panama: Sixteen Years of Struggle Against Drug Traffic_. Panama City: Impreso en Editora Renovaicon, S.A., 1986.

Greve, Frank. "U.S. Quits War With Panama Bankers." Miami Herald, February 22, 1990, pp. 1A, 16A.

"Gunning for Noriega." The Economist (December 23, 1989): 29-30.

Healy, Melissa. "Combat in Panama: Panamanian Military 'Decapitated' by Coordinated American Strike." Los Angeles Times, December 21, 1989, p. A4.

_____. "Pentagon Puts Panama Civilian Deaths at 220; Invasion: Estimate Suggests 10 Died for Each U.S. Soldier Who Fell. Defense Force Losses Are Put at 314." Los Angeles Times, January 10, 1990, p. A1.

Hedges, Michael. "To Gen. Noriega with Love: Letters from America's Top Drug Enforcers." Washington Times, January 17, 1990, p. A1.

Hersh, Seymour M. "Our Man in Panama." Life (March 1990): 81-93.

Hoffman, David and Bob Woodward. "President Launched Invasion with Little View to Aftermath." Washington Post, December 24, 1989, p. A1.

Hughes, David. "Night Airdrop in Panama Surprises Noriega's Forces." Aviation Week & Space Technology (January 1, 1990): 30.

_____. "Night Invasion of Panama Required Special Operations Aircraft, Training." Aviation Week and Space Technology (January 1, 1990): 30-31.

International Institute for Strategic Studies. The Military Balance, 1988-1989. London: The International Institute for Strategic Studies, 1988.

Jehl, Douglas. "Ranger Force Bore Brunt of Panama Toll." Los Angeles Times, January 7, 1990, p. A1.

"Just Cause: How Well Did We Do?" National Review (January 22, 1990): 14.

Kaplan, Fred. "Pentagon Salvation in Panama--Military Seized Key PR Weapon in Budget Fight." Boston Globe, January 14, 1990.

Kempe, Frederick. Divorcing the Dictator: America's Bungled Affair with Noriega. New York: G.P. Putnam's Sons, 1990.

Koch, Peter. "Panamanian Forces Quickly Overwhelmed." Army Times (January 1, 1990): R8.

238

Koster, R.M. "In Panama, We're Rebuilding Frankenstein." _New York Times_, December 29, 1989, p. A35.

Labaton, Stephen. "Panama is Resisting U.S. Pressure to Alter Inadequate Bank Laws." _New York Times_, February 6, 1990, p. A1, D24.

LaFeber, Walter. _The Panama Canal: The Crisis in Historical Perspective_. New York: Oxford University Press, 1978.

Larmer, Brook. "Police Grapple With Crime Wave." _Christian Science Monitor_, April 3, 1990. p. 3.

"Legislation to End Money Laundering Approved." Foreign Broadcast Information Service, _Daily Report: Latin America_ (February 15, 1990): 29.

"Linares Criticizes Amendment to Canal Treaty." Foreign Broadcast Information Service, _Daily Report: Latin America_ (April 2, 1990): 46.

Luttwak, Edward N. "Just Cause--a Military Score Sheet." _Washington Post_, December 31, 1989, p. C4.

_____. "'Operation Just Cause'--What Went Right, Wrong." _Navy Times_ (December 31, 1989): C4.

Magnuson, Ed. "Sowing Dragon's Teeth." _Time_ (January 1, 1990): 24-27.

Maraniss, David. "A Trooper's 4 Days in Action: from Fort Bragg Cold to a Leg Wound." _Washington Post_, December 28, 1989, p. A1.

McClintok, John M. "U.S. Troops Left Embassy Unguarded: Vatican Envoy Consulted U.S. General on Giving Sanctuary to Noriega." _Baltimore Sun_, December 26, 1989, p. A1.

McDowell, Bart. "The Panama Canal Today." _National Geographic_ (February 1978): 278-294.

McGrath, Marcos G., C.S.C. (Archbishop of Panama). "The Panama Canal: A Test Case." In _The Panama Canal and Social Justice_. Edited by Margaret D. Wilde. Washington: United States Catholic Conference, 1976, pp. 5-11.

McManus, Doyle. "Combat in Panama; U.S. Widens Hunt for Noriega to Mountains of Western Panama; Tactics: the General Is 'Turning Out To Be a Lot Tougher Than We Anticipated,' a U.S. Official Concedes." _Los Angeles Times_, December 23, 1989, Home Edition, p. A3.

Miles, Donna. "Operation Just Cause." Soldiers (February 1990): 20-24.

Miller, David Norman. "Panama and U.S. Policy." Global Affairs (Summer 1989): 136.

Millet, Richard. "Looking Beyond Noriega." Foreign Policy (Summer 1988): 46-63.

_____. "Once the Cheering Stops." Miami Herald, December 24, 1989, pp. 1C, 4C.

Morgenthau, Tom, et al. "Anatomy of a Fiasco." Newsweek (June 6, 1988): 39.

Moore, Molly. "U.S. Seeks to Rebuild Structure: Some Units Spread Propaganda." Washington Post, December 30, 1989, p. A1.

Morley, Jefferson. "Bush's Drug Problem--and Ours." The Nation, August 27/September 3, 1988, pp. 1, 165-169.

Morrocco, John D. "F-117A Fighter Used in Combat for First Time in Panama." Aviation Week and Space Technology (January 1, 1990): 32.

Nelson, Soraya. "'All of the Blood...'." Army Times (January 22, 1990): 10.

"Noriega Loyalists Hit Back at U.S. Military as Chaos Grips Streets." Los Angeles Times, December 24, 1989, p. A1.

Omang, Joanne. "Neutrality For Panama Suggested." Washington Post, December 30, 1989, p. A17.

"Operation Just Cause, 459th Assists in Panama Invasion." Capital Flier. Gaithersburg, MD: Morkap Publishing Co., January 1990.

Oppenheimer, Andres. "Panama May Restrict Cash Laundering." Miami Herald, January 18, 1990. p. 13A.

"The Panama Blitz." Newsweek (January 1, 1990): 16-17.

Panama Canal Commission. 10 Year Report: FY 1980 to FY 1989, A Decade of Progress in Canal Operations and Treaty Implementations. Washington, D.C., 1990.

"The Panama Canal: Old Myths and New Realities." The Defense Monitor (August 1976): 1-8.

Pedreschi, Carlos Bolivar. "Carta sobre la Ley Organica de las Fuerzas de Defensa." Matutino, October 21, 1983. Reprinted in Pedreschi, De la proteccion del

Canal a la militarizacion del pais. Panama, 1987, pp. 65-69.

_____. "Las enmiendas y la intervencion norteamericana en Panama." Matutino, March 30, 1978. Reprinted in Pedreschi, De la proteccion del Canal a la militarizacion del pais. Panama, 1987.

Pichirallo, Joe, and Goshko, John M. "New Ambassador to Panama Named." Washington Post, January 3, 1990, pp. A1, A24.

"Poll Reports Public's View of U.S. Invasion." Foreign Broadcast Information Service, Daily Report: Latin America (January 22, 1990): 39.

"Possible Leasing of Bases." Foreign Broadcast Information Service, Daily Report: Latin America, February 5, 1990. pp. 54-55.

Prater, SSgt Phil. "Combat in the Streets: Securing Panama City Required a Lot of Skill." Soldiers (February 1990): 25-32.

Priest, Dana and Kamen, Al. "U.S. in 'Real War' in Panama, General Says; Anarchy Continues to Rule Streets of Capital." Washington Post, December 23, 1989, p. A1.

Rafshoon, Ellen. "Some U.S. Civilians Caught in the Wrong Place at the Wrong Time." Air Force Times (January 1, 1990): R7.

Robinson, Linda. "Dwindling Options in Panama." Foreign Affairs (Winter 1989-90): 187-205.

Robinson, Walter V. and Bennett, Philip. "The Harrowing Tales of an Untidy Invasion." Boston Globe, December 28, 1989, p. 1.

Ropelewski, Robert R. "How Panama Worked: Planning, Precision, and Surprise Led to Panama Successes." Armed Forces Journal International (February 1990): 28, 32.

Ropp, Steve C. Panamanian Politics: From Guarded Nation to National Guard. New York: Praeger. 1982.

Rosenthal, Andrew. "American Troops Press Hunt for Noriega; Order Breaks Down; Looting Widespread: Curfew is Defied: Bush Urges New Leader to Take Control--Fighting Persists." New York Times, December 22, 1989, p. A1.

Roth, Margaret. "Panama: An Attack Plan for the Future."

Army Times (January 8, 1990): 10.

Rother, Larry. "America's Blind Eye: The U.S. for Years Has Ignored Corruption in Panama." *The New York Times Magazine*, May 28, 1988, pp. 25+.

Samuel, Peter. "Panama--Putting the Pineapple in the Can." *Defense 2000* (Australia) (February 1990).

Scarborough, Rowan. "Controversial Night Goggles Hailed in Panama." *Washington Times*, January 15, 1990.

Schemmer, Benjamin F. "Panama and Just Cause: The Rebirth of Professional Soldiering." *Armed Forces Journal International* (February 1990): 5.

Scicchitano, Paul. "On Patrol: Panama: Stories of Friends Made, of Friends Lost, of Friends Left Behind." *Army Times* (January 8, 1990): 6.

Simpson, Ross. "Devil in Disguise." *Soldier of Fortune* (May 1990): 45.

Soler, Ricaurte. *Pensamiento Panameno y Concepcion de la Nacionalidad durante el Siglo XIX*. Panama: Libreria Cultural Panameno, 1971.

Steele, Dennis. "Operation Just Cause." *Army* (February 1990): 35-44.

Summ, G. Harvey and Kelly, Tom, eds. *The Good Neighbors: America, Panama, and the 1977 Canal Treaties*. Athens: Ohio University Center for International Studies, 1988.

"'Surgical Firepower' Trashed Noriega Post." *Washington Times*, January 11, 1990.

"Task Forces Demonstrate Range of Army Capabilities." *Army Times* (January 1, 1990): R34.

Tice, Jim. "Helicopters, Repairs Get High Marks in Panama Fight." *Army Times* (January 22, 1990): 14.

Trainor, Bernard E. "Gaps in Vital Intelligence Hampered U.S. Troops." *New York Times*, December 21, 1989, p. A21.

Tyler, Patrick E. "U.S. Commander Decries Leak on Panama Invasion." *Washington Post*, February 27, 1990, p. A7.

_____, and Moore, Molly. "Strike Force Struck Out: Special Teams Failed to Find Noriega." *Washington Post*, December 23, 1989, p. A1.

242

_____. "U.S. Paratroopers May Have Seen Noriega Escape During Invasion." Washington Post, January 7, 1990, p. A1.

United States. Congress. Congressional Record. March 3, 1978; February 22, 1988; March 24, 1988; and March 25, 1988.

United States. Congress. House of Representatives. Committee on Foreign Affairs. Urgent Assistance for Democracy in Panama Act of 1990. Report to accompany H.R. 3952. United States House of Representatives, 101st Congress, 2nd sess., February 7, 1990. House Report 101-401, Part 1.

United States. Congress. Senate. Committee on Foreign Relations. Drugs, Law Enforcement, and Foreign Policy: The Cartel, Haiti and Central America. Hearings before the Subcommittee on Terrorism, Narcotics, and International Communications, United States Senate, 100th Congress, 2nd sess., 1988.

_____. Drugs, Law Enforcement, and Foreign Policy: Panama. Senate Hearing 100-773. Hearings before the Subcommittee on Terrorism, Narcotics, and International Communications, United States Senate, 100th Congress, 2nd sess., 1988.

_____. Resolution Pertaining to the Presidential Certification that Panama has Fully Cooperated with the United States Anti-Drug Efforts. March 27, 1987. S.Rpt. 100-25. United States Senate, 100th Congress, 1st sess., 1988.

_____. Restricting United States Assistance to Panama. December 15, 1987. S.Rpt. 100-257. United States Senate, 100th Congress, 1st sess., 1988.

United States. Congress. Senate. Committee on Government Operations. Permanent Subcommittee on Investigations. Drugs and Money Laundering in Panama. Senate Hearing 100-654. United States Senate, 100th Congress, 2nd sess., 1988.

United States. Department of the Army. Panama, A Country Study. Sandra W. Meditz and Dennis M. Hanratty, eds. Washington, D.C.: Headquarters, Department of the Army, 1989.

United States. Department of Defense. "Just Cause and the War Powers Resolution." Defense Issues 5, no 6. Washington, D.C.: GPO, 1990.

_____. "Memorandum for Correspondents." Washington, D.C.:

Office of the Assistant Secretary of Defense Public
Affairs, March 20,1990.

_____. News Briefing by General Kelly and Admiral
Schaeffer. Pentagon, December 21, 1989, 12:10 p.m.

_____. News Briefing by General T.W. Kelly, Director of
Operations, Joint Staff." News Briefing. Washington,
D.C.: Department of Defense, December 20, 1989.

_____. News Briefing by Secretary of Defense Dick Cheney,
General Colin Powell, USA, Chairman, Joint Chiefs of
Staff. News Briefing. Washington, D.C.: Department
of Defense, December 20, 1989.

_____. Review of Panama Pool Deployment, December 1989.
Prepared by Fred S. Hoffman. Washington, D.C.: Office
of the Assistant Secretary of Defense Public Affairs,
1990.

_____. "Units Deployed for Operation Just Cause." Dated
December 22, 1989.

United States. Department of Justice. Office of Justice
Programs, Bureau of Justice Statistics. NCJ-118312.
Drugs and Crime Facts, 1988. Washington, D.C.:
Department of Justice, September 1989.

United States. Department of Justice. Office of the United
States District Attorney for the Middle District of
Florida. News release dated February 5, 1988.

United States. Department of Justice. Office of the United
States District Attorney for the Southern District of
Florida. News release dated February 5, 1988.

United States. Department of State. The Defense and
Neutrality of the Panama Canal Under the New Treaties.
Special Report No. 37. Washington: Bureau of Public
Affairs, Department of State, 1977.

United States. Department of State. Bureau of
International Narcotics Matters. International
Narcotics Control Strategy Report. Washington, D.C.:
Department of State, March 1, 1987.

United States. Department of State. Bureau of
International Narcotics Matters. International
Narcotics Control Strategy Report. Washington, D.C.:
Department of State, March 1, 1988.

United States. Department of State. Bureau of
International Narcotics Matters. International
Narcotics Control Strategy Report. Washington, D.C.:

Department of State, March 1990.

United States. General Accounting Office. Controlling Drug
     Abuse: A Status Report. GAO/GGD-88-39. Washington,
     D.C.: General Accounting Office, 1988.

United States. Library of Congress. Congressional Research
     Service. Congress and U.S. Policy Toward Central
     America and Panama in 1988. Maureen Taft-Morales and
     Mark P. Sullivan. Washington, D.C., September 25,
     1989. CRS Report 89-560 F.

_____. Panama's Political Crisis: Prospects and U.S.
     Policy Concerns. Mark P. Sullivan. Washington, D.C.,
     December 16, 1989. CRS Archives Issue Brief 87230.

_____. Panama: U.S. Policy after the May 1989 Elections.
     Mark P. Sullivan. Washington, D.C., December 16, 1989.
     CRS Archives Issue Brief 89106.

_____. Panama-U.S. Relations: Issues for Congress. Mark
     P. Sullivan. Washington, D.C., March 21, 1990. CRS
     Issue Brief 90044.

_____. War Powers Resolution: Presidential Compliance.
     Ellen C. Collier. Washington, D.C., February 16, 1990.
     CRS Issue Brief 81050.

United States. National Narcotics Intelligence Consumers
     Committee (NNICC). Narcotics Intelligence Estimate
     1983. Washington, D.C.: NNICC, 1983.

_____. Narcotics Intelligence Estimate 1985-1986.
     Washington, D.C.: NNICC, 1986.

United States. Panama Canal Commission. The Panama Canal:
     Today and Yesterday. Washington, D.C.: Panama Canal
     Commission, n.d.

United States. White House. Nixon, Richard M. "Special
     Message to Congress on Control of Narcotics and
     Dangerous Drugs, July 14, 1969." In Public Papers of
     the Presidents of the United States: Containing the
     Public Messages, Speeches, and Statements of the
     President, 1969. Washington, D.C.: Government
     Printing Office, 1971.

_____. Office of the Press Secretary. Statement by the
     President. Washington, D.C.: The White House, January
     3, 1990.

United States, White House, Office of the Press Secretary.
     Statement by the President, 7:20 A.M., December 20,
     1989.

Watson, Russell. "Invasion." Newsweek (January 1, 1990): 12-22.

"'We Will Chase Him and We Will Find Him:' Noriega Defiant as Fight Goes On." Washington Times, December 21, 1989, p. A1.

Wilson, George C. "Panamanian Commanders Fled Their Posts, Thurman Says." Washington Post, January 6, 1990, p. A13.

_____. "SouthCom Commander Rewrote Contingency Plans for Action." Washington Post, January 7, 1989, p. A1.

Zuckerman, Lawrence. "Wanted: Noriega." Time Magazine (February 15, 1988): 16-17.